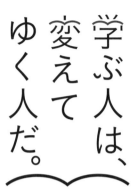

学ぶ人は、
変えて
ゆく人だ。

目の前にある問題はもちろん、

人生の問いや、

社会の課題を自ら見つけ、

学ぶことができる世の中へ。

旺文社

文部科学省後援

英検®1級

テーマ別

ぶんたん
文で覚える
単熟語

[4訂版]

英検®は、公益財団法人 日本英語検定協会の登録商標です。

旺文社

はじめに

　本書は「例文を通して文脈の中で単熟語を覚える」というコンセプトでご好評をいただいていた『英検 文で覚える単熟語』の 4 訂版です。英検でよく出題される単熟語を 5 のテーマに分類し，約 1,580 の見出し語を収録しています。改訂にあたって収録内容を見直し，一部の長文や収録語に入れ替えや変更を施しました。

本書の特長
....

長文を読みながら単熟語が覚えられる

　英検 1 級レベルの長文の中で，文脈を通じて単熟語を覚えられます。単語学習と同時に，読解力も身につけることができます。

学習をサポートする無料音声つき

　音声ダウンロード・アプリ対応なので，スマホやパソコンで簡単に音声をお聞きいただけます。

学習効果がわかる確認テストつき

　長文テーマごとに，見出し語を覚えたかを確認できるチェックテストがついています。

　本書での単語学習が皆さんの英検合格につながることを心より願っています。
　最後に，本書の刊行にあたり多大なご協力をいただきました Ed Jacob 先生に深く感謝の意を表します。

※本書に掲載されている英文の内容は，最新の情報でないもの，架空のものや事実と異なるものを含んでいます。ご了承ください。

もくじ

文化・歴史

政治・経済

教育・心理・社会

執筆：Ed Jacob
編集協力：斉藤敦，株式会社シー・レップス，斎藤なが子（Minos English），鹿島由紀子，株式会社 鷗来堂
データ分析協力：幸和印刷株式会社
装幀・本文デザイン：相馬敬徳（Rafters）
イラスト：TOKUMA（bowlgraphics）
録音：ユニバ合同会社
ナレーション：Howard Colefield，Emma Howard，大武芙由美

本書の構成

文化・歴史 1

Hidden Messages in Horror Movies

As well as frightening audiences, some horror movies also try to make people think about various social issues.

❶
Look beyond the ¹bloodshed and screams in many horror movies, and you may just discover some ²incisive social commentary. The horror ³genre frequently serves as a ⁴vehicle to address issues ranging from politics to consumer culture.

A classic example is *Invasion of the Body Snatchers*. Released when anti-communist ⁵paranoia was at its height, the film is often said to be an ⁶allegory representing the spread of ⁷communism or the dangers of ⁸conformity. In the film, aliens ⁹disintegrate humans in their sleep and replace them with emotionless ¹⁰replicas, a ¹¹metaphor for the ¹²insidious spread of a dangerous idea through a complacent society.

Similarly, George Romero's critically ¹³acclaimed ¹⁴masterpiece, *Dawn of the Dead*, is often said to be a metaphor for the ¹⁵ills of modern consumer society. Set in the days following a zombie apocalypse, it tells the story of human survivors sheltering in a shopping mall. The plot of the film ¹⁶revolves around how the survivors' and the zombies' mutual ¹⁷obsession with the mall and the consumer goods inside it leads to the survivors' demise.

These are just two of many examples of hidden messages ¹⁸concealed in films of the horror genre. The next time you are ¹⁹cowering on your sofa as the zombies close in, ask yourself if the director might be making a point about the society you yourself inhabit. **❷** (320 words)

❸
ℓ.13 apocalypse：黙示録、世の終末
ℓ.20 make a point：主張する、強調する

14

文化・歴史 1

ホラー映画に隠されたメッセージ

ホラー映画の中には観客を怖がらせるだけでなく、人々にさまざまな社会問題について考えさせようとするものもある。

❹
多くのホラー映画の ¹流血と悲鳴の先を見れば、あなたは ²鋭利な社会的批評を見いだすかもしれない。ホラーという ³ジャンルは、しばしば政治から消費者文化に至るまでの問題に取り組む ⁴手段としての機能を果たす。

『ボディ・スナッチャー／恐怖の街』はその古典的な例である。反共産主義的 ⁵妄想が最高潮のときに公開されたこの映画は、しばしば ⁷共産主義の拡散や、⁸服従の危険性を表す ⁶寓意だと言われる。映画の中では、人間が眠っている間に異星人が彼らを ⁹分解して感情のない ¹⁰複製と取り替える。すなわち無頓着な社会を通して危険な思想が ¹²知らぬ間に広がることの ¹¹隠喩である。

同様に、ジョージ・ロメロの批評家に ¹³絶賛された ¹⁴傑作、『ドーン・オブ・ザ・デッド』はしばしば現代の消費社会の ¹⁵弊害の暗喩だと言われる。ゾンビによる世界の終わりに続く時代を舞台とするこの映画は、生き残った人間たちがショッピングモールに避難する物語である。映画の筋書きは、ショッピングモールとその中にある消費財に対する生き残った人間とゾンビの双方の ¹⁷固執が生存者の死の原因となるさまを中心に ¹⁶展開する。

これらはホラー映画というジャンルに ¹⁸隠された多くの密かなメッセージのほんの2つの例である。次にゾンビが詰め寄ってきたあなたがソファーの上で ¹⁹縮こまっているときには、監督があなた自身が生きている社会について主張をしているのではないかと自分に問うてみるといい。

比喩のいろいろ

figure of speech（比喩）の代表的なものは simile（直喩）で、Life is like a journey.（人生は旅のようなものだ）のように、like や as などを用いて何かを別の何かに例える技法である。metaphor（隠喩）は、Life is a journey.（人生は旅だ）のように、何かを別の概念で直接表現する。metonymy（換喩）は、例えば「ペンタゴン」＝「アメリカ国防総省」のように、密接な関係がある事柄（国防総省の建物が五角形）からの連想で何かを表現する。allegory（アレゴリー）は、具体的なイメージを用いて抽象的な概念を表現する芸術上の技法を言う。例えば、冷戦時代の映画で描かれた異星人の密かな侵略を、共産主義の浸透のアレゴリーと考えることもできる。

15

Hidden Messages in Horror Movies **❻**

❺
1 ☐☐ **bloodshed** [blʌ́dʃèd]	🔵 流血（の惨事）
	🔵 shed blood（血を流す、流血の惨事を起こす）からできた名詞

2 ☐☐ **incisive** [ɪnsáɪsɪv]	▶ keen, piercing, trenchant
	🔵（批評などが）鋭敏な、（頭脳が）明敏な
	🔵 in-（中に）+cis（切る）+ive（形容詞語尾）

3 ☐☐ **genre** [ʒáːnrə]	▶ a particular style of literature or art
	🔵 ジャンル

4 ☐☐ **vehicle** [víːəkl] 🔵	▶ medium
	🔵（思想・感情などの）伝達手段、表現手段

5 ☐☐ **paranoia** [pærənɔ́ɪə]	🔵 被害妄想、パラノイア
	🔵 paranoid（パラノイアの（人））

6 ☐☐ **allegory** [ǽləɡɔ̀ːri]	🔵 寓話、寓意、アレゴリー
	🔵 allegorical

7 ☐☐ **communism** [kɑ́ːmjunɪ̀zm]	🔵 共産主義
	🔵 communist（共産主義者；共産主義の）

8 ☐☐ **conformity** [kənfɔ́ːrməti]	▶ obedience, submission
	🔵 服従、追随
	🔵 conform 🔵 conformist 🔵 nonconformist

9 ☐☐ **disintegrate** [dɪsíntəɡrèɪt]	▶ break up, break down, decompose
	🔵（を）分解する、を崩壊させる
	🔵 disintegration

10 ☐☐ **replica** [réplɪkə]	▶ exact copy, replication
	🔵 複製、レプリカ

11 ☐☐ **metaphor** [métəfɔ̀ːr]	🔵 暗喩、隠喩
	🔵 metaphorical

16

文化・歴史 1

12 ☐☐ **insidious** [ɪnsídiəs]	🔵（病気などが）知らないうちに進行する、潜行性の

13 ☐☐ **acclaim** [əkléɪm]	▶ praise, applaud, laud
	🔵 を称賛する 🔵 称賛
	🔵 critically acclaimed は「批評家に称賛された」の意味

14 ☐☐ **masterpiece** [mǽstərpìːs]	▶ masterwork
	🔵 傑作、名作

15 ☐☐ **ill** [íl]	▶ malady, evil
	🔵 弊害、（通例-s）不幸、困難

16 ☐☐ **revolve** [rɪvɑ́ːlv]	🔵 展開する、回る（around ～を中心に）
	🔵 believe that the world revolves around oneself（世界は自分を中心に回っていると考える）

17 ☐☐ **obsession** [əbséʃən]	🔵 delusion, fixation
	🔵 妄想、強迫観念
	🔵 obsess 🔵 obsessive

18 ☐☐ **conceal** [kənsíːl]	▶ hide, cover up, hush up
	🔵 を隠しておく、を秘密にする
	🔵 concealment 🔵 reveal

19 ☐☐ **cower** [káʊər]	▶ cringe, recoil
	🔵（恐怖などで）縮こまる、すくむ

❼
☐☐ **convey** [kənvéɪ] 🔵	▶ communicate, express, put across
	🔵（情報・メッセージなど）を伝える

☐☐ **horrific** [hɔːrífɪk]	▶ appalling, frightful, horrendous
	🔵 恐ろしい、ぞっとする
	🔵 horror 🔵 horrify

☐☐ **hideous** [hídiəs] 🔵	▶ ugly, unsightly, unattractive
	🔵 見苦しい、醜い
	🔵 sightly（見た目の良い）

17

テーマを知る
各テーマについて，英検での出題傾向やおさえておきたい背景知識，キーワードなどをまとめています。

本編

❶長文……英文中の重要な単熟語が赤字になっており，数字は単熟語ページの見出し語に対応しています。

❷音声ナレーター……長文の読み上げ音声（p.8 参照）がアメリカ英語かイギリス英語かを国旗のマークで示しています。見出し語の読み上げは全てアメリカ英語です。

❸注……長文の中に出てくる注意すべき語句や構文について説明しています。

❹全訳……長文の日本語訳です。

❺発音記号……見出し語の読み方を表す記号です（詳細はp.10 参照）。とくに発音・アクセントに注意が必要な語に ❶を付けています。

❻語義その他……英検合格に必要なものを取り上げています。他動詞の語義には基本的に小文字で「を」「に」などを示しています。「を」「に」などがない動詞は自動詞です。その他，英英定義，派生関係にある語や補足，用例などを掲載しています。

❼関連語……見出し語や長文トピックに関連する語句です。長文には出てきませんが，あわせて覚えるようにしましょう。

確認テスト
各テーマで学習した単熟語の確認ができるチェックテストです。記憶が曖昧だったものは，各ページに戻って復習しましょう。

表記について

▶ 同義語・類義語や英英定義

動 動 動詞　　　**名** 名 名詞
形 形 形容詞　　**副** 副 副詞

➡ 反意語　　● 補足説明，用例など

（　　）……省略可能／補足説明
［　　］……直前の語句と言い換え可能
〈　　〉……コロケーション／文型表示

A, B ……*A, B* に異なる語句が入る
one's, oneself ……人を表す語句が入る
doing ……動名詞，現在分詞が入る
to *do* ……不定詞が入る

音声について

本書に掲載されている以下の音声をスマートフォン等でお聞きいただけます。

収録内容

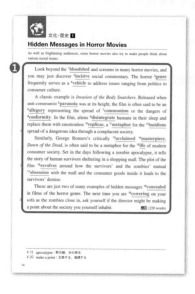

❶ 長文（英語）

❷ 見出し語（英語）

❸ 見出し語の訳（※）

※赤字部分のうち，最初に掲載している
品詞の訳を読み上げています。

音声のご利用方法

2種類の方法で音声をお聞きいただけます。

パソコンで音声データ（MP3）をダウンロード

❶ 以下の URL から，Web 特典にアクセス

https://eiken.obunsha.co.jp/1q/

❷ 本書を選び，以下のパスワードを入力してダウンロード

okycwz ※全て半角アルファベット小文字

❸ ファイルを展開して，オーディオプレーヤーで再生
音声ファイルは zip 形式にまとめられた形でダウンロードされます。展開後，
デジタルオーディオプレーヤーなどで再生してください。

※音声の再生には MP3 を再生できる機器などが必要です。
※ご利用機器，音声再生ソフト等に関する技術的なご質問は，ハードメーカーもしくはソフト
　メーカーにお願いいたします。
※本サービスは予告なく終了することがあります。

公式アプリ「英語の友」（iOS／Android）で再生

❶「英語の友」公式サイトより，アプリをインストール

https://eigonotomo.com/

 左の2次元コードから読み込めます。

❷ アプリ内のライブラリより本書を選び，「追加」ボタンをタップ

※本アプリの機能の一部は有料ですが，本書の音声は無料でお聞きいただけます。
※詳しいご利用方法は「英語の友」公式サイト，あるいはアプリ内のヘルプをご参照ください。
※本サービスは予告なく終了することがあります。

発音記号表

本書では代表的な発音を 1 つだけ掲載しています。
発音記号はあくまで参考であることをご了承ください。

母音

発音記号	例	発音記号	例
[i:]	eat [i:t]	[u]	casual [kǽʒuəl]
[i]	happy [hǽpi]	[u:]	school [sku:l]
[ɪ]	sit [sɪt]	[eɪ]	cake [keɪk]
[e]	bed [bed]	[aɪ]	eye [aɪ]
[æ]	cat [kæt]	[ɔɪ]	boy [bɔɪ]
[ɑ:]	palm [pɑ:*l*m]	[aʊ]	house [haʊs]
[ʌ]	cut [kʌt]	[oʊ]	go [goʊ]
[ə:*r*]	bird [bə:*r*d]	[ɪə*r*]	ear [ɪə*r*]
[ə]	above [əbʌ́v]	[eə*r*]	air [eə*r*]
[ə*r*]	doctor [dá(:)ktə*r*]	[ɑ:*r*]	heart [hɑ:*r*t]
[ɔ:]	law [lɔ:]	[ɔ:*r*]	morning [mɔ́:*r*nɪŋ]
[ʊ]	pull [pʊl]	[ʊə*r*]	poor [pʊə*r*]

※母音の後の [*r*] は，アメリカ英語では直前の母音が r の音色を持つことを示し，イギリス
英語では省略されることを示す。

子音

発音記号	例	発音記号	例
[p]	pen [pen]	[v]	very [véri]
[b]	book [bʊk]	[θ]	three [θri:]
[m]	man [mæn]	[ð]	this [ðɪs]
[t]	top [tɑ(:)p]	[s]	sea [si:]
[t̬]	water [wɔ́:t̬ə*r*]	[z]	zoo [zu:]
[d]	dog [dɔ(:)g]	[ʃ]	ship [ʃɪp]
[n]	name [neɪm]	[ʒ]	vision [víʒən]
[k]	cake [keɪk]	[h]	hot [hɑ(:)t]
[g]	good [gʊd]	[l]	lion [láɪən]
[ŋ]	ink [ɪŋk]	[r]	rain [reɪn]
[tʃ]	chair [tʃeə*r*]	[w]	wet [wet]
[dʒ]	June [dʒu:n]	[*hw*]	white [*hw*aɪt]
[f]	five [faɪv]	[j]	young [jʌŋ]

※ [t̬] はアメリカ英語で弾音（日本語のラ行に近い音）になることを示す。
※斜体および [(:)] は省略可能であることを示す。

文化・歴史

文化・歴史

テーマを知る

　文化・歴史の英文では，さまざまな歴史上の出来事とその影響やそれに対する評価，考古学的な発見，ある地域の文化，イベントの説明やその起源などの話題が扱われる。科学的な方法による分析などが紹介されることも多い。あまりなじみのない話題が取り上げられることもあるが，前提知識を要求するようなものは多くないため，歴史や文化を説明する文章のスタイルに慣れておくことが対策となる。

キーワード・表現

□ **copyright**	著作権，版権	p.20
□ **medieval**	中世の	p.24
□ **manuscript**	（手書きの）写本，手書き本	p.24
□ **artifact**	（過去の）工芸品，人工遺物	p.24
□ **craftsmanship**	職人技，技巧	p.25
□ **strife**	争い，不和	p.28
□ **venue**	開催地	p.36
□ **hub**	拠点，（活動の）中心地	p.36
□ **invoke**	（神など）に加護を祈る	p.37
□ **curse**	呪い	p.37
□ **skull**	頭蓋骨，頭骨	p.40
□ **hominid**	ヒト科の動物	p.40
□ **Homo erectus**	ホモエレクトゥス，原人類	p.40
□ **forerunner**	先祖，先触れ	p.40
□ **metallurgy**	冶金（術），金属加工（の技術）	p.44
□ **irrigation**	灌漑，（農業のために）水を引くこと	p.45

☐ **commemorate**	を記念する	p.48
☐ **festivity**	祭り，祭典	p.49
☐ **settlement**	集落，入植地	p.52
☐ **unearth**	を発掘する，を掘り出す	p.52
☐ **excavator**	発掘者	p.52
☐ **scribe**	写字生，写本を書き写す人	p.52
☐ **garrison**	（守備隊のいる）要塞，駐屯地	p.53
☐ **ritualistic**	儀式の	p.56
☐ **radiocarbon dating**	放射性炭素年代測定（法）	p.56
☐ **Neolithic Age**	新石器時代	p.56
☐ **anthropologist**	（文化）人類学者	p.60
☐ **remnant**	遺跡，残存物	p.60
☐ **rudimentary**	原始的な，初歩的な	p.60
☐ **apocalypse**	この世の終わり（の日）	p.64
☐ **nomadic**	遊牧民の，放浪生活の	p.65

Hidden Messages in Horror Movies

As well as frightening audiences, some horror movies also try to make people think about various social issues.

1　　Look beyond the ¹**bloodshed** and screams in many horror movies, and you may just discover ²**incisive** social commentary. The horror ³**genre** frequently serves as a ⁴**vehicle** to address issues ranging from politics to consumer culture.

5　　A classic example is *Invasion of the Body Snatchers*. Released when anti-communist ⁵**paranoia** was at its height, the film is often said to be an ⁶**allegory** representing the spread of ⁷**communism** or the dangers of ⁸**conformity**. In the film, aliens ⁹**disintegrate** humans in their sleep and replace them with emotionless ¹⁰**replicas**, a ¹¹**metaphor** for the ¹²**insidious**
10　spread of a dangerous idea through a complacent society.

　　Similarly, George Romero's critically ¹³**acclaimed** ¹⁴**masterpiece**, *Dawn of the Dead*, is often said to be a metaphor for the ¹⁵**ills** of modern consumer society. Set in the days following a zombie apocalypse, it tells the story of human survivors sheltering in a shopping mall. The plot of the
15　film ¹⁶**revolves** around how the survivors' and the zombies' mutual ¹⁷**obsession** with the mall and the consumer goods inside it leads to the survivors' demise.

　　These are just two of many examples of hidden messages ¹⁸**concealed** in films of the horror genre. The next time you are ¹⁹**cowering** on your
20　sofa as the zombies close in, ask yourself if the director might be making a point about the society you yourself inhabit.　　　　　■≣ (220 words)

ℓ.13　apocalypse：黙示録，世の終末
ℓ.20　make a point：主張する，強調する

ホラー映画に隠されたメッセージ

ホラー映画の中には観客を怖がらせるだけでなく，人々にさまざまな社会問題について考えさせようとするものもある。

　多くのホラー映画の ¹流血と悲鳴の先を見れば，あなたは ²鋭利な社会的批評を見いだすかもしれない。ホラーという ³ジャンルは，しばしば政治から消費者文化に至るまでの問題に取り組む ⁴手段としての機能を果たす。

　『ボディー・スナッチャー／恐怖の街』はその古典的な例である。反共産主義的 ⁵妄想が最高潮のときに公開されたこの映画は，しばしば ⁷共産主義の拡散や，⁸服従の危険性を表す ⁶寓喩だと言われる。映画の中では，人間が眠っている間に異星人が彼ら ⁹を分解して感情のない ¹⁰複製と取り替える，すなわち無頓着な社会を通して危険な思想が ¹²知らぬ間に広がることの ¹¹暗喩である。

　同様に，ジョージ・ロメロの批評家に ¹³絶賛された ¹⁴傑作，『ドーン・オブ・ザ・デッド』はしばしば現代の消費社会の ¹⁵罪悪の暗喩だと言われる。ゾンビによる世界の終わりに続く時代を舞台とするこの映画は，生き残った人間たちがショッピングモールに避難する物語である。映画の筋書きは，ショッピングモールとその中にある消費財に対する生き残った人間とゾンビの双方の ¹⁷固執が生存者の死の原因となるさまを中心に ¹⁶展開する。

　これらはホラー映画というジャンルに ¹⁸隠された多くの密かなメッセージのほんの2つの例である。次にゾンビが詰め寄ってきてあなたがソファーの上で ¹⁹縮こまっているときには，監督があなた自身が生きている社会について主張をしているのではないかと自分に問うてみるといい。

比喩のいろいろ

figure of speech（比喩）の代表的なものは simile（直喩）で，Life is like a journey.（人生は旅のようなものだ）のように，like や as などを用いて何かを別の何かに例える技法である。metaphor（隠喩）は，Life is a journey.（人生は旅だ）のように，何かを別の概念で直接表現する。metonymy（換喩）は，例えば「ペンタゴン」→「アメリカ国防総省」のように，密接な関係がある要素（国防総省の建物が五角形）からの連想で何かを表現する。allegory（アレゴリー）は，具体的なイメージを用いて抽象的な概念を表現する芸術上の技法を言う。例えば，冷戦時代の映画で描かれた異星人の密かな侵略を，共産主義の浸透のアレゴリーと考えることもできる。

Hidden Messages in Horror Movies

1 ☐☐ **bloodshed** [bládʃèd]	名 流血（の惨事） ● shed blood（血を流す，流血の惨事を起こす）からできた名詞
2 ☐☐ **incisive** [ɪnsáɪsɪv]	▶ keen, piercing, trenchant 形（批評などが）鋭利な，（頭脳が）明敏な ● in-（中に）＋cis（切る）＋ive（形容詞語尾）
3 ☐☐ **genre** [ʒáːnrə]	▶ a particular style of literature or art 名 ジャンル
4 ☐☐ **vehicle** [víːəkl] ❶	▶ medium 名（思想・感情などの）伝達手段，表現手段
5 ☐☐ **paranoia** [pæ̀rənɔ́ɪə]	名 被害妄想，パラノイア 形 名 paranoid（パラノイアの（人））
6 ☐☐ **allegory** [ǽləgɔ̀ːri]	名 寓喩，寓意，アレゴリー 形 allegorical
7 ☐☐ **communism** [ká(ː)mjunìzm]	名 共産主義 名 形 communist（共産主義者；共産主義の）
8 ☐☐ **conformity** [kənfɔ́ːrməti]	▶ obedience, submission 名 服従，追随 動 conform 名 形 conformist ⬌ nonconformity
9 ☐☐ **disintegrate** [dɪsíntəgrèɪt]	▶ break up, break down, decompose 動（を）分解する，を崩壊させる 名 disintegration
10 ☐☐ **replica** [réplɪkə]	▶ exact copy, replication 名 複製，レプリカ
11 ☐☐ **metaphor** [méṭəfɔ̀(ː)r]	名 暗喩，隠喩 形 metaphorical

12 ☐☐ **insidious** [ɪnsídiəs]	形（病気などが）知らないうちに進行する，潜行性の

13 ☐☐ **acclaim** [əkléɪm]	▶ praise, applaud, laud 動 を称賛する　名 称賛 ● critically acclaimed は「批評家に称賛された」の意味

14 ☐☐ **masterpiece** [mǽstərpìːs]	▶ masterwork 名 傑作，名作

15 ☐☐ **ill** [ɪl]	▶ malady, evil 名 罪悪，（通例 -s）不幸，困難

16 ☐☐ **revolve** [rɪvá(ː)lv]	動 展開する，回る〈around 〜を中心に〉 ● believe that the world revolves around *oneself*（世界は自分を中心に回っていると考える）

17 ☐☐ **obsession** [əbséʃən]	▶ delusion, fixation 名 妄想，強迫観念 動 obsess　形 obsessive

18 ☐☐ **conceal** [kənsíːl]	▶ hide, cover up, hush up 動 を隠しておく，を秘密にする 名 concealment　⇔ reveal

19 ☐☐ **cower** [káʊər]	▶ cringe, recoil 動（恐怖などで）縮こまる，すくむ

☐☐ **convey** [kənvéɪ] ●	▶ communicate, express, put across 動（情報・メッセージなど）を伝える

☐☐ **horrific** [hɔ(ː)rífɪk]	▶ appalling, frightful, horrendous 形 恐ろしい，ぞっとする 名 horror　動 horrify

☐☐ **hideous** [hídiəs] ●	▶ ugly, unsightly, unattractive 形 見苦しい，醜い ⇔ sightly（見た目の良い）

文化・歴史 **2**

Savior of the Video Recorder

In the 1970s, a children's TV show host helped makers of video recorders overcome objections that the new technology would hurt the TV and movie industries.

1   Today, we take the ability to record our favorite movies and TV programs for granted. However, if it were not for a [1]**precedent**-setting court case and the intervention of a [2]**beloved** children's TV show host, the outcome may have been very different.

5   When the first [3]**commercially** successful video recorder was released in the 1970s in the US, there was tremendous opposition from media companies, which worried that this then-[4]**groundbreaking** technology would lead to [5]**copyright** [6]**violations** involving the [7]**unauthorized** [8]**duplication** and distribution of their broadcasts. They began a [9]**lawsuit**

10 against the manufacturer that eventually reached [10]**the Supreme Court**, and a verdict in favor of the media companies would likely have been a [11]**death knell** for the product.

    However, Fred Rogers, host of the long-running kids' show *Mister Rogers' Neighborhood*, [12]**testified** in favor of video recorders, asserting

15 that they would be a tool which [13]**empowered** viewers, enabling them to become more active in scheduling television viewing, thereby lessening the degree to which television influenced people's lives. Rogers was so highly [14]**esteemed**, and his [15]**testimony** was so [16]**persuasive**, that in 1983 he played a significant role in swaying the court in favor of the video

20 recorder's manufacturer. (194 words)

ビデオレコーダーの救世主

1970 年代，ビデオレコーダーのメーカーが「新技術はテレビや映画業界に損害を与えるだろう」という反対意見を克服するのを，子供向け番組の司会者が支援した。

今日，我々は気に入った映画やテレビ番組を録画できることを当たり前だと思っている。しかしながら，もし ¹前例となる裁判と子供たちが ²大好きなテレビ番組のホストの介入がなければ，結果は非常に違ったものであったかもしれない。

³商業的に成功した最初のビデオレコーダーがアメリカで 1970 年代に発売されたとき，当時 ⁴画期的であったこの技術が，彼らの放送の ⁷無認可の ⁸複製と流通を含む ⁵著作権 ⁶侵害につながるのではないかと心配したメディア企業からとてつもない反対があった。彼らは製造企業を相手取った ⁹訴訟を起こし，最終的には ¹⁰最高裁にまで行ったが，メディア企業に好意的な評決が出たらこの製品は ¹¹終わりになるところだった。

しかしながら，長寿番組である子供番組，『ミスター・ロジャース・ネイバーフッド』のホストであるフレッド・ロジャースはビデオレコーダーに好意的な ¹²意見を述べて，この機械が視聴者 ¹³に決定権を与え，テレビ視聴のスケジュール作りをより積極的に行えるようにし，その結果，テレビが人々の生活に与える影響の程度を小さくする道具になるだろうと断言した。ロジャースは非常に高い ¹⁴評価を受けており，彼の ¹⁵証言はとても ¹⁶説得力があったので，1983 年に裁判所がビデオレコーダーの製造企業に好意的に傾くのに重要な役割を果たした。

エンパワーメント

2015 年に国連総会で採択された 17 の Sustainable Development Goals（持続可能な開発目標, SDGs）の第 5 の目標は Achieve gender equality and empower all women and girls. である。では「力を与える」とはどういうことか。empowerment（エンパワーメント）は civil rights movement（公民権運動）や feminist movement（フェミニズム運動）を経て一般化した概念で，自分の生活を自分でコントロール・決定し，正当な権利を主張し，能力を発揮できるようにすることなどを言う。パッセージでは，テレビに時間を支配されるのではなく，録画することによって自分の使う時間を自分でコントロールできるようにする，という意味で用いられている。

Savior of the Video Recorder

1 ☐☐ **precedent** [présɪdənt]	名 前例，先例 動 precede（に先立つ）　名 precedence（先行） ● set a precedent for ～（～の先例を作る）
2 ☐☐ **beloved** [bɪlʌ́vɪd] ❶	▶ adored, cherished, dear 形 最愛の，いとしい
3 ☐☐ **commercially** [kəmə́ːrʃəli]	副 商業的に 名 commerce　形 commercial
4 ☐☐ **groundbreaking** [ɡráʊndbrèɪkɪŋ]	▶ epoch-making, revolutionary 形 画期的な，草分け的な ● break new ground（新分野を切り開く）
5 ☐☐ **copyright** [kɑ́(ː)pàɪrɪt]	名 著作権，版権 ● hold the copyright of [in, on, to] ～（～の著作権を持っている）
6 ☐☐ **violation** [vàɪəléɪʃən]	▶ breach, infringement, infraction 名 侵害，違反 動 violate
7 ☐☐ **unauthorized** [ʌnɔ́ːθəràɪzd]	▶ not officially permitted 形 無認可の，非公認の ⇔ authorized
8 ☐☐ **duplication** [djùːplɪkéɪʃən]	▶ replication, reproduction 名 複製（すること），複写 動 duplicate
9 ☐☐ **lawsuit** [lɔ́ːsjùːt]	▶ suit, action, litigation 名 訴訟〈against ～に対する〉 ● file [bring, launch] a lawsuit（訴訟を起こす）
10 ☐☐ **the Supreme Court**	最高裁判所 ● 米国では最高裁判所の下に Court of Appeals（控訴裁判所），district court（地方裁判所）などがある
11 ☐☐ **death knell**	終末［破滅］の前兆 ● knell [nel] は「弔鐘」（死者のために鳴らす鐘）の意味

12 ☐☐ **testify** [téstɪfàɪ]	▶ attest, witness **動** 証言する ● testify for 〜（〜に有利な証言をする）
13 ☐☐ **empower** [ɪmpáʊər]	**動** に力［権限］を与える **名** empowerment
14 ☐☐ **esteem** [ɪstí:m] ❶	▶ admire, respect, venerate **動** を尊敬する, を尊重する　**名** 尊敬, 尊重 **形** esteemed
15 ☐☐ **testimony** [téstəmòʊni]	▶ attestation, witness **名** 証言 ● give testimony in court（法廷で証言する）
16 ☐☐ **persuasive** [pərswéɪsɪv]	▶ convincing, compelling **形** 説得力のある **動** persuade　**名** persuasion
☐☐ **piracy** [páɪərəsi] ❶	**名** 著作権侵害 **動 名** pirate ●「海賊行為」が本義
☐☐ **intellectual property**	知的財産（権）
☐☐ **plaintiff** [pléɪnṭəf]	**名** 原告
☐☐ **defendant** [dɪféndənt]	**名** 被告
☐☐ **plagiarize** [pléɪdʒəràɪz]	▶ rip off **動** を剽窃する, を盗用する **名** plagiarism（剽窃）, plagiarist（剽窃者）
☐☐ **encroach** [ɪnkróʊtʃ]	▶ impinge, infringe, trespass **動** 侵害する〈on, upon 他人の権利などを〉 **名** encroachment

文化・歴史 **3**

Chromium Steel

Researchers have discovered that an important modern manufacturing material called chromium steel was actually invented hundreds of years ago in ancient Persia.

1   Tool steel has become an ¹**indispensable** manufacturing material in modern society due to its hardness and resistance to ²**abrasion** and ³**corrosion**, and it is a ⁴**component** in everything from pocket knives to drill bits. Often made with an element called chromium, it was long
5   thought to have been invented in the twentieth century. Recently, however, scientists have discovered that ⁵**medieval** Persians created an ⁶**alloy** resembling tool steel nearly a millennium ago.

An ancient ⁷**manuscript** whose title translates as "A ⁸**Compendium** to Know the Gems" contains an account of the process for ⁹**forging** steel
10 with chromium. While the recipe was ¹⁰**ambiguous** in places, traces of chromium were discovered in ¹¹**artifacts** from the site where the manuscript was found. Using radiocarbon dating, researchers have determined that the steel ¹²**dates back** to at least the twelfth century.

The steel was likely used to manufacture armor and swords and would
15 not have contained the ¹³**impurities** of other ancient metals. However, because the ancient blacksmiths also added phosphorus in order to lower the metal's melting point, the items would have been more ¹⁴**brittle** than the tool steel of today. Nonetheless, the items produced by medieval Persians were known for their ¹⁵**exquisite** ¹⁶**craftsmanship**, and this
20 amazing discovery demonstrates once again the ingenuity and ¹⁷**resourcefulness** of our ancestors.　　　　　　　　　　(211 words)

ℓ.16 phosphorus：リン

クロム鋼

研究者たちは，クロム鋼と呼ばれる重要な現代の製造のための原料が実は数百年前に古代ペルシャで発明されたことを発見した。

工具鋼は，その硬度と²摩耗や³腐食に対する強さから，現代社会では製造のための原料として¹不可欠なものとなり，ポケットナイフからドリルの先端まであらゆるものの⁴部品である。それはしばしばクロムという元素から作られるため，長い間 20 世紀に発明されたものだと思われてきた。しかし，最近になって，科学者たちは⁵中世のペルシャ人たちが 1000 年近くも前に工具鋼に似た⁶合金を作り出したことを発見した。

「宝石を知るための⁸概要」と訳される題名が付いた古代の⁷書物には，クロムから鋼⁹を鍛造する過程についての説明が記されている。その作り方は所々¹⁰不明瞭ではあったが，書物が見つかった場所にあった¹¹工芸品からはわずかにクロムが発見された。研究者たちは放射性炭素年代測定法を使って，この鋼が少なくとも 12 世紀に¹²さかのぼると断定した。

その鋼は甲冑や刀剣を製造するのに使われたものらしく，他の古代の金属の¹³不純物は含んでいなかっただろう。しかし，古代の鍛冶屋は金属の融点を下げるためにリンも加えたために，それらの製品は今日の工具鋼よりも¹⁴もろかったであろう。それにもかかわらず，中世ペルシャ人たちが作った品物はその¹⁵精緻な¹⁶職人技で知られていた。そしてこの驚くべき発見は，再び我々に祖先の創意工夫と¹⁷機知とを示している。

Chromium Steel

1 ☐☐ **indispensable** [ìndɪspénsəbl]	▶ essential, imperative, vital 形 不可欠な, なくてはならない ⇔ dispensable
2 ☐☐ **abrasion** [əbréɪʒən]	▶ wear 名 摩耗 動 abrade 形 abrasive
3 ☐☐ **corrosion** [kəróʊʒən]	▶ erosion 名 腐食, 浸食 動 corrode 形 corrosive
4 ☐☐ **component** [kəmpóʊnənt]	▶ part, piece, constituent 名 部品, 構成要素
5 ☐☐ **medieval** [mì:díí:vəl] ❶	形 中世の ● 「中世」は the Middle Ages と言う
6 ☐☐ **alloy** [ǽlɔɪ]	▶ a mixture of two or more metals 名 合金 ● aluminum alloy（アルミニウム合金）
7 ☐☐ **manuscript** [mǽnjuskrìpt]	名（手書きの）写本, 手書き本 ● manu-（手で）＋script（書かれたもの）
8 ☐☐ **compendium** [kəmpéndiəm]	▶ summary, survey 名 概説, 概論 ● 1つのテーマに関する網羅的な情報をまとめた本
9 ☐☐ **forge** [fɔ:rdʒ]	動（鉄など）を鍛造する ● 金属を熱してたたき成形すること
10 ☐☐ **ambiguous** [æmbígjuəs]	▶ equivocal, unclear 形 曖昧な, 両義 [多義] 的な 名 ambiguity 副 ambiguously
11 ☐☐ **artifact** [á:rtɪfækt]	名（過去の）工芸品, 人工遺物 ● artefact とも綴る

12 □□ **date back** 	▶ go back さかのぼる 〈to ある時代に〉 ● date back a decade（10年さかのぼる）
13 □□ **impurity** [ɪmpjúərəti]	**名** 不純物 **形** impure ● free of impurities（不純物を含まない）
14 □□ **brittle** [brítl]	▶ fragile, breakable **形** もろい, 砕けやすい
15 □□ **exquisite** [ɪkskwízɪt]	▶ elegant, graceful **形** 精緻な, 優美な
16 □□ **craftsmanship** [krǽftsmənʃìp]	▶ artistry, workmanship **名** 職人技, 技巧 **名** craftsman
17 □□ **resourcefulness** [rɪsɔ́ːrsfələs]	▶ ingenuity **名** 臨機応変の才があること, 才覚に富むこと **形** resourceful
□□ **ore** [ɔːr]	**名** 鉱石 ● iron ore（鉄鉱石）
□□ **originate** [ərídʒənèɪt] ❶	▶ arise, derive, spring **動** 生じる, 起こる 〈from ～から, in ～において〉 **名** origin（起源）
□□ **earthenware** [ə́ːrθənwèər]	**名** 土器

The Presidency of Andrew Johnson

This passage is a look at the many problems of President Andrew Johnson during his time in office in the late 1860s.

1   Following the ¹**assassination** of Abraham Lincoln in 1865, Andrew Johnson ²**assumed** the office of president, but he was, most historians agree, ³**woefully** ⁴**unqualified** for the role. Optimism that Lincoln's ⁵**successor** would close the terrible ⁶**rift** created by four years of the Civil
5   War quickly faded as what were perceived as ⁷**rigid** policies, ⁸**incompetence**, and racism extended the period of ⁹**strife** that ¹⁰**engulfed** the nation.

Most notably, Johnson's ¹¹**administration** ¹²**obstructed** desperately needed reforms, such as redistribution of land to former slaves, and
10   refused to condemn or ¹³**abolish** racist laws in Southern states called "Black Codes" that, despite the end of slavery, severely limited the freedom and economic prospects of African Americans. Johnson's ¹⁴**abandonment** of former slaves and general incompetence caused him to lose the trust of powerful men in Congress.

15   A power struggle ¹⁵**ensued** in which Congress attempted to ¹⁶**strip** Johnson **of** various powers, and he was ¹⁷**impeached**, but remained in office by only a single vote. Many historians believe that had Johnson abolished the Black Codes and supported the meaningful reforms that many were proposing, African Americans may not have had to face so
20   much of the discrimination and ¹⁸**grinding** poverty that ¹⁹**afflicted** American society at the time.   🏴󠁧󠁢󠁥󠁮󠁧󠁿 (198 words)

アンドリュー・ジョンソン政権時代

この文章は，1860 年代後半のアンドリュー・ジョンソン大統領の任期中の数多くの問題を示している。

　1865 年のエイブラハム・リンカーンの [1]暗殺を受けて，アンドリュー・ジョンソンが大統領 [2]に就任したが，彼はほとんどの歴史家が同意するように，その役職には [3]痛ましいほどに [4]資質を欠いていた。南北戦争の 4 年間が生み出したひどい [6]亀裂を，リンカーンの [5]後継者が埋めてくれるだろうという楽観論は，[7]柔軟性に欠ける政策，[8]無能力，それに人種差別として認識されるものが国 [10]を飲み込んだ [9]争いの時期を長引かせるにつれて，急速に色あせていった。

　最も顕著だったのは，ジョンソン [11]政権は，例えば解放奴隷たちに土地を再分配するなどの切実に必要な改革 [12]を妨げ，奴隷制の終結にもかかわらず，アフリカ系アメリカ人の自由と経済的な見通しを厳しく制限する「黒人取締法」と呼ばれた南部諸州の人種差別的な法律を非難したり，[13]廃止したりすることを拒否したことである。ジョンソンが解放奴隷を [14]見捨てたことや全体的な無能の結果，彼は議会で有力者たちの信頼を失った。

　[15]続いて権力闘争が起こり，議会はジョンソンからさまざまな権限 [16]を剥奪しようと試み，彼は [17]弾劾されたが，一票の僅差で大統領職にとどまった。多くの歴史家たちは，もしジョンソンが黒人取締法を廃止し，多くが提案していた意味のある改革を支持していたなら，アフリカ系アメリカ人たちは当時アメリカ社会 [19]を悩ませていた，これほどまでの差別や [18]過酷な貧困に直面しなくて済んだだろうと信じている。

グラインドとミル

形容詞 grinding は動詞 grind（を粉にひく）から派生した語。穀物や豆をひく手作業が延々と続くことから名詞 grind に「退屈で骨の折れる仕事」という意味が生じたように，grinding には，苦しいことがいつまでも終わらないというニュアンスがある。動詞 grind には grind down 〜（〜をじわじわと苦しめる）という句動詞もある。同じ「粉にひく」でも，「コーヒーミル」や「ペッパーミル」の mill にそうしたネガティブな意味合いはない。句動詞 mill around [about] は「（大勢の人が）うろうろ動き回る」という意味で，例えばコーヒーミルの中でたくさんの豆が不規則に跳ねている様子をイメージすると良い。

The Presidency of Andrew Johnson

1 ☐☐
assassination
[əsæsınéıʃən]

▶ the murder of an important person usually for political reasons
名 暗殺　**動** assassinate　**名** assassin（暗殺者）

2 ☐☐
assume
[əsjúːm]

▶ accept, take on
動（責任のある地位）に就く，を引き受ける
名 assumption　● assume office（就任する）

3 ☐☐
woefully
[wóufəli]

▶ deplorably, miserably, pitifully
副 嘆かわしいほど，悲痛なほど
名 woe（悲痛）　**形** woeful

4 ☐☐
unqualified
[ʌnkwá(ː)lıfàıd]

形 適性［資質］を欠いて〈for ～に必要な〉
⇔ qualified

5 ☐☐
successor
[səksésər]

▶ heir
名 後継者，後任
動 succeed　**名** succession　**⇔** predecessor

6 ☐☐
rift
[rıft]

▶ breach, division, split
名 亀裂，（友好関係の）ひび
● 「（岩などの）裂け目」が本義

7 ☐☐
rigid
[rídʒıd] ❶

▶ strict, inflexible
形 厳格な，融通の利かない
名 rigidity　**⇔** flexible

8 ☐☐
incompetence
[ınká(ː)mpətəns]

▶ inability, incapacity, ineptitude
名 無能，不適格
形 incompetent　**⇔** competence

9 ☐☐
strife
[straıf]

▶ conflict, discord
名 争い，不和
● civil strife（内乱）

10 ☐☐
engulf
[ıngʌ́lf]

▶ overwhelm, swallow up
動 を飲み込む，を覆い尽くす

11 ☐☐
administration
[ədmìnıstréıʃən]

▶ government
名 政権，政府

12 ☐☐ **obstruct** [əbstrΛkt]	▶ hinder, impede, hold back 動 を妨げる，を妨害する 名 obstruction　形 obstructive
13 ☐☐ **abolish** [əbá(:)lɪʃ]	▶ do away with 動 （法律・制度など）を廃止する 名 abolition　● abolish slavery（奴隷制を廃止する）
14 ☐☐ **abandonment** [əbǽndənmənt]	▶ renunciation, relinquishment 名 見捨てること，放棄 動 abandon
15 ☐☐ **ensue** [ɪnsjúː]	▶ follow, result 動 続いて起こる，結果として起こる 形 ensuing
16 ☐☐ **strip _A_ of _B_**	▶ deprive _A_ of _B_, take away _B_ from _A_ A から B を剥奪［没収］する
17 ☐☐ **impeach** [ɪmpíːtʃ]	▶ accuse, charge, indict 動 を弾劾する，を告発する 名 impeachment
18 ☐☐ **grinding** [gráɪndɪŋ]	▶ harsh 形 過酷な，ひどい
19 ☐☐ **afflict** [əflíkt]	▶ torment, plague, torture 動 を苦しめる，を悩ます 名 affliction
☐☐ **reconcile** [rékənsàɪl] ●	▶ reunite 動 を和解させる〈with ～と〉，和解する 名 reconciliation　形 reconcilable
☐☐ **suffrage** [sΛfrɪdʒ]	▶ the right to vote in elections 名 選挙権，参政権 ● deny suffrage to Blacks（黒人に選挙権を与えない）
☐☐ **supremacy** [supréməsi]	名 優越，優位 形 supreme　名 supremacist（優越論者） ● white supremacy（白人至上主義）

Looking at Neanderthals in a New Light

The discovery of a skeleton in Spain has shown that Neanderthals ate plants as well as meat, and may even have used plants for medicine.

1   For most people, the word Neanderthal ¹**conjures up** images of a ²**clumsy** ³**brute** who could not compete with our more ⁴**versatile** human ancestors. Scientists, too, have been guilty of reinforcing our false ⁵**perceptions**. The Neanderthal was said to be strictly ⁶**carnivorous**, for
5   example, while humans could ⁷**draw on** a variety of food sources. One wonders if this ⁸**smear** campaign was inspired by modern-day human ⁹**arrogance** and ¹⁰**self-interest**.

Recent findings ¹¹**debunk** such concepts. A recent study of 50,000-year-old Neanderthal skeletal remains in Spain disclosed some
10   surprising discoveries about our ancient cousin. A chemical analysis of the teeth, for example, showed ¹²**traces** of ¹³**starch** and ¹⁴**carbohydrates**, providing clear evidence that at least some Neanderthals ate a variety of plants.

Perhaps the most interesting finding was that the Neanderthals also
15   consumed chamomile and yarrow, plants that offer few nutrients. Archaeologist Karen Hardy believes that since the Neanderthals would have found the plants bitter, they were likely selected for reasons other than taste. According to Hardy, the plants may have been used as early ¹⁵**pharmaceuticals** to treat a variety of physical ¹⁶**ailments**. People still
20   use them for stress and ¹⁷**digestive** ¹⁸**disorders** to this day.

These findings paint a picture that is ¹⁹**incongruous** with earlier stereotypes. Perhaps a fresh perception of the Neanderthal is long ²⁰**overdue**.   ▤ (211 words)

ℓ.15 chamomile：カモミール。camomile とも言う。
ℓ.15 yarrow：ノコギリソウ。

ネアンデルタール人を考え直す

スペインでの骸骨の発見は，ネアンデルタール人が植物および肉を食べ，植物を薬として利用した可能性さえも示している。

　大半の人にとって，ネアンデルタール人という言葉はもっと [4]いろいろなことができる私たちヒトの祖先とは比較にならない，[2]不器用な [3]獣のイメージ [1]を想像させる。科学者たちにも私たちの誤った [5]認識を助長してきた責任がある。例えば，ヒトはいろいろな食料源 [7]を利用できたが，ネアンデルタール人は完全に [6]肉食性だったとされていた。こうした組織的 [8]中傷は現代人の [9]傲慢と [10]利己主義によって引き起こされたのだろうか。

　最近の発見はそういった考え [11]の誤りを暴いている。スペインの５万年前のネアンデルタール人の骸骨に関する最近の研究から，私たちの古代の近縁種についていくつかの驚くべき発見が明らかにされた。例えば，歯の化学的分析から [13]でんぷんや [14]炭水化物の [12]痕跡が検出され，少なくとも一部のネアンデルタール人はさまざまな植物を食べていたという明白な証拠が出た。

　おそらく最も興味深い発見は，ネアンデルタール人がほとんど栄養分を含まない植物であるカモミールやノコギリソウも食べていたことだった。考古学者のカレン・ハーディは，ネアンデルタール人はこれらの植物を苦いと知っていただろうから，それらは味以外の目的で選ばれたようだと考える。ハーディによれば，これらの植物はさまざまな身体の [16]病気を治療するために，初期の [15]薬として利用されていたかもしれない。人間は今でもそれらをストレスや [17]消化 [18]不良に用いている。

　これらの発見が表す実態は，従来の固定観念とは [19]矛盾する。おそらく，ネアンデルタール人についての新たな認識が [20]あってしかるべきなのかもしれない。

---

smear

smear campaign（中傷キャンペーン）は，嘘やでっち上げを流布させて相手にダメージを与える戦略を言う。相手のマイナス面を強調する negative campaigning（ネガティブキャンペーン）の一種だが，意図的に虚偽の情報を流す点でいっそう悪質だと言える。smear campaign が最もよく見られるのは選挙戦で，特に米国の選挙ではおなじみである。
この英文では，ネアンデルタール人は肉食性だったという誤った情報が現生人類との差異を強調するために用いられ，ネアンデルタール人の獣的なイメージを定着させる結果となった，という文脈で smear campaign という表現が用いられている。

Looking at Neanderthals in a New Light

1 ☐☐ **conjure up 〜**	▶ imagine, visualize 〜を思い浮かべる，〜を想像する
2 ☐☐ **clumsy** [klʌ́mzi]	▶ awkward 形 不器用な，ぎこちない
3 ☐☐ **brute** [bru:t]	▶ beast, animal 名 (人間に対する) 獣，動物
4 ☐☐ **versatile** [və́:rsəṭəl]	▶ all-around, resourceful, flexible 形 多才な，何でもできる 名 versatility
5 ☐☐ **perception** [pərsépʃən]	▶ conception, idea, understanding, recognition 名 認識，見方 動 perceive (を知覚する，を認識する)
6 ☐☐ **carnivorous** [kɑːrnívərəs]	▶ meat-eating, predatory 形 肉食性の 名 carnivore (肉食動物) 🔄 herbivorous
7 ☐☐ **draw on 〜**	▶ rely on, employ, avail *oneself* of (資源など) を利用する，〜に頼る
8 ☐☐ **smear** [smɪər]	▶ slander, slur, defamation, calumny 名 中傷，誹謗，名誉毀損 動 を汚す ● 動詞 smear *one's* good name は「(人の) 名を汚す」
9 ☐☐ **arrogance** [ǽrəgəns]	▶ haughtiness, egoism, pompousness 名 傲慢，尊大 形 arrogant
10 ☐☐ **self-interest** [sèlfíntərəst]	▶ egocentrism, selfishness, self-seeking 名 利己主義，利己心 形 self-interested
11 ☐☐ **debunk** [dìːbʌ́ŋk]	▶ disprove, negate, discredit 動 の誤りを暴く

12 ☐☐ **trace** [treɪs]	▶ vestige, mark, indication **名** 痕跡，形跡
13 ☐☐ **starch** [stɑːrtʃ]	**名** でんぷん **形** starchy
14 ☐☐ **carbohydrate** [kὰːrbouháɪdreɪt]	**名** 炭水化物 ● carbo-（炭素）＋ hydrate（水化物）
15 ☐☐ **pharmaceutical** [fὰːrməsúːṭɪkəl]	**名**（通例 -s）薬剤　**形** 製薬の **名** pharmacist（薬剤師） ● pharmaceutical company（製薬会社）
16 ☐☐ **ailment** [éɪlmənt]	▶ disease, illness, disorder, malady **名**（軽いまたは慢性の）病気 **動** ail（患う）
17 ☐☐ **digestive** [daɪdʒéstɪv]	▶ alimentary **形** 消化の **名** digestion（消化）
18 ☐☐ **disorder** [dɪsɔ́ːrdər]	▶ malady, ailment, disease, condition **名**（心身の）不調，疾患 ● dis-（無，非）＋ order（正常な状態）
19 ☐☐ **incongruous** [ɪnká(ː)ŋgruəs]	▶ incompatible, conflicting, discordant **形** 一致しない，つじつまが合わない〈with ～と〉 **名** incongruity（不一致，不調和）
20 ☐☐ **overdue** [òuvərdjúː]	▶ that should have happened or been done before now **形** 延び延びになった，支払期限を過ぎた

The Origins of the Summer Olympics

This passage is about the ancient Olympics in Greece and discusses preparations for the Games as well as early attempts at cheating.

1　　The ¹**venue** for the first Olympic Games, held in 776 BC, was Olympia, Greece, an ²**idyllic** rural setting with a stadium, three sacred temples, and only one inn for guests. The quiet village would become a ³**boisterous** ⁴**hub** of ancient sports and entertainment every four years.

5　⁵**Peripheral** ⁶**distractions** included artistic and literary events, as well as more ⁷**frivolous** entertainments such as fortune-telling and fire-eating displays.

　　Athletes showed up at the nearby city of Elis one month before the Games. They ⁸**underwent** a ⁹**stringent** training ¹⁰**regimen** and weaker

10　athletic candidates, who **were** not ¹¹**cut out for** Olympic competitions, would be ¹²**weeded out**. Before entering the stadium for the Games, athletes went to a temple to ¹³**swear an oath** they would ¹⁴**abide by** Game rules. Athletes would also ¹⁵**invoke** the gods, ¹⁶**pleading for** power to ¹⁷**vanquish** their opponents.

15　Olympic officials worried that athletes would turn elsewhere in their efforts to win. It was said that some athletes used powerful ¹⁸**potions** to enhance their performance. Others placed ¹⁹**curses** on their opponents. ²⁰**Corruption** entered the Games in other forms from the 4th century BC. Eupolus, a boxer, was caught ²¹**bribing** his opponents, who had been

20　asked to ²²**throw their matches**. Although the early Olympic Games are considered to have been clean and fair overall, wrongdoing has a fairly long history.

(216 words)

夏季オリンピックの起源

この文章はギリシャの古代オリンピックについてのもので，大会の準備だけでなく初期の不正行為の試みについても論じている。

　紀元前 776 年に開かれた最初のオリンピック競技会の ¹開催地はギリシャのオリンピアだった。²牧歌的な農村地で，競技場が 1 つと神聖な神殿が 3 つあり，観客が泊まる宿は 1 軒しかなかった。4 年に 1 度，この静かな村が古代のスポーツと娯楽の ³騒々しい ⁴拠点となった。⁵周辺の ⁶娯楽には，芸術や文学の催しから占いや火を口に入れる実演といったもっと ⁷気楽な余興もあった。

　選手たちは競技の 1 カ月前に近隣のエリスの町にやって来た。彼らは ⁹厳しいトレーニング ¹⁰指導 ⁸を受け，オリンピックの競争 ¹¹に向いていない弱い選手候補者は ¹²除外されることになっていた。試合のために競技場に入場する前に選手たちは神殿に行き，オリンピックの規則 ¹⁴に従うこと ¹³を誓った。また，対戦相手 ¹⁷を打ち破る力 ¹⁶を願い，神々 ¹⁵に加護を祈った。

　オリンピックの運営者たちは選手たちが勝つための努力を他のところへ向けてしまうことを心配した。身体能力を高めるために強壮 ¹⁸剤を使う選手もいたと言われていた。対戦相手に ¹⁹呪いをかける選手もいた。紀元前 4 世紀から別の形で ²⁰不正行為が競技に入ってきた。ボクシング選手のユーポラスは相手選手たちを ²²試合にわざと負けるよう ²¹買収しているところを見つかった。古代オリンピック競技会は全般的に正々堂々とした公正なものであったと考えられているが，不正行為にはかなり長い歴史があるのだ。

The Origins of the Summer Olympics

1 ☐☐ **venue** [vénju:]	▶ a place for an organized meeting, concert, etc. 名 開催地 〈for 試合・会合などの〉
2 ☐☐ **idyllic** [aɪdílɪk]	▶ beautiful and peaceful with no problems 形 牧歌的な 名 idyll (牧歌, 田園詩)
3 ☐☐ **boisterous** [bɔ́ɪstərəs]	▶ lively, exuberant, animated, spirited 形 陽気で騒がしい ⇔ restrained (抑制した)
4 ☐☐ **hub** [hʌb]	▶ center, core, focus, heart 名 拠点, (活動の) 中心地
5 ☐☐ **peripheral** [pərífərəl]	▶ surrounding, outlying 形 周囲の, 末梢的な
6 ☐☐ **distraction** [dɪstrǽkʃən]	▶ entertainment, recreation, amusement 名 娯楽, 気晴らし 動 distract ((人) の退屈を紛らす, を楽しませる)
7 ☐☐ **frivolous** [frívələs]	▶ trivial, trifling 形 取るに足らない, くだらない
8 ☐☐ **undergo** [ʌndərgóu] ❶	▶ experience, go through 動 (試練・変化) を経験する
9 ☐☐ **stringent** [stríndʒənt]	▶ harsh, severe, rigorous 形 厳しい, 過酷な
10 ☐☐ **regimen** [rédʒɪmən]	▶ a special plan of exercise intended to improve your strength or skills 名 運動療法, 健康増進法
11 ☐☐ **be cut out for ~**	▶ be fitted for, be suited to ~に適している

12 ☐☐ **weed out ~**	▶ filter out, separate out, eliminate （有害なもの）を排除する，〜を取り除く ● 動詞 weed は「雑草を取り除く」という意味
13 ☐☐ **swear an oath**	誓いを立てる，宣誓する
14 ☐☐ **abide by ~**	▶ comply with, conform to, follow, obey （規則・法律など）に従う，〜を守る
15 ☐☐ **invoke** [ɪnvóuk]	▶ pray to **動** （神など）に加護を祈る **名** invocation（神への祈願，祈り）
16 ☐☐ **plead for ~**	▶ beg, beseech, implore, entreat 〜を懇願する，〜を嘆願する
17 ☐☐ **vanquish** [væŋkwɪʃ]	▶ defeat, conquer **動** を破る，に勝つ
18 ☐☐ **potion** [póuʃən]	▶ a drink with magical powers **名** （魔力のある）飲み薬，（毒薬などの）1 服
19 ☐☐ **curse** [kəːrs]	▶ malediction, imprecation **名** 呪い ● put [place] a curse on ~（（人）に呪いをかける）
20 ☐☐ **corruption** [kərʌ́pʃən]	▶ depravity, degeneracy, decadence **名** 堕落，汚職
21 ☐☐ **bribe** [braɪb]	▶ buy off, pay off, suborn, square **動** を買収する，に賄賂を送る　**名** 賄賂 **名** bribery（贈賄，収賄）
22 ☐☐ **throw a match**	▶ deliberately lose 試合にわざと負ける

New Human Species Found

When Richard Leakey discovered the skull of what he believed was a relative of early humans, many experts doubted him. It has now been confirmed as a new species.

1　　A ¹**skull** of an early ²**hominid** was discovered by anthropologist Richard Leakey, the ³**premier** ⁴**authority** in early human evolution, in Kenya in 1972. The skull was determined to be almost two million years old, and had ⁵**physiological** differences from ⁶**Homo erectus**, our human
5 ⁷**forerunner**, which lived at the same time and in the same area. The ⁸**specimen** showed a larger brain casing and a flatter face than other known hominids, leading Leakey to believe this was a new human species. However, the skull did not include a jaw, which was ⁹**integral** to ¹⁰**verify** if it was indeed a new species and not merely an ¹¹**aberrant** Homo
10 erectus. Many anthropologists voiced skepticism of Leakey's claim, and the skull's connotation remained ¹²**contentious** for several decades. Leakey's wife even admitted that the skull was an ¹³**enigma**.

　　New fossils were discovered in 2007 and 2009 that confirmed Leakey's earlier assessment, including an ¹⁴**intact** skull, complete with a
15 lower jaw. The new findings are ¹⁵**unambiguous** and ¹⁶**allay** the concerns of skeptics, who have been ¹⁷**swayed** by the fossil evidence. The flat face was accepted as a reality based on the new fossils. Anthropologists have now ¹⁸**reached a consensus** that at least one, and perhaps even more, human species lived near each other in Kenya some two million years ago.

（214 words）

ℓ.7　leading Leakey to believe ...：「そしてそのことがリーキーに…だと考えさせた」という分詞
　　　構文。which led Leakey to believe ... と言い換えられる。

新人類発見

リチャード・リーキーが初期人類の近縁種と彼が考える頭蓋骨を発見したとき, 多くの専門家は彼を疑った。現在ではそれは新種であることが確認されている。

　古人類進化に関する³第一の⁴権威である人類学者リチャード・リーキーは, 初期の²ヒト科の¹頭蓋骨を 1972 年にケニアで発見した。この頭蓋骨はほぼ 200 万年前のものと断定され, 同時期に同じ地域に生存した我々現生人類の⁷祖先である⁶ホモエレクトゥスとは⁵生理学的に異なる点があった。その⁸標本は既知のヒト科より脳頭蓋が大きく, 顔の凹凸が少なかったことから, リーキーは新種の人類であると考えた。しかし, それが本当に新種であり, ただのホモエレクトゥスの¹¹異常な個体ではないと¹⁰立証するために⁹不可欠な部分である顎がその頭蓋骨には欠けていた。多くの人類学者がリーキーの主張に懐疑的な態度を表明し, 数十年間依然としてその頭蓋骨の意味することについて¹²議論の的となっていた。リーキーの妻でさえ, この頭蓋骨は¹³謎だと認めた。

　2007 年と 2009 年に発見された新たな化石は下顎までそろった¹⁴完全な頭蓋骨を含み, 以前のリーキーの判断を裏づけた。新たな発見には¹⁵疑いの余地はなく, 化石の証拠に¹⁷振り回されてきた懐疑論者たちの懸念¹⁶を払拭する。平らな顔は新たな化石に基づく現実として受け入れられた。今日人類学者は, およそ 200 万年前にケニアには少なくとも 1 種, おそらく 2 種以上の人類が互いに近くで生きていたということで¹⁸意見が一致している。

人類と学名

Homo erectus (ホモエレクトゥス) はラテン語で upright man (直立した人) という意味で, 2 本足で直立して歩いていたことが判明している最古の人類の祖先である。英語の erect はこのラテン語 erectus が語源になっている。現生人類の学名は Homo sapiens (ホモサピエンス) だが, これはラテン語で wise man (知恵のある人) の意味である。sapiens は sapience という英語になっており, 文語で「知恵」の意味。形容詞 sapient (知恵のある, 賢い) という語もある。

New Human Species Found

1 ☐☐ **skull** [skʌl]	▶ cranium 名 頭蓋骨，頭骨
2 ☐☐ **hominid** [há(ː)mənɪd]	▶ Hominidae 名 ヒト科の動物 ● homin-（人）+-id（～科の）
3 ☐☐ **premier** [prɪmíər]	▶ leading, outstanding, foremost, principal 形 最高の，一流の，主要な
4 ☐☐ **authority** [əːθɔ́ːrəṭi] ❶	▶ expert, specialist, pundit 名 権威者，大家 形 authoritative（権威のある，信頼できる）
5 ☐☐ **physiological** [fɪ̀ziəlá(ː)dʒɪkəl]	形 生理学的な，生理学上の 名 physiology（生理学，生理機能） ● physio-（身体の）+ -logy（学問）
6 ☐☐ **Homo erectus**	ホモエレクトゥス，原人類 ● homo（人）+ erect（直立した）
7 ☐☐ **forerunner** [fɔ́ːrrʌ̀nər]	▶ ancestor, antecedents, forefather, forebear, predecessor 名 先祖，前触れ
8 ☐☐ **specimen** [spésəmɪn]	▶ sample 名 標本
9 ☐☐ **integral** [ínt̬ɪɡrəl] ❶	▶ essential, vital, necessary, requisite 形 不可欠な，必須の
10 ☐☐ **verify** [vérɪfàɪ]	▶ corroborate, substantiate, prove 動 を実証する，を検証する 名 verification
11 ☐☐ **aberrant** [æbérənt]	▶ anomalous, irregular, atypical 形 （生物学的・医学的に）異常な 名 aberration（（生物学的・医学的な）異常（型））

12 ☐☐ **contentious** [kənténʃəs]	▶ controversial, debatable, disputable 形 議論を呼ぶ，異論の余地がある 動 contend（論争する） 名 contention（論争）
13 ☐☐ **enigma** [ɪnígmə]	▶ mystery, puzzle 名 謎，不可解なもの
14 ☐☐ **intact** [ɪnt&kt] ❶	▶ unimpaired, undamaged, unbroken, whole, complete 形 完全な，損なわれていない
15 ☐☐ **unambiguous** [ʌnæmbígjuəs]	▶ clear, evident, plain, unmistakable, indisputable 形 曖昧でない，解釈が1つしかない
16 ☐☐ **allay** [əléɪ]	▶ alleviate, diminish, soothe, assuage, reduce 動 (疑念など)を鎮める，を和らげる
17 ☐☐ **sway** [sweɪ]	▶ influence, affect 動 を動揺させる，(人・意見など)に影響を与える ● be swayed by ~（～に心を揺さぶられる）
18 ☐☐ **reach a consensus**	意見が一致する
☐☐ **cranium** [kréɪniəm]	名 頭蓋骨
☐☐ **skeleton** [skélɪtən]	▶ (structure of) bones 名 骨格，骸骨
☐☐ **Homo sapiens**	▶ the species of human that exists now ホモサピエンス ● homo（人）＋sapiens（知恵のある）

文化・歴史 **8**

Lost Civilization of the Sahara

Ancient castles discovered in Libya are believed to be evidence that the indigenous Garamantes civilization that built them was surprisingly advanced.

1   ¹**Poring over** satellite images of ²**barren** desert in Libya, archaeologists discovered a ³**cluster** of ancient castles located about 1,000 kilometers south of Tripoli. The ⁴**fortresses**, with their detailed, straight-line construction, could easily be mistaken for Roman ⁵**outposts**, but they
5   were situated beyond the frontiers of that era's superpower. David Mattingly from England's University of Leicester, who led a team of researchers to the sites, believes they were built by a powerful native African kingdom. Using samples of ⁶**pottery**, they ⁷**ascertained** the fortresses and surrounding villages were built by an ⁸**elusive** people
10   known as the Garamantes, who were ⁹**indigenous** to Libya.

Mattingly was astonished to see how well the sites were preserved. The architectural remains and artifacts are a ¹⁰**testament** to the high level of civilization the Garamantes achieved, which included ¹¹**metallurgy**, very high-quality ¹²**textiles**, and a writing system, indicating an organized,
15   state-level society. The site also showed that the residents had an advanced ¹³**irrigation** system that allowed them to cultivate a variety of crops. The water for the irrigation system came from underground ¹⁴**channels**. Mattingly suspects the ¹⁵**demise** of the civilization was brought on by a shortage of water, a ¹⁶**prerequisite** for any civilization. Once underground
20   ¹⁷**reservoirs** were ¹⁸**tapped** and used up, maintaining ¹⁹**cohesive** communities was no longer ²⁰**feasible**.   🏴󠁧󠁢󠁥󠁮󠁧󠁿 (209 words)

失われたサハラの文明

リビアで発見された古代の城は，それを建造した先住民族のガラマンテス文明が驚くほど先進的であった証拠だと信じられている。

　リビアの[2]不毛な砂漠の衛星画像[1]を詳細に調べ，考古学者たちはトリポリの約1,000キロ南の地点に古代の城郭[3]群を発見した。精密な直線の建築様式を備えた[4]要塞は，ローマ帝国の[5]前哨地に間違えられやすいが，当時の超大国の国境を越えた先に位置していた。研究班を率いて現地を訪れた英国レスター大学のデイビッド・マッティングリーは，それらは有力なアフリカ原住民の王国によって建造されたと考える。[6]陶器類の標本を使って，彼らはその要塞と周辺の村落は，リビア地域[9]土着のガラマンテス人として知られる[8]謎に包まれた民族によって造られたこと[7]を突き止めた。

　マッティングリーは遺跡の保存状態の良さを目の当たりにして驚いた。建築遺構や工芸品はガラマンテス人が持っていた高度な文明を[10]証明するものであり，[11]冶金術，非常に質の良い[12]織物，書記体系などは組織立った国家水準の共同体であることを示している。その遺跡からは居住者たちが高度な[13]灌漑システムを使ってさまざまな穀物を栽培できたこともわかった。灌漑用の水は地下[14]水路から取られていた。マッティングリーはこの文明の[15]終焉は，どんな文明にも[16]必須である水の不足によってもたらされたと考えている。地下[17]貯水池から水[18]を取り出しそれが使い果たされると，共同体の[19]結束を維持することはもはや不[20]可能となったのである。

Lost Civilization of the Sahara

1 ☐☐ **pore over 〜** 	▶ scrutinize, peruse, examine, scan, go over 〜を詳細に調べる, 〜をじっくり見る
2 ☐☐ **barren** [bǽrən]	▶ infertile, sterile, dry, unproductive 形 (土地が) 不毛な, 作物が育たない ⇔ fertile (肥沃な)
3 ☐☐ **cluster** [klʌ́stər]	▶ bunch, bundle, clump 名 集まり, 集団
4 ☐☐ **fortress** [fɔ́:rtrəs]	▶ fort, redoubt, bastion 名 要塞
5 ☐☐ **outpost** [áutpòust]	▶ borderland, frontier, march(land), outland 名 前哨地, 辺境の植民地
6 ☐☐ **pottery** [pá(:)ṭəri]	▶ earthenware, porcelain, china, crockery, ceramics 名 陶器類, 陶磁器類
7 ☐☐ **ascertain** [æ̀sərtéɪn] ❶	▶ discover, establish, determine, confirm, find out 動 を突き止める, を確認する
8 ☐☐ **elusive** [ɪlú:sɪv]	▶ inscrutable, unidentifiable, mysterious 形 理解しにくい, 捕まえにくい 動 elude (を逃れる) 名 elusion (回避)
9 ☐☐ **indigenous** [ɪndídʒənəs]	▶ native, aboriginal, domestic, original 形 土着の, 原産の 〈to 〜に〉 名 indigene (先住民, 固有種)
10 ☐☐ **testament** [téstəmənt]	▶ testimony, evidence, attestation 名 証明するもの, 証拠 〈to 〜の [を]〉
11 ☐☐ **metallurgy** [méṭəlɜ̀:rdʒi]	名 冶金 (術), 金属加工 (の技術) 形 metallurgical ● metal (金属) +-urgy (操作 [生産] 技術)

12 ☐☐ **textile** [tékstaɪl]	▶ woven fabric, cloth 名 織物，布地
13 ☐☐ **irrigation** [ìrɪɡéɪʃən]	名 灌漑，（農業のために）水を引くこと 動 irrigate（（土地）を灌漑する，（作物）に水をやる）
14 ☐☐ **channel** [tʃǽnəl] ❶	▶ conduit, race, sluice, gutter 名 水路
15 ☐☐ **demise** [dɪmáɪz]	▶ end, termination, disintegration, collapse 名 終焉，消滅
16 ☐☐ **prerequisite** [priːrékwəzɪt]	▶ essential, necessity, must, requirement 名 欠くことのできないもの，必須条件，前提条件〈for 〜に［の］〉
17 ☐☐ **reservoir** [rézərvwàːr] ❶	▶ pool, pond, cistern 名 貯水池，貯水槽
18 ☐☐ **tap** [tæp]	▶ pump up, pump out, draw up 動（液体）を取り出す，を流す 名 栓，蛇口
19 ☐☐ **cohesive** [koʊhíːsɪv]	▶ united, solid, combined, banded, coherent 形 団結した，結合した 名 cohesion, coherence（団結，結合）
20 ☐☐ **feasible** [fíːzəbl]	▶ viable, possible, practicable, achievable 形 実現［実行］可能な

Celebrating Mexico's Cinco de Mayo — in America

Cinco de Mayo is a Mexican holiday celebrating a military victory, but it has become much more famous in the United States.

1　　On May 5, 1862, a ¹**ragtag** Mexican army defeated French forces ²**deployed** by France's Napoleon III at the Battle of Puebla. The victory inspired Mexican ³**troops** in their struggle to prevent France from ⁴**toppling** Mexico's ⁵**legitimate** government and ⁶**installing** a European

5　emperor. Though it suffered various defeats after the Battle of Puebla, Mexico eventually assured its ⁷**autonomy**, and the battle's date was ⁸**commemorated** by the festival of Cinco de Mayo, which means "the fifth of May."

　　Today, the festival is celebrated only ⁹**sporadically** in Mexico, but it

10　has millions of ¹⁰**adherents** among the United States' large Hispanic population. In fact, it is so well known in America that though the holiday ¹¹**has nothing to do with** official ¹²**proclamations** or constitutions, it is widely assumed to be Mexican Independence Day.

　　The American celebration has its roots in its Good Neighbor Policy of

15　the 1930s, when the government sought to ¹³**foster** closer relations with Mexico. It was meant to help bridge the two cultures. Cinco de Mayo has proven to be more than just ¹⁴**durable**. While at first ¹⁵**catering** primarily **to** Mexican American communities in ¹⁶**a handful of** cities, the celebrations have since ¹⁷**fanned out** to thousands of communities across

20　the US, even including areas with few Hispanics. It has recently become more commercialized, with ¹⁸**ubiquitous** ¹⁹**vendors** ²⁰**cashing in on** the ²¹**festivities**.　　　　　　　　　　　　　　■ (220 words)

ℓ.14　Good Neighbor Policy：善隣外交政策。Franklin D. Roosevelt 大統領が唱えた，中南米諸国との友好関係を目指す政策のこと。

アメリカでメキシコのシンコ・デ・マヨを祝う

シンコ・デ・マヨは軍の勝利を祝うメキシコの祝日だが，アメリカにおいてはるかに有名になった。

1862年5月5日，プエブラの会戦において，[1]寄せ集めのメキシコ軍がフランスのナポレオン三世によって[2]展開されたフランス軍を打ち負かした。その勝利は，フランスがメキシコの[5]正当な政権[4]を倒し，ヨーロッパ人の皇帝[6]を就任させようとするのを阻止するための戦いにおいて，メキシコ[3]軍を鼓舞した。プエブラの会戦の後，数々の敗北を喫したにもかかわらず，最終的にメキシコは[7]自治権を確実なものとし，戦いの日は「5月5日」を意味するシンコ・デ・マヨの祭りによって[8]記念された。

今日では，祭りはメキシコで[9]散発的に祝われているにすぎないが，アメリカの多くのラテン系アメリカ人住民たちの間で数百万もの[10]支持者を持つ。実際，その祭日はアメリカではとてもよく知られているので，正式な[12]宣言や憲法[11]とは何の関係もないにもかかわらず，メキシコの独立記念日だと広く考えられている。

アメリカにおける祝典は1930年代の善隣外交政策に端を発する。このころアメリカ政府はメキシコとより緊密な関係[13]を促進しようとしていた。祝典は2つの文化の橋渡しをすることを意図していた。シンコ・デ・マヨは単に[14]息の長い祭り以上のものであることがわかった。初めのうちは[16]一握りの都市で主としてメキシコ系アメリカ人コミュニティー[15]の要望に応えたものだったが，それ以来この祭典はラテン系アメリカ人がほとんどいない地域をも含めて全米数千の都市に[17]広まっている。最近では[21]祭り[20]に便乗して儲けよう[19]という商人が[18]至る所に現れ，商業的意味合いが強まっている。

最も有名な proclamation

proclamation は公式な「宣言」の意味で，この英文からは the proclamation of independence「独立宣言」という表現がまず連想される。1776年の米国の独立宣言は the Declaration of Independence と declaration が使われているが，一般的には proclamation を用いることも多い。歴史上最も有名な proclamation は，米国大統領リンカーンが1862年に布告した the Emancipation Proclamation「奴隷解放宣言」だろう。

Celebrating Mexico's Cinco de Mayo — in America

1 ☐☐ **ragtag** [rǽgtæg]	▶ scratch, pickup 形 (集団・組織が) 寄せ集めの
2 ☐☐ **deploy** [dɪplɔ́ɪ]	▶ station, position, place 動 (軍隊など) を展開する，を配置する 名 deployment
3 ☐☐ **troop** [tru:p]	▶ army, armed forces, soldiers 名 (通例 -s) 軍隊
4 ☐☐ **topple** [tá(:)pl]	▶ oust, overturn 動 (政府・権力者など) を倒す，をぐらつかせる
5 ☐☐ **legitimate** [lɪdʒítəmət] ❶	▶ legal, lawful, licit 形 正当な，合法的な ⇔ illegitimate, illegal, illicit (違法な)
6 ☐☐ **install** [ɪnstɔ́:l]	▶ instate, induct, inaugurate 動 を就任させる ⟨as ～として⟩ 名 installation
7 ☐☐ **autonomy** [ɔ:tá(:)nəmi]	▶ independence, sovereignty, self-government 名 自治 形 autonomous
8 ☐☐ **commemorate** [kəmémərèɪt]	▶ celebrate, honor 動 を記念する 名 commemoration
9 ☐☐ **sporadically** [spərǽdɪkəli]	▶ occasionally, intermittently, periodically 副 散発的に，時々 形 sporadic ⇔ frequently (頻繁に)
10 ☐☐ **adherent** [ədhíərənt]	▶ advocate, upholder, follower, believer 名 支持者，信奉者 ● 動詞 adhere to ～ で「～に固執する」の意味
11 ☐☐ **have nothing to do with ～**	～と何の関係もない ● have something to do with ～ (～と何らかの関係がある)

12 ☐☐ **proclamation** [prà(:)kləméɪʃən]	▶ declaration, statement, announcement **名** 宣言, 布告 **動** proclaim
13 ☐☐ **foster** [fá(:)stər]	▶ promote, advance, forward, encourage, nurture **動** を促進する, を育む
14 ☐☐ **durable** [djúərəbl]	▶ long-lasting, enduring **形** 永続性のある, 長持ちする **名** duration（持続期間）
15 ☐☐ **cater to ～**	▶ gratify, satisfy, fulfill, indulge ～の要求に応じる
16 ☐☐ **a handful of ～**	▶ a few of, a small amount [number] of 一握りの～, ごくわずかな～
17 ☐☐ **fan out**	▶ spread, diffuse, scatter （扇形に）広がる
18 ☐☐ **ubiquitous** [jubíkwətəs] ❶	▶ omnipresent, present everywhere **形** 至る所に存在する, どこにでもある［いる］ **名** ubiquity（遍在）
19 ☐☐ **vendor** [véndər]	▶ merchant, dealer, trader, seller, retailer **名** 商人, 売主 **動** vend
20 ☐☐ **cash in on ～**	▶ profit from, make money from, take advantage of, exploit ～に便乗する, ～で儲ける, ～を利用する
21 ☐☐ **festivity** [festívəti]	▶ celebration, festival, fete, jamboree **名** 祭り, 祭典 **形** festive

Viking Community Discovered in Germany

Historians are excited about the discovery of a large Viking settlement called Sliasthorp that was probably a military headquarters.

1   An 8th century Viking military ¹**settlement**, recently ²**unearthed** in Germany, is ³**causing a stir among** historians. From initial clues, lead ⁴**excavator** Andres Dobat from Aarhus University in Denmark, believes the site is the legendary Viking colony of Sliasthorp, first described by
5 royal ⁵**scribes** of the ⁶**eminent** Frankish king Charlemagne. The site includes 200 buildings, including an enormous 30-meter-long, 9-meter-wide longhouse.

The Viking settlement is in ⁷**proximity** to a ⁸**fortification** called the Danevirke, an ⁹**imposing** 30-kilometer-long defensive ¹⁰**earthwork**
10 ¹¹**erected** by Danes around AD 700. The earliest account of Sliasthorp describes it as a military headquarters for the region and a base used by Viking king Godfred. Godfred stayed in the ¹²**garrison** in order to repair the Danevirke, which was required to ¹³**thwart** the advancement of the Frankish empire. The settlement also ¹⁴**likely** ¹⁵**accommodated** laborers
15 who worked on the Danevirke.

The town was also located near the port of Hedeby, which served as a trading center during Viking times. Historians ¹⁶**infer** that Vikings controlled the ¹⁷**lucrative** international shipping trade that took place at Hedeby.

20   The settlement itself was not heavily fortified, but it was surrounded by ¹⁸**marshes** that would have ¹⁹**deterred** approaching enemies. In order to attack, they would have had to ²⁰**skirt around** the natural ²¹**buffer** and cross a narrow, heavily guarded strip of land.   🇬🇧 (214 words)

ドイツで発見されたバイキングの居住地

歴史家たちは，おそらく軍事上の中枢であったであろう，スリエストルプと呼ばれる大きなバイキングの集落の発見に興奮している。

　8世紀のバイキングの軍用 [1]集落が先ごろドイツで [2]発掘され，歴史家たち [3]の間で物議を醸している。[4]発掘責任者であるデンマークのオーフス大学のアンドレス・ドバットは，初期の手がかりからこの遺跡が伝説のバイキング居留地であるスリエストルプだと考えている。スリエストルプは [6]高名なフランク王カール大帝に仕えた王室 [5]写字生たちによって初めて記述されている。遺跡には 200 の建築物があり，奥行き 30 メートル，間口 9 メートルの巨大な共同住居もある。

　このバイキングの集落は，デーン人が西暦 700 年ごろに [11]建てた [9]壮大な全長 30 キロメートルの防衛 [10]土塁であるダーネビルケと呼ばれる [8]要塞の [7]近くにある。スリエストルプについての最も古い文書には，それがこの地方の軍事上の中枢で，バイキングの王ゴトフレドが利用した軍事基地だったという記述がある。フランク帝国の進出 [13]を阻むのに必要なダーネビルケを修復するために，ゴトフレドはその [12]要塞にとどまった。また，ダーネビルケで作業にあたった人夫たちも [14]おそらくこの集落に [15]宿泊した。

　その町はまた，バイキングの時代に交易の要衝の役目を果たしたヘーゼビュー港の近くに位置していた。歴史学者たちはバイキングがヘーゼビューで行われた [17]利益性の高い国際海運事業の実権を握っていた [16]と推測する。

　集落そのものは堅固に要塞化されていなかったが，敵が近づくの [19]を阻止したであろう [18]湿地に囲まれていた。攻撃するにはその自然の [21]盾 [20]を回避し，厳重に警備された狭い道を突破するしかなかっただろう。

バイキング

「バイキング」と聞くと，並んだ食事の中から好きなものを好きなだけとって食べる形式を思い浮かべるが，これは和製英語。英語では buffet meal, all-you-can-eat restaurant, smorgasbord などと言う。

この他，サラリーマン（英語では office worker），ノートパソコン（英語では laptop computer），フロント（英語では reception），クレーム（英語では complaint）が和製英語としてよく知られている。

Viking Community Discovered in Germany

1 ☐☐ **settlement** [sétlmənt]	▶ colony, outpost, community, habitation 名 集落，入植地 動 settle
2 ☐☐ **unearth** [ʌnə́ːrθ]	▶ dig up, excavate, uncover 動 を発掘する，を掘り出す
3 ☐☐ **cause a stir among ～**	～の間で物議を醸す，騒ぎになる ● stir は「物議，騒動」を意味する名詞
4 ☐☐ **excavator** [ékskəvèitər]	名 発掘者 動 excavate（を発掘する）　名 excavation（発掘）
5 ☐☐ **scribe** [skraɪb]	▶ transcriber, copyist 名 写字生，写本を書き写す人
6 ☐☐ **eminent** [émɪnənt]	▶ renowned, esteemed, notable, distinguished, illustrious 形 高名な，著名な
7 ☐☐ **proximity** [prɑ(ː)ksíməti]	▶ closeness, vicinity 名 近いこと〈to ～に〉，近接〈to ～への〉 ● in close proximity to ～（～のすぐ近くに）
8 ☐☐ **fortification** [fɔ̀ːrtəfɪkéɪʃən]	▶ rampart, bastion, fort, fortress 名 要塞，防壁 動 fortify（の防御を固める，を要塞化する）
9 ☐☐ **imposing** [ɪmpóuzɪŋ]	形 壮大な，堂々たる 動 impose（を強いる）
10 ☐☐ **earthwork** [ə́ːrθwə̀ːrk]	▶ mound, bulwark 名 （軍事的な防御のための）土塁
11 ☐☐ **erect** [ɪrékt]	▶ build, construct, put up 動 を建てる，を直立させる 名 erection（建設，直立）

12 ☐☐ **garrison** [gǽrɪsən]	▶ fortification, fort, stronghold 名（守備隊のいる）要塞，駐屯地
13 ☐☐ **thwart** [θwɔ:rt]	▶ frustrate, block, prevent 動（人・計画など）を阻止する，を妨害する
14 ☐☐ **likely** [láɪkli]	▶ probably, presumably 副 おそらく，たぶん
15 ☐☐ **accommodate** [əká(:)mədèɪt]	▶ lodge, put up 動 を宿泊させる，（人）を収容する
16 ☐☐ **infer** [ɪnfə́:r]	▶ deduce, reason, gather 動 と（根拠に基づいて）推論する 名 inference（推論）
17 ☐☐ **lucrative** [lú:krətɪv]	▶ profitable, moneymaking, remunerative 形 利益の上がる，儲かる ● lucrative business（儲かるビジネス）
18 ☐☐ **marsh** [mɑ:rʃ]	▶ swamp, morass 名 湿地，沼
19 ☐☐ **deter** [dɪtə́:r] ❶	▶ stop, prevent, discourage, dissuade 動 を阻止する，を抑止する 名 deterrent（（核兵器などの）戦争抑止力）
20 ☐☐ **skirt around ～**	▶ avoid, circumvent, evade ～を回避する
21 ☐☐ **buffer** [bʌ́fər]	▶ barrier, guard, shield, cushion 名 緩衝物 ● buffer zone（緩衝地帯）

The Forerunner of Stonehenge

An archaeological site discovered on an island in northern Britain is helping researchers to better understand the famous monument, Stonehenge.

1   Excavations on one of the Orkney Islands off the tip of northern Great Britain have unearthed an ¹**intriguing** ancient religious ²**complex**. This may have been the original model for Stonehenge and other ³**ritualistic** complexes located further south. ⁴**Radiocarbon dating** shows that the
5 complex, known as the Ness of Brodgar, was ⁵**occupied** in about 3200 BC. Though only 10 percent of the Ness complex has ⁶**as yet** emerged from the ground, historians estimate it included 100 buildings with a massive wall around the complex's ⁷**perimeter**. The huge stones of Stonehenge, ⁸**icons** of Great Britain's ⁹**Neolithic Age**, were not set down
10 on Salisbury Plain until about 2500 BC.

       Excavation leader Nick Card said he believes Orkney is one of the keys to understanding the development of Neolithic religion. While researchers have not yet ¹⁰**fleshed out** in detail what the rituals at Ness were like, archaeological evidence leads them to believe they ¹¹**set**
15 **precedents for** subsequent rituals at Stonehenge and elsewhere. Farmers from near and far are believed to have gathered at the Ness complex for ¹²**communal** rites to commemorate the dead and celebrate seasonal changes.

       Bones from ¹³**livestock** dated at about 2300 BC were found near the
20 ¹⁴**exquisitely** decorated central temple. The bones are ¹⁵**ostensibly** the remains of a ¹⁶**lavish** feast held at the time to ¹⁷**decommission** the temple. Rituals at Ness most likely either ¹⁸**wound down** or ¹⁹**ceased** after the feast.

(230 words)

ℓ.12　keys to understanding：この to は前置詞であるため，後ろには名詞・動名詞が続く。to 不定詞ではないので，key to do という言い方はしない。

ストーンヘンジのモデル

英国北部の島で発見された考古学的遺跡は，研究者たちが有名な遺跡であるストーンヘンジをより
よく理解するのに役立っている。

　グレートブリテン島北端の沖にあるオークニー諸島の1つの島の発掘調査で[1]興味
深い古代の宗教[2]建造物群が発掘された。これはずっと南にあるストーンヘンジやそ
の他の[3]儀式用建造物群の原型だったかもしれない。[4]放射性炭素年代測定法による
と，ネス・オブ・ブロッガーとして知られているその建造物群は紀元前3200年ごろ
に[5]使われていた。[6]今のところ，ネス建造物群の10％しか土から出ていないが，歴史
家たちは100の建物があり，その[7]周囲には巨大な壁があったと推定している。グレ
ートブリテン島の[9]新石器時代の[8]象徴であるストーンヘンジの巨石はおよそ紀元前
2500年までソールズベリー平原には設置されていなかった。

　発掘調査を率いるニック・カードは，オークニーは新石器時代の宗教の発展を理解
する上で重要な場所の1つだと言った。研究者たちはネスでの儀式がどのようなもの
だったかをまだ詳細に[10]具体化していないが，考古学的証拠によってその儀式がスト
ーンヘンジや他の場所でその後に行われた儀式[11]の先例になったと考えている。農夫
たちは近隣からも遠方からも，死者を追悼し季節の変化を祝う[12]共同体の儀式のため
にネスの建造物群に集ったと考えられている。

　およそ紀元前2300年のものとされる[13]家畜の骨が[14]非常に美しく装飾された中央
神殿の近くで見つかった。その骨は[15]見たところ，神殿[17]を閉鎖する際に行われた
[16]豪華な宴の残物である。ネスの儀式はその宴の後，[18]下火になったか，[19]途絶えて
しまった可能性が高い。

The Forerunner of Stonehenge

1 ☐☐ **intriguing** [ɪntríːgɪŋ]	▶ interesting, captivating, fascinating 形 興味をそそる，魅力的な 動 intrigue（の興味を引く）
2 ☐☐ **complex** [ká(:)mplèks]	▶ nexus, aggregation, combination 名 建築物の集合体，複合施設
3 ☐☐ **ritualistic** [rìtʃuəlístɪk]	▶ connected with religious ceremonies 形 儀式の 名 ritual, rite（儀式）　形 ritual（儀式の）
4 ☐☐ **radiocarbon dating**	放射性炭素年代測定（法） ● carbon dating とも言う
5 ☐☐ **occupy** [á(:)kjupàɪ] ❶	▶ employ, utilize 動 （場所）を使用する
6 ☐☐ **as yet**	▶ so far, thus far, up to now これまでのところ，今までに
7 ☐☐ **perimeter** [pərímətər]	▶ circumference, periphery 名 周囲，外周部
8 ☐☐ **icon** [áɪkɑ(:)n]	▶ symbol, token 名 象徴，肖像 形 iconic（象徴的な，肖像画の）
9 ☐☐ **Neolithic Age**	▶ the latter part of the Stone Age, the New Stone Age 新石器時代
10 ☐☐ **flesh out ～**	▶ expand on, elaborate on ～を具体的に説明する，～を肉付けする
11 ☐☐ **set a precedent for ～**	～の先例となる

12 ☐☐ **communal** [kəmjúːnəl]	▶ relating to all the people living in a particular community 形 共同体の，コミュニティーの
13 ☐☐ **livestock** [láɪvstɑ̀(ː)k] ❶	▶ animals that are kept on a farm 名 家畜 ● 集合名詞
14 ☐☐ **exquisitely** [ɪkskwízɪtli]	▶ elegantly, finely, excellently, beautifully 副 非常に美しく，精巧に
15 ☐☐ **ostensibly** [ɑ(ː)sténsəbli]	▶ supposedly, seemingly, apparently 副 見た目では，表面上は 形 ostensible
16 ☐☐ **lavish** [lǽvɪʃ]	▶ luxurious, sumptuous, opulent, splendid 形 豪華な，ぜいたくな
17 ☐☐ **decommission** [dìːkəmíʃən]	▶ stop using, deactivate 動 （施設・道具など）の使用を中止する，の役を解く
18 ☐☐ **wind down**	▶ slow down, tail off 徐々に終わる
19 ☐☐ **cease** [siːs] ❶	▶ terminate, halt, stop 動 止まる
☐☐ **sanctum** [sǽŋktəm]	▶ sanctuary, holy place 名 神聖な場所
☐☐ **archipelago** [ɑ̀ːrkəpéləɡoʊ]	名 群島，諸島

文化・歴史 **12**

The Gobi's Great Wall

Genghis Khan's Wall is an ancient structure in the Gobi Desert similar to the Great Wall of China. It was probably built to control the movement of Mongolian tribes.

1   Using satellite images to ¹**zero in on** parts of Mongolia's Gobi Desert, ²**anthropologists** located ³**hitherto** unknown ⁴**remnants** of the Great Wall of China. These structures, known ⁵**collectively** as Genghis Khan's Wall, stand up to 2.75 meters in height. Some stretches are made up of
5   ⁶**rudimentary** mud blocks, while other sections ⁷**comprise** quarried volcanic rock. Historians believe the wall once stretched for vast distances, but ⁸**eroded** over the centuries.

Ancient Mongolian records say the wall was built by Genghis Khan's son, Ögedei, to ⁹**confine** wild herds of gazelle on his land. However, the
10   hostile Gobi Desert could not have supported gazelle, ¹⁰**casting doubt on** this claim. Chinese researchers have ¹¹**conjectured** that the wall was erected by the Han ¹²**dynasty** in about 115 BC, but radiocarbon dating of wall ¹³**fragments** shows it was built between AD 1040 and 1160. Since this was a time of frequent ¹⁴**warfare**, some researchers suggested it was
15   constructed to ¹⁵**repel** Mongol tribes making ¹⁶**forays** to the south, but more recent research suggests its purpose was to limit the movement of nomadic peoples.

Mongolians would prefer to ¹⁷**hang on to** the name "Genghis Khan's Wall," since ¹⁸**conceding** that it was once part of the Great Wall would be
20   ¹⁹**tantamount** to admitting the region was once held by China, an idea they ²⁰**chafe at**.   🏴 (215 words)

. . . .

ℓ.9   gazelle：ガゼル。鹿のような動物。

ゴビ砂漠の巨大な壁

チンギス・ハンの壁はゴビ砂漠にある中国の万里の長城に似た古代建造物だ。それはおそらくモンゴル部族の動きを制御するために建設された。

　衛星画像を使ってモンゴルのゴビ砂漠 [1]に注目することで，[2]文化人類学者たちは[3]これまで知られていなかった中国の万里の長城の[4]遺跡を見つけた。これらの建造物は[5]まとめてチンギス・ハンの壁として知られており，高さ 2.75 メートルに達する。[6]原始的な泥のブロックを使った区間がある一方で，切り出された火山岩[7]でできている区間もある。その壁はかつて広大な距離に及んだが，その後何世紀ものうちに[8]浸食されたと歴史研究家たちは信じている。

　古代モンゴルの記録によると，その壁はチンギス・ハンの息子，オゴデイが領土に野生のガゼルの群れ[9]を閉じ込めるために建てたものだという。しかしゴビ砂漠の厳しい環境ではガゼルは生息できなかっただろうから，この主張[10]には疑問がある。中国人の研究家たちは，壁は漢[12]王朝が紀元前 115 年ごろに建てた[11]と推測してきたが，壁の[13]かけらの放射性炭素年代測定では西暦 1040 年から 1160 年の間に建てられたという結果が出ている。研究者の中には，これは[14]争いの絶えない時代であったために，南に[16]侵略していったモンゴル部族[15]を撃退すべく建てられたと示唆する者もいたが，さらに最近の研究は，その目的は遊牧民の動きを制限することだったことを示唆している。

　モンゴル人としては「チンギス・ハンの壁」の名称[17]に執着があるようだ。その壁がかつて万里の長城の一部であった[18]と認めることは，その地方をかつて中国が征服していたこと，すなわちモンゴル人にとって[20]しゃくにさわる意見を認めることに[19]等しいからである。

The Gobi's Great Wall

1 ☐☐ **zero in on ～**	▶ focus on, zoom in on, center on ～に（カメラなどの）焦点を合わせる，～に集中する
2 ☐☐ **anthropologist** [æ̀nθrəpá(:)lədʒɪst]	名（文化）人類学者 名 anthropology 形 anthropological
3 ☐☐ **hitherto** [hìðərtúː]	▶ formerly, previously, so far, to date 副 従来，これまで（のところ） ⇔ hereafter, henceforth（これ以降）
4 ☐☐ **remnant** [rémnənt]	▶ remains, relic 名 遺跡，残存物
5 ☐☐ **collectively** [kəléktɪvli]	副 ひとまとめにして，集合的に
6 ☐☐ **rudimentary** [rùːdɪméntəri]	▶ primitive, simple, crude, basic 形 原始的な，初歩的な
7 ☐☐ **comprise** [kəmpráɪz]	▶ consist of, be composed of, be made up of 動（全体が）～から構成される，～から成る ●「（部分が）（全体）を構成する」という意味もある
8 ☐☐ **erode** [ɪróʊd]	▶ corrode, be eaten away, wear away 動 浸食される 名 erosion（浸食）
9 ☐☐ **confine** [kənfáɪn]	▶ enclose, impound, imprison 動 を閉じ込める 名 confinement
10 ☐☐ **cast doubt on [upon] ～**	▶ throw doubt on [upon], question, impeach ～に疑問を投げかける
11 ☐☐ **conjecture** [kəndʒéktʃər]	▶ guess, presume, surmise, infer 動 を推測する，を推量する 名 推測，推量

12 ☐☐ **dynasty** [dáɪnəsti]	▶ reign, regime, rule, empire, sovereignty 名 王朝
13 ☐☐ **fragment** [frǽgmənt] ❶	▶ piece, fraction 名 断片，かけら 形 fragmentary（断片の，断片的な）
14 ☐☐ **warfare** [wɔ́ːrfèər] ❶	▶ war, hostilities 名 戦争，交戦状態
15 ☐☐ **repel** [rɪpél]	▶ repulse, drive away, fight off 動 を撃退する，を追い払う
16 ☐☐ **foray** [fɔ́(ː)reɪ]	▶ invasion, raid, incursion 名 侵略，急襲 動 侵略する ● make a foray（急襲する）
17 ☐☐ **hang on to ～**	▶ cling to, hold on to ～を持ち続ける，～にしがみつく
18 ☐☐ **concede** [kənsíːd]	▶ admit, acknowledge, accept 動 を（しぶしぶ）正しいと認める 名 concession（容認，譲歩）
19 ☐☐ **tantamount** [tǽntəmàʊnt]	▶ equal, equivalent, commensurate, comparable 形 同等の，等しい〈to ～と〉
20 ☐☐ **chafe at ～**	▶ be annoyed [incensed, irritated] at ～にいら立つ

文化・歴史 **13**

The Great Mayan Mix-Up

Around 2012, there were stories saying that the ancient Mayans had predicted that the world was going to end soon. However, it was based on a misunderstanding.

1　　The media ¹**played up** the possible end of the world in the year 2012, which was ²**prophesied** by the Mayan calendar. However, this ³**chimera** was a result of confusing two different cultures. The Aztec Stone of the Sun, a familiar symbol of ancient Latin America, was ⁴**depicted** in stories

5　on the Internet and other media about the Mayan calendar, but the ⁵**carved**, ⁶**circular** stone is Aztec, and it is not a calendar.

　　The Aztec and Mayan civilizations existed 500 years apart and were vastly different. The Mayans were an older civilization, and rather than an empire, they were a collection of autonomous states. They were ⁷**notable**

10　for their innovation, including their mathematics which ⁸**surpassed** Europe's at that time. Their art was also ahead of its time, depicting people realistically, often with ⁹**subtle** expressions. The year 2012 was a year when their calendars would have reset, much like the year 2000 on contemporary calendars. Though a significant year, it had nothing to do

15　with ¹⁰**foreseeing** an ¹¹**apocalypse**.

　　Once ¹²**nomadic**, the Aztecs settled in the area that is now Mexico City. They were known for their ¹³**aggression** and tyranny, ¹⁴**suppressing** nearby states. For them, the world was full of menace, and they were obsessed with the apocalypse. ¹⁵**As such**, their art depicts scenes of death

20　and ¹⁶**cataclysmic** destruction. However, their calendar was circular and would reset to zero at the end of each cycle, meaning they had no means to predict events as far away as 2012.　　　　　　　　(245 words)

・・
タイトル　mix-up：混乱。
ℓ.6　　　circular：ここでは「円形の」の意味で，ℓ.20 の circular は「循環の」という意味。

マヤについての大きな混乱

2012 年ごろ，世界はもうすぐ終わると古代マヤ人が予言していた，という話があった。しかし，それは誤解に基づくものだった。

　メディアはマヤ暦が [2]予言した 2012 年に起きる世界の終末の可能性 [1]について大きく取り上げた。しかし，この [3]妄想は 2 つの異なる文化を混同した結果として起きた。一般になじみのある古代ラテン・アメリカの象徴，アステカの太陽の石がインターネットや他のメディアのマヤ暦についての物語の中 [4]に描かれていたが，その [5]彫刻が施された [6]円形の石はアステカ族のものであり，暦ではない。

　アステカ文明とマヤ文明が存在した時代は 500 年離れており，（2 つの文明は）非常に異なっていた。マヤ族の方が古い文明で，帝国というよりは自治権を持つ小国家の集合体であった。彼らは新しいことを取り入れることで [7]知られ，そこには当時のヨーロッパ [8]より優れていた数学が含まれていた。彼らの絵もまた時代に先駆けており，人物を写実的に，しばしば [9]繊細な表情も描いていた。2012 年は現代の暦の 2000 年のように彼らの暦がリセットする年であった。重要な年ではあるが，それは [11]この世の終わり [10]を予知することとは関連がなかった。

　かつて [12]遊牧民だったアステカ族は，現在のメキシコ・シティのある地域に定住した。彼らは [13]好戦性や専制政治で知られており，近隣する都市国家 [14]を抑圧していた。彼らにとって世界は脅威に満ちており，終末思想に取り憑かれていた。[15]それゆえに，彼らの絵は死や [16]激変的破壊の場面を描いている。しかし，彼らの暦は循環するもので，周期の終わりごとにリセットしてゼロになる。つまり，2012 年というはるか遠い未来の出来事を予測する手段などなかったということだ。

The Great Mayan Mix-Up

1 ☐☐
play up ～
▶ emphasize, accentuate, stress
～を強調する

2 ☐☐
prophesy
[prá(:)fəsàɪ] ❶
▶ predict, foretell
動 を予［預］言する
名 prophet（預言者）

3 ☐☐
chimera
[kaɪmíərə] ❶
▶ fancy, illusion
名 妄想, 奇怪な幻想

4 ☐☐
depict
[dɪpíkt]
▶ describe, portray, delineate
動 を描写する, を叙述する
名 depiction

5 ☐☐
carve
[kɑːrv]
▶ sculpt
動 に彫刻を施す

6 ☐☐
circular
[sə́ːrkjulər]
▶ round
形 円形の, 循環の
名 circle

7 ☐☐
notable
[nóʊţəbl]
▶ eminent, prominent, famed, distinguished
形 著名な, 卓越した
動 note（に注目する）

8 ☐☐
surpass
[sərpǽs]
▶ excel, outdo, exceed
動 に勝る, をしのぐ

9 ☐☐
subtle
[sʌ́ţl] ❶
▶ fine
形 繊細な, 微妙な

10 ☐☐
foresee
[fɔːrsíː]
▶ predict, envisage, envision, prophesy
動 を予知する, を予見する
形 foreseeable（予知できる）

11 ☐☐
apocalypse
[əpá(:)kəlìps]
▶ doomsday
名 この世の終わり（の日）
形 apocalyptic（この世の終わりの）

12 ☐☐ **nomadic** [noʊmǽdɪk]	▶ wandering, migrant, itinerant 形 遊牧民の，放浪生活の 名 nomad（遊牧民）
13 ☐☐ **aggression** [əgréʃən]	▶ pugnaciousness, belligerence, violence 名 好戦性，攻撃性 形 aggressive
14 ☐☐ **suppress** [səprés] ❶	▶ subdue, repress, conquer 動 を抑圧する 名 suppression
15 ☐☐ **as such**	▶ therefore, thus, so それゆえに
16 ☐☐ **cataclysmic** [kæ̀ʈəklízmɪk]	▶ catastrophic, disastrous, devastating 形 激変的な，大災害の 名 cataclysm（突然の大災害）
☐☐ **eschatology** [èskətá(:)lədʒi]	▶ apocalypticism 名 終末論，終末思想
☐☐ **theocracy** [θiá(:)krəsi]	▶ a social system or state controlled by religious leaders 名 神権政治，神政
☐☐ **solar deity**	▶ sun god(dess) 太陽神
☐☐ **human sacrifice**	▶ (sacrificial) victim 人身御供，人柱
☐☐ **astronomy** [əstrá(:)nəmi]	▶ the scientific study of the stars and planets 名 天文学 名 astronomer（天文学者）
☐☐ **astrology** [əstrá(:)lədʒi]	▶ horoscope, horoscopy 名 占星術 名 astrologer（占星術師）

The Birth of Earth Day

This passage looks at how Earth Day originated in 1970 as a way to bring attention to the world's environmental problems.

1   Earth Day is a popular holiday that was ¹**conceived** in the US in 1970. It is now commonly celebrated on April 22 by more than a billion people in over 180 countries around the world. There are some rumors on why this date was chosen. One ²**persistent** rumor ³**holds** that the date was

5   selected for being the birthday of Vladimir Lenin, whose goals were said to have been shared by some environmentalists at that time. However, the date was selected in 1970 because it ⁴**fell on** a Wednesday, an ideal day for encouraging a large ⁵**turnout** for ⁶**rallies**. It was an ⁷**auspicious** choice, for 20 million people eventually took part.

10   Earth Day is a ⁸**by-product** of 1960s activism and concern for a ⁹**ravaged** environment. US Senator Gaylord Nelson became frustrated with the ¹⁰**apathy** in the American Congress, which did not seem ¹¹**disposed to** take action, so he collaborated with others to form a ¹²**coalition** of ¹³**like-minded** people. They aimed to hold rallies across the

15   country, and their efforts to ¹⁴**fire up** the American public about the environment ¹⁵**resonated**. Earth Day was a ¹⁶**spectacular** success, ¹⁷**exceeding** all expectations.

Environmentalism is no longer ¹⁸**relegated** to a ¹⁹**fringe** issue. However, environmentalists remain concerned that people are becoming

20   ²⁰**complacent** and that enthusiasm is ²¹**giving out**. Environmental problems such as polluted rivers and smog in the 1970s were more ²²**transparent** than the elusive concerns today, such as global warming.

(234 words)

アースデイの始まり

この文章では，世界の環境問題に注意を向けさせる方法としてアースデイが 1970 年にどのように始まったかを見ていく。

アースデイは 1970 年にアメリカで ¹創設された有名な祝日である。今では一般的に世界 180 カ国以上で 10 億人を超える人が 4 月 22 日にアースデイを祝っている。なぜこの日が選ばれたかについてはさまざまな噂がある。その日はウラジミール・レーニンの誕生日で，彼の目的が当時の一部の環境保護論者に共有されていたと言われていて選ばれた ³と考える 1 つの ²なかなか消えない噂がある。しかし，1970 年にその日にちが選ばれたのは，⁶集会に大勢の ⁵参加者を行く気にさせるのに理想的な日である水曜日 ⁴に当たったからであった。最終的に 2,000 万人が参加したのだから，それは ⁷幸先の良い選択だった。

アースデイは 1960 年代の行動主義と，環境 ⁹破壊への懸念の ⁸副産物である。米国上院議員のゲイロード・ネルソンは行動を起こす ¹¹気配を見せない議会の ¹⁰無関心な態度に不満を抱いていたので，他の人たちと協力して ¹³同じ意見を持つ人たちの ¹²連合体を作った。彼らは国中で集会を開くことを目指し，アメリカの人々に環境問題への関心 ¹⁴を燃え立たせる彼らの努力は ¹⁵共感を呼んだ。アースデイは ¹⁶目覚ましい成功を収め，それはあらゆる予想 ¹⁷を超えるものだった。

環境保護主義はもはや ¹⁹些末な問題と ¹⁸片づけられるものではない。それでも環境保護論者たちは人々が ²⁰満足しつつあり，情熱が ²¹尽きてきているとの懸念を持ち続けている。1970 年代の河川の汚染や光化学スモッグといった環境問題は，地球温暖化のような今日のとらえどころがない懸念よりも ²²わかりやすかったのだ。

The Birth of Earth Day

1 ☐☐ **conceive** [kənsíːv]	動 を創設する，を思いつく
2 ☐☐ **persistent** [pərsístənt]	形 なかなかなくならない，しつこい 動 persist（（好ましくないものが）存続する） 名 persistence（しつこさ，持続性）
3 ☐☐ **hold** [hoʊld]	▶ believe, think, maintain, deem, reckon 動 と考える，と主張する
4 ☐☐ **fall on 〜**	▶ happen on （記念日など）に当たる
5 ☐☐ **turnout** [tə́ːrnàʊt]	▶ attendance, assembly, throng 名 参加者（数），（催しの）人出
6 ☐☐ **rally** [rǽli]	▶ gathering, assembly, demonstration 名 集会，集結
7 ☐☐ **auspicious** [ɔːspíʃəs]	▶ promising, propitious, favorable, fortunate 形 幸先の良い，縁起の良い 名 auspice（（通例 -s）後援，吉兆，前兆）
8 ☐☐ **by-product** [báɪprɑ̀(ː)dʌkt]	▶ fallout, outgrowth 名 副産物
9 ☐☐ **ravage** [rǽvɪdʒ] 🔊	▶ devastate, ruin, destroy 動 を破壊し尽くす
10 ☐☐ **apathy** [ǽpəθi]	▶ indifference, unconcern 名 無関心，冷淡 形 apathetic
11 ☐☐ **be disposed to *do***	▶ be willing to *do*, be inclined to *do* 〜（しようと）する気がある

12 □□ **coalition** [kòʊəlíʃən]	▶ alliance, partnership, association, union **名** 連合, 提携
13 □□ **like-minded** [làɪkmáɪndɪd]	▶ having similar interests and opinions **形** 同じ意見の
14 □□ **fire up 〜**	▶ inspire, motivate, rouse (人) を鼓舞する, 〜を刺激する
15 □□ **resonate** [rézənèɪt]	▶ impress, get sympathy **動** 共感を呼ぶ, 賛同を得る **名** resonance (反響) **形** resonant (鳴り響く)
16 □□ **spectacular** [spektǽkjələr] ❶	▶ remarkable, impressive, outstanding **形** 目覚ましい, 壮大な **名** spectacle (壮観, 眺め)
17 □□ **exceed** [ɪksíːd] ❶	▶ surpass, outdo, go beyond **動** を超える **名** excess (超過)
18 □□ **relegate** [réləgèɪt]	▶ degrade, downgrade, demote, lower, put down **動** を追いやる 〈to 低い地位に〉, を退ける
19 □□ **fringe** [frɪndʒ]	▶ unimportant, trivial, minor **形** 些末な, 周辺的な
20 □□ **complacent** [kəmpléɪsənt]	▶ content, satisfied **形** 満足した **名** complacency (自己満足)
21 □□ **give out**	▶ run out, be used up 尽きる, なくなる, 終わる ● 「〜を配る」や「〜を放出する」の意味もある
22 □□ **transparent** [trænspǽrənt] ❶	▶ obvious, plain, evident, unequivocal **形** わかりやすい, 明白な

文化·歴史 **15**

How the Moon May Have Sunk the Titanic

The Titanic disaster may have occurred because the sun, moon, and Earth were lined up, raising tides and thereby increasing the number of icebergs.

1   The sinking of the Titanic on April 14, 1912 was the world's most famous ¹**maritime** disaster, with over 1,500 ²**fatalities**. The ³**hull** of the Titanic had been ⁴**breached** by an ⁵**iceberg**. Icebergs often ⁶**hamper** ships crossing the Atlantic Ocean in spring. However, the spring of 1912 saw an
5   unusual number of them ⁷**cluttering** shipping lanes, which has always been a ⁸**riddle** to historians.

Astronomer Donald Olson of Texas State University believes he has the answer. A rare ⁹**alignment** of the sun, the full moon and Earth, plus the closest lunar approach to Earth since AD 796, caused extremely high
10   tides on January 4, 1912. The full moon and its proximity to Earth created a "supermoon." Olson believes the high tide refloated a ¹⁰**horde** of icebergs that had ¹¹**run aground** in the shallow seas just offshore from Canada's eastern ¹²**seaboard** and sent them in the path of the Titanic. The icebergs reached the area of the Titanic three months later, ¹³**sealing its**
15   **fate**. Olson's theory is supported by reports of record high tides around the world in January 1912.

The timing of the moon's changes in 1912 was ¹⁴**anything but** ¹⁵**propitious**. The disaster happened on a moonless night, when the iceberg was ¹⁶**inconspicuous** — and the moon ¹⁷**set** a series of events **in**
20   **motion** three months earlier that led to the passenger ship's ¹⁸**wreck**.

(222 words)

タイタニックを沈めたかもしれない月の進行

タイタニック号の大惨事が起きたのは，太陽と月と地球が一直線に並ぶことで潮位が上がり，それによって氷山の数が増えたためかもしれない。

1912 年 4 月 14 日のタイタニック号沈没は世界で最も有名な [1]海難事故で，1,500 人以上の [2]死者を出した。タイタニック号の [3]船体は [5]氷山によって [4]穴を開けられた。春期に氷山はしばしば大西洋を渡る船 [6]を妨げていたのだ。しかし，1912 年の春に航路 [7]をふさぐ氷山の数は並外れていた。そのことは歴史家にとってずっと [8]謎であった。

テキサス州立大学の天文学者ドナルド・オルソンは答えを見つけたと考えている。1912 年 1 月 4 日に太陽と満月と地球がまれなことに [9]一直線に並び，さらに西暦 796 年以来，月が地球に最も近づいたことで，潮位が非常に高くなった。満月であることとそれが地球に近づくことで「スーパームーン」が生じた。オルソンは高い潮位がカナダの東 [12]海岸沖すぐの浅瀬に [11]乗り上げていた [10]大量の氷山を再浮上させ，それらをタイタニック号の航路に運んだと考えている。氷山は 3 カ月後にタイタニックのいる場所に到着し，[13]その運命を決したのだ。オルソンの仮説は，1912 年 1 月の全世界的な記録的潮位の報告から裏づけられている。

1912 年の月の変化のタイミングは [14]まったく [15]幸先の良い ものではなかった。大惨事は氷山が [16]目につきにくい月のない夜に起こった。そして月は 3 カ月前から客船の [18]難破を引き起こす一連の動き [17]を始めていた。

How the Moon May Have Sunk the Titanic

1 ☐☐ **maritime** [mǽrɪtàɪm]	▶ oceanic, marine, nautical 形 海の，船の
2 ☐☐ **fatality** [feɪtǽləţi]	▶ casualty, mortality 名 死者（数） 形 fatal（致命的な，致死的な）
3 ☐☐ **hull** [hʌl]	▶ body of a ship 名 船体，船殻
4 ☐☐ **breach** [briːtʃ]	▶ hole, rip, stave 動 に穴を開ける，（法律など）を破る
5 ☐☐ **iceberg** [áɪsbə̀ːrg]	▶ ice floe 名 氷山
6 ☐☐ **hamper** [hǽmpər]	▶ impede, hinder, encumber 動 の動きを妨げる，を邪魔する
7 ☐☐ **clutter** [klʌ́ţər]	▶ jumble up, block up 動 （場所）を雑然とふさぐ 名 散乱（したもの）
8 ☐☐ **riddle** [rídl]	▶ enigma, mystery 名 謎，難問，不可解なこと
9 ☐☐ **alignment** [əláɪnmənt]	▶ lining up 名 一列に並ぶこと 動 align（を整列させる，を提携させる）
10 ☐☐ **horde** [hɔːrd]	▶ throng, drove, swarm 名 大量，大群
11 ☐☐ **run aground**	▶ be driven ashore, strike a reef 浅瀬に乗り上げる，座礁する

12 ☐☐ **seaboard** [síːbɔ̀ːrd]	▶ coast, coastline, shoreline **名** 海岸，海岸線
13 ☐☐ **seal *one's* fate**	▶ dictate *one's* destiny 〜の運命を決する
14 ☐☐ **anything but 〜**	▶ by no means, not 〜 at all まったく〜でない
15 ☐☐ **propitious** [prəpíʃəs]	▶ advantageous, auspicious, favorable **形** 幸先の良い
16 ☐☐ **inconspicuous** [ìnkənspíkjuəs]	▶ unnoticeable, unobtrusive **形** 目につきにくい，目立たない **⇔** conspicuous（目立つ）
17 ☐☐ **set 〜 in motion**	▶ start, activate, initiate 〜を始める
18 ☐☐ **wreck** [rek] ❶	▶ shipwreck, wreckage **名** 難破 **動** を難破させる
☐☐ **glacier** [gléɪʃər]	**名** 氷河 **形** glacial
☐☐ **spring tide**	大潮

文化・歴史
確認テスト

1 次の日本語の意味の単語を下の❶〜⓰の中から選んで書きなさい。

（1）寓喩，寓意 　　　　　　　（　　：　　　　　　　　　　　）

（2）原告 　　　　　　　　　　（　　：　　　　　　　　　　　）

（3）もろい，砕けやすい 　　　（　　：　　　　　　　　　　　）

（4）を弾劾する，を告発する 　（　　：　　　　　　　　　　　）

（5）でんぷん 　　　　　　　　（　　：　　　　　　　　　　　）

（6）（神など）に加護を祈る 　（　　：　　　　　　　　　　　）

（7）呪い 　　　　　　　　　　（　　：　　　　　　　　　　　）

（8）完全な，損なわれていない （　　：　　　　　　　　　　　）

（9）織物，布地 　　　　　　　（　　：　　　　　　　　　　　）

（10）支持者，信奉者 　　　　　（　　：　　　　　　　　　　　）

（11）緩衝物 　　　　　　　　　（　　：　　　　　　　　　　　）

（12）家畜 　　　　　　　　　　（　　：　　　　　　　　　　　）

（13）従来，これまで（のところ）（　　：　　　　　　　　　　　）

（14）に勝る，をしのぐ 　　　　（　　：　　　　　　　　　　　）

（15）連合，提携 　　　　　　　（　　：　　　　　　　　　　　）

（16）幸先の良い 　　　　　　　（　　：　　　　　　　　　　　）

---

❶ intact	❷ livestock	❸ plaintiff	❹ hitherto
❺ curse	❻ propitious	❼ brittle	❽ allegory
❾ adherent	❿ coalition	⓫ surpass	⓬ invoke
⓭ impeach	⓮ buffer	⓯ starch	⓰ textile

2 次の日本語の意味の単語を下の❶〜⓬の中から選んで書きなさい。

（1）傑作，名作 　　　　　　　　　　　　（　　：　　　　　　　　　　　　　）

（2）複製（すること），複写 　　　　　　（　　：　　　　　　　　　　　　　）

（3）中傷，誹謗，名誉毀損 　　　　　　　（　　：　　　　　　　　　　　　　）

（4）牧歌的な 　　　　　　　　　　　　　（　　：　　　　　　　　　　　　　）

（5）先祖，前触れ 　　　　　　　　　　　（　　：　　　　　　　　　　　　　）

（6）終焉，消滅 　　　　　　　　　　　　（　　：　　　　　　　　　　　　　）

（7）〜に便乗する，〜で儲ける 　　　　　（　　：　　　　　　　　　　　　　）

（8）〜を回避する 　　　　　　　　　　　（　　：　　　　　　　　　　　　　）

（9）〜に集中する 　　　　　　　　　　　（　　：　　　　　　　　　　　　　）

（10）遊牧民の，放浪生活の 　　　　　　　（　　：　　　　　　　　　　　　　）

（11）なかなかなくならない 　　　　　　　（　　：　　　　　　　　　　　　　）

（12）船体，船殻 　　　　　　　　　　　　（　　：　　　　　　　　　　　　　）

---

❶ idyllic	❷ demise	❸ masterpiece	❹ cash in on 〜
❺ persistent	❻ zero in on 〜	❼ forerunner	❽ duplication
❾ hull	❿ smear	⓫ nomadic	⓬ skirt around 〜

解答

1　（1）❽ (→p. 16)　（2）❸ (→p. 21)　（3）❼ (→p. 25)　（4）⓭ (→p. 29)

　　（5）⓯ (→p. 33)　（6）⓬ (→p. 37)　（7）❺ (→p. 37)　（8）❶ (→p. 41)

　　（9）⓰ (→p. 45)　（10）❾ (→p. 48)　（11）⓮ (→p. 53)　（12）❷ (→p. 57)

　　（13）❹ (→p. 60)　（14）⓫ (→p. 64)　（15）❿ (→p. 69)　（16）❻ (→p. 73)

2　（1）❸ (→p. 17)　（2）❽ (→p. 20)　（3）❿ (→p. 32)　（4）❶ (→p. 36)

　　（5）❼ (→p. 40)　（6）❷ (→p. 45)　（7）❹ (→p. 49)　（8）⓬ (→p. 53)

　　（9）❻ (→p. 60)　（10）⓫ (→p. 65)　（11）❺ (→p. 68)　（12）❾ (→p. 72)

3 次の単語の意味に最も近いものをそれぞれ❶〜❹の中から1つ選びなさい。

（1）acclaim

❶ applaud
❷ occupy
❸ plagiarize
❹ hinder

（2）testify

❶ attest
❷ allay
❸ convey
❹ overwhelm

（3）compendium

❶ artifact
❷ survey
❸ renunciation
❹ venue

（4）rift

❶ attestation
❷ proximity
❸ mystery
❹ breach

（5）strife

❶ conflict
❷ indication
❸ apocalypse
❹ ore

（6）clumsy

❶ persuasive
❷ awkward
❸ severe
❹ durable

（7）ailment

❶ specimen
❷ bloodshed
❸ illness
❹ cranium

（8）weed out 〜

❶ eliminate
❷ ensue
❸ conceive
❹ comprise

（9）authority

❶ cluster
❷ obsession
❸ gutter
❹ expert

（10）integral

❶ equivalent
❷ fringe
❸ intriguing
❹ requisite

（11）elusive

❶ inscrutable
❷ nautical
❸ solid
❹ aberrant

（12）indigenous

❶ digestive
❷ equivocal
❸ domestic
❹ beloved

(13) topple　❶ oust　❷ disprove　❸ empower　❹ revolve

(14) eminent　❶ incisive　❷ lucrative　❸ esteemed　❹ boisterous

(15) earthwork　❶ rally　❷ mound　❸ swamp　❹ regimen

(16) cease　❶ substantiate　❷ erect　❸ respect　❹ halt

(17) confine　❶ promote　❷ impound　❸ admit　❹ surmise

(18) foray　❶ raid　❷ ingenuity　❸ brute　❹ conformity

(19) depict　❶ portray　❷ engulf　❸ excavate　❹ ravage

(20) auspicious　❶ evident　❷ promising　❸ prominent　❹ horrific

(21) apathy　❶ suit　❷ suffrage　❸ indifference　❹ reservoir

(22) horde　❶ disorder　❷ eschatology　❸ fort　❹ throng

文化・歴史

確認テスト

解答

3 （1）❶（→p. 17）（2）❶（→p. 21）（3）❷（→p. 24）（4）❹（→p. 28）
（5）❶（→p. 28）（6）❷（→p. 32）（7）❸（→p. 33）（8）❶（→p. 37）
（9）❹（→p. 40）（10）❹（→p. 40）（11）❶（→p. 44）（12）❸（→p. 44）
（13）❶（→p. 48）（14）❸（→p. 52）（15）❷（→p. 52）（16）❹（→p. 57）
（17）❷（→p. 60）（18）❶（→p. 61）（19）❶（→p. 64）（20）❷（→p. 68）
（21）❸（→p. 68）（22）❹（→p. 72）

(13) topple　　⑩ oust　　⑩ disapprove
　　　　　　　⑨ empower　　⑩ revive
(14) eminent　　⑩ incisive　　⑩ lucrative
　　　　　　　⑩ esteemed　　⑩ boisterous
the earthwork　　⑩ rally　　⑩ rebound
　　　　　　　⑩ amp...　　⑩ regimen
(16) cease　　⑩ sustainable　　⑩ snarl
　　　　　　　⑩ respect　　⑩ halt
(17) confine　　⑩ promote　　⑩ impound
　　　　　　　⑩ admit　　⑩ sunrise
(18) to lay　　⑩ raid　　⑩ ingenuity
　　　　　　　⑩ bribe　　⑩ conformity
(19) deplor...　　⑩ portray　　⑩ engulf
　　　　　　　⑩ excavate　　⑩ ravage
(20) auspicious　　⑩ evident　　⑩ promising
　　　　　　　⑩ prominent　　⑩ haughty
(21) apathy　　⑩ suit　　⑩ subfloda
　　　　　　　⑩ indifference　　⑩ reservoir
(22) horde　　⑩ discover　　⑩ eschatology
　　　　　　　⑩ fort　　⑩ throng

政治・経済

政治・経済

テーマを知る

　政治・経済は出題頻度が特に高く，また，やや専門的な話題が扱われることも多い。法律，国や地域の社会問題，国際問題，マクロ・ミクロの経済問題，人口問題，エネルギー問題など，さまざまな話題が取り上げられる。日ごろから英語の新聞・雑誌の主要記事に目を通して，注目されている話題やそれに関連した語彙や概念を理解しておくことが有効である。

注目用語

rights and duties 権利と義務

人々が持つ rights（権利）と人々に課される duties（義務）はしばしば各国の constitution（憲法）において定められている。その内容は国によってさまざまで，日本では選挙への参加は the right to vote（選挙権）として国民が有する権利だが，本書の「政治・経済 6. Compulsory Voting」では選挙への参加が義務となっている例が紹介されている。また，「政治・経済 4. Nonhuman Rights」では人間以外の権利について扱っている。

refugee 難民

一般に，国籍を持つ国で race（人種）や religion（宗教），political opinion（政治的意見）等を理由に迫害される恐れのある人を political refugee（政治難民）と呼ぶ。1951 年に採択された Convention Relating to the Status of Refugees（難民の地位に関する条約）等によって国際社会は難民に対して基本的な権利や保護を与えるべきと定められている。しかし，asylum（亡命）に関する法整備や，難民受け入れに対する反発感情など難民を取り巻く問題は多い。

wealth gap 貧富の差

近年，少数の人々がますます多くの富を所有するようになる一方で，多くの人々の生活水準は向上しない，または悪化しており wealth gap（貧富の差）が広がり過ぎているとして問題視されている。

キーワード・表現

□ **productivity**	生産性，生産力	p.84
□ **logistics**	物流（管理システム）	p.84
□ **stagnant**	（経済などが）停滞した，低迷した	p.84
□ **subsidize**	に補助金［助成金］を支給する	p.88
□ **enforcement**	（法の）執行，施行	p.93
□ **tyrannize**	に暴政［暴虐］を行う	p.93
□ **litigate**	訴訟を起こす	p.96
□ **legislature**	立法機関	p.96
□ **authoritarian regime**	権威主義体制	p.108
□ **pledge**	公約，約束	p.112
□ **manifesto**	（政党などの）宣言（書），マニフェスト	p.113
□ **influence peddling**	あっ旋収賄	p.116
□ **embezzlement**	横領，着服	p.116
□ **meritocracy**	能力［実力］主義（社会）	p.117
□ **referendum**	国民投票	p.120
□ **electorate**	有権者	p.120
□ **remit**	（借金など）を免除する	p.128
□ **bail out ～**	（経済的危機にある会社など）を救う	p.129
□ **conglomerate**	複合企業	p.132
□ **poverty line**	貧困線	p.137
□ **subvention**	（政府などからの）補助金，助成金	p.137
□ **remuneration**	報酬，給与	p.141

Baumol's Cost Disease

William Baumol's famous "cost disease" theory explains why workers whose productivity does not increase continue to receive increases in salary.

1   In the 1960s, economist William Baumol became ¹**intrigued** with the question of why the remuneration for professions such as classical music performers had continued to rise steadily even though the music they were producing was exactly the same as it had been a century or more ago.

5   Such labor-²**intensive** jobs, Baumol realized, have extremely low ³**productivity** growth, while industries such as electronics manufacturing or ⁴**logistics** have been the ⁵**beneficiaries** of technological innovations that have led to ⁶**colossal** improvements in their productivity that bring about both lower prices and better wages.

10   Baumol realized that musicians' wages had risen because when pay in the manufacturing sector rose, it created incentives for workers in other industries to move into those jobs. As a result, occupations without productivity gains were forced to raise their wages in order to ⁷**retain** their workers. While this is good for people like musicians, economists

15   ⁸**perceive** it as a "disease" because industries with ⁹**stagnant** productivity growth are seen as reducing the economy's overall efficiency.

    Today, ¹⁰**skyrocketing** college tuitions and ¹¹**soaring** healthcare costs are often ¹²**proclaimed** to be ¹³**manifestations** of cost disease. Some economists accept Baumol's explanation, while others ¹⁴**contend** that high

20   tuitions are more the result of lavish facilities and funding cuts, and that healthcare cost increases are more ¹⁵**attributable to** the huge profits being ¹⁶**reaped** by the pharmaceutical industry.   (221 words)

ℓ.5   labor-intensive：労働集約型の（コスト全体に占める人件費の割合が大きい）

ボーモルのコスト病

ウィリアム・ボーモルの有名な「コスト病」理論は，生産性の上がらない労働者の給料がなぜ上がり続けるのかを説明している。

1960年代に，経済学者のウィリアム・ボーモルは，例えばクラシック音楽の演奏家などの専門的職業に対する報酬は，彼らが作り出している音楽は1世紀以上前からまったく同じなのに，なぜ着実に上がり続けるのかという疑問に [1]興味をそそられた。そのような労働 [2]集約型の仕事は [3]生産性の伸びが非常に低い一方，電子機器製造や [4]物流などの産業は，低価格と高賃金の両方を実現するような，生産性の [6]壮大な改善につながった技術革新の [5]受益者であることをボーモルは知った。

ボーモルは，音楽家の賃金が上がったのは，製造部門の報酬が上がったときには，他の産業の労働者たちがこれらの職業に参入してくる誘因を作り出したからだということに気づいた。その結果，生産性向上のない職業が，自分たちの労働者 [7]をつなぎ止めておくために賃金を上げざるを得なかった。このことは音楽家のような人々にとっては良いことだが，生産性向上が [9]停滞気味である産業は経済の全体的な効率を低下させていると見なされるため，経済学者たちはこのことを「病気」と [8]理解する。

今日，[10]うなぎ登りの大学の授業料と [11]高騰する医療費は，しばしばコスト病の [13]兆候だと [12]宣告されている。経済学者の中にはボーモルの説明を受け入れる者もいるが，高額な授業料はむしろぜいたくな設備と財源の削減の結果であり，医療費の増加はむしろ製薬業界が [16]得る莫大な利益 [15]に起因する [14]と強く主張する者もいる。

Baumol's Cost Disease

1 ☐☐ **intrigue** [ɪntríːg]	▶ engage, interest 動 の好奇心［興味］をそそる　形 intriguing ● be intrigued with [by] 〜（〜に興味をそそられる）
2 ☐☐ **intensive** [ɪnténsɪv]	形（〜を）集約的に用いる ● capital-intensive（資本集約的な）
3 ☐☐ **productivity** [pròʊdʌktívəti]	名 生産性，生産力 形 productive
4 ☐☐ **logistics** [loʊdʒístɪks]	名 物流（管理システム） 形 logistic, logistical ● 単数または複数扱い
5 ☐☐ **beneficiary** [bènɪfíʃièri]	名 受益者 形 beneficial（有益な）
6 ☐☐ **colossal** [kəlá(ː)səl]	▶ huge, enormous, massive 形 壮大な，途方もない ● 「巨像」を意味する colossus が語源
7 ☐☐ **retain** [rɪtéɪn]	▶ keep, maintain 動 を雇用し続ける，を保持する 名 retention
8 ☐☐ **perceive** [pərsíːv]	▶ understand, see, think of 動 を理解する，を考える〈as 〜と〉 名 perception
9 ☐☐ **stagnant** [stǽgnənt]	▶ sluggish, static 形（経済などが）停滞した，低迷した 名 stagnancy　動 stagnate
10 ☐☐ **skyrocket** [skáɪrà(ː)kət]	▶ soar, shoot up, zoom (up) 動（物価などが）急騰する，急上昇する ⇔ plummet, plunge, nosedive
11 ☐☐ **soar** [sɔːr] ●	▶ skyrocket, shoot up, zoom (up) 動（物価などが）急騰する，急上昇する ⇔ plummet, plunge, nosedive

12 ▢▢ **proclaim** [prəkléɪm] ❶	▶ declare, profess **動** を宣言する〈to be ～だと〉 **名** proclamation
13 ▢▢ **manifestation** [mæ̀nɪfestéɪʃən]	▶ indication, sign **名** 兆候, 表れ〈of ～の〉 **動** manifest
14 ▢▢ **contend** [kənténd]	▶ maintain, assert, affirm, allege **動** と強く主張する **名** contention
15 ▢▢ **attributable to ～**	▶ ascribable to ～に起因する, ～に帰すことができる
16 ▢▢ **reap** [ri:p]	▶ obtain, receive **動** (報酬など) を獲得する, を得る
▢▢ **turnover** [tə́:rnòʊvər]	**名** 離職率, (従業員の) 回転率 ● turnover rate とも言う
▢▢ **workforce** [wə́:rkfɔ̀:rs]	▶ labor force **名** (国などの) 労働人口, (企業などの) 総従業員
▢▢ **expenditure** [ɪkspéndɪtʃər]	▶ spending, expense, outlay **名** 歳出, 支出, 費用

政治・経済 **2**

Electric Vehicle Subsidies

Governments sometimes pay subsidies to help consumers afford electric cars, but some critics complain that these payments are wasteful and no longer provide a benefit.

1   Ending the ¹**long-standing** ²**dominance** of the internal ³**combustion** engine has been an ⁴**uphill** struggle, largely due to the prohibitive price tags of the electric vehicles (EVs) that are expected to replace them. However, as the climate crisis has worsened, many governments have
5   responded by ⁵**subsidizing** EVs to ⁶**kick-start** production and stimulate demand.

Subsidies have ⁷**bolstered** both the production and purchase of EVs, but some critics ⁸**allege** that governments are ⁹**squandering** money that could be used to combat climate change more effectively. According to
10   one study, most purchasers of EVs belong to affluent households and would have ¹⁰**shelled out** for an EV even without a subsidy. Furthermore, the majority of EVs purchased were bought ¹¹**in lieu of** highly efficient fossil-fuel or hybrid vehicles, as buyers of EVs are not usually the type of people who would buy ¹²**gas-guzzling** vehicles in the first place.

15   Another argument against subsidies is that the EV market is about to reach a tipping point. Every major automaker has committed to EVs, and ¹³**astronomical** sums are being devoted to research and development already.   Steep declines in battery prices mean that EVs will soon achieve price ¹⁴**parity** with traditional automobiles, and charging stations are
20   quickly becoming ubiquitous. Many experts therefore believe that a more effective way to combat climate change would be to ¹⁵**divert** money from EV subsidies to public transportation.   ＞＜ (223 words)

••

ℓ.18   achieve price parity with 〜：〜と同じ価格になる

電気自動車への補助金

政府は，消費者が電気自動車を購入できるように補助金を支払うことがあるが，批判的な人々の中には，こうした支払いは無駄であり，もはや利益をもたらさないと不満を述べる者もいる。

[1]長年にわたる内[3]燃機関の[2]支配を終わらせることが[4]苦しい戦いであったのは，それらに取って代わるはずである電気自動車（EV）の法外な値段が大きな理由であった。しかしながら，気候危機がひどくなるにつれて，多くの政府は EV の生産[6]に弾みをつけ，需要を刺激するために EV [5]に補助金をつけることで対応した。

補助金は EV の生産と購入の両方[7]を高めたが，批判的な人々の中には，政府がもっと効果的に気候変動と戦うために使えるはずの資金[9]を浪費している[8]と主張する者もいる。ある研究によると，EV を購入している人のほとんどは裕福な家庭であり，補助金なしでも EV に[10]大金を払っただろうということだ。さらに，購入された EV の大半は非常に効率の良い化石燃料かハイブリッドの自動車[11]の代わりに買われた。EV の購入者たちは普通，そもそも[12]ガソリンを大量に消費する車を買うタイプの人たちではないのだ。

補助金に反対するまた別の議論は，EV 市場は転換点に到達しようとしているというものだ。すべての大手自動車メーカーは EV に尽力しており，すでに研究開発に[13]天文学的な金額が投入されている。急激なバッテリー価格の低落は，EV がまもなく従来の自動車と[14]同じ価格に達するということを表しており，充電スタンドは急速に普及しつつある。そのため，多くの専門家たちは気候変動と戦うより効果的な方法は，EV への補助金から公共交通機関に資金[15]を回すことだと考えている。

Electric Vehicle Subsidies

1 ☐☐
long-standing
[lɔ̀(:)ŋstǽndɪŋ]

▶ abiding, enduring, long-lasting
形 長年の，長期にわたる
⇄ short-lived（短命の）

2 ☐☐
dominance
[dá(:)mɪnəns]

▶ supremacy, predominance, ascendancy
名 支配，優勢
動 dominate　形 dominant

3 ☐☐
combustion
[kəmbʌ́stʃən]

▶ burning, fire, inflammation
名 燃焼
動 combust

4 ☐☐
uphill
[ʌ̀phíl]

▶ arduous, laborious, strenuous
形 骨の折れる，困難な
⇄ easy, facile, effortless

5 ☐☐
subsidize
[sʌ́bsɪdàɪz]

動 に補助金［助成金］を支給する
名 subsidy（補助金），subsidization（補助金支給）

6 ☐☐
kick-start
[kíkstàːrt]

▶ spur, stimulate, jump-start
動 に弾みをつける，を促進する
● バイクのレバーを踏んで起動することから

7 ☐☐
bolster
[bóulstər]

▶ boost, reinforce, strengthen
動 を高める，を強化する
⇄ weaken, undermine

8 ☐☐
allege
[əlédʒ]

▶ assert, claim
動 を（十分な証拠なしに）主張する
名 allegation　形 alleged

9 ☐☐
squander
[skwá(:)ndər]

▶ waste, fritter away
動 を浪費する，を無駄に使う
名 squanderer（浪費家）

10 ☐☐
shell out

▶ fork out
大金を払う〈for ～に〉

11 ☐☐
in lieu of ～

▶ instead of, in place of
～の代わりに
● lieu [ljuː] は place の意味の古語

88

12 ☐☐ **gas-guzzling** [ɡǽsɡʌ̀zlɪŋ]	🔣 ガソリンを食う，燃費の悪い 🔣 gas guzzler（燃費の悪い車） ● gas（ガソリン）＋guzzling（をがつがつ食べる）
13 ☐☐ **astronomical** [æ̀strəná(:)mɪkəl]	▶ huge, enormous, immense 🔣 天文学的な，膨大な 🔣 astronomically
14 ☐☐ **parity** [pǽrəti]	▶ equality, equivalence, par 🔣 同等，対等〈with ～との〉
15 ☐☐ **divert** [dəvə́:rt]	▶ redirect 🔣（資金など）を転用する〈from ～から，to ～に〉 🔣 diversion
☐☐ **pollutant** [pəlú:tənt]	▶ contaminant 🔣 汚染物質 🔣 pollute
☐☐ **fume** [fju:m]	🔣（有害で悪臭のする）煙，ガス ● exhaust fumes（排気ガス）

The Confederate Monument Controversy

Today, monuments to Southern leaders from the Civil War in the 1860s are seen as symbols of racism and slavery, so some want them taken down.

1   For some White Southerners, Confederate monuments to Civil War generals, such as Robert E. Lee, are a ¹**commemoration** of what they see as a tragic yet glorious conflict. Many Black Americans, however, view them as symbols of White ²**oppression** and ³**bigotry** because the political

5   and social system the South was fighting to ⁴**perpetuate** was based on the ⁵**subjugation** and ⁶**enslavement** of Blacks.

⁷**In the wake of** police ⁸**brutality**, ⁹**homicides**, and ¹⁰**unjustified** use of force involving Black citizens, a "Black Lives Matter" movement has ¹¹**sprung up**, and Confederate monuments have become a focus of Black

10   ¹²**ire** toward what many Blacks feel is a law ¹³**enforcement** system that has long ¹⁴**trampled** on Black ¹⁵**civil rights**. A significant proportion of monuments are on courthouse grounds, and are therefore perceived by some people as symbols of how ¹⁶**entrenched** racism is thought to be in the legal and policing system.

15   Research has indicated that rather than being benign monuments intended to ¹⁷**pay tribute to** the sacrifices of Southern military personnel, the overwhelming majority of statues were erected in the early 1900s, nearly half a century after the war had ended. During this period, ¹⁸**sweeping** laws designed to suppress Black civil rights were being

20   ¹⁹**enacted**, and the statues are seen by some people as ²⁰**menacing** symbols intentionally constructed to ²¹**tyrannize** Black citizens. Dozens of the statues have been torn down, but a significant number remain.

■ (229 words)

ℓ.1   Southerner：（ここでは）米国南部の人

南部連合の記念像についての議論

1860年代に起きた南北戦争の南部の指導者たちの記念像は今日，人種差別と奴隷制度の象徴として見られているため，その取り壊しを望んでいる人もいる。

　南部の一部の白人たちにとっては，南北戦争の将軍たち，例えばロバート・E・リーなどの南部連合の記念像は彼らが悲劇的ではあるが栄光に満ちた戦いと見るものの[1]記念碑である。しかし，南部が[4]存続させるために戦っていた政治・社会制度は，黒人たちを[5]服従させ[6]隷属させることに基づいていたため，多くのアメリカ黒人たちはそれらを白人による[2]圧制と[3]偏狭のシンボルと見る。

　黒人市民たちに関わる警察の[8]残虐行為，[9]殺人，それに[10]不当な権力行使[7]の結果，「ブラック・ライブズ・マター」運動が[11]誕生し，南部連合の記念像は，多くの黒人たちが長きにわたって自分たちの[15]公民権を[14]踏みにじってきた法[13]執行制度と感じるものに対する黒人の[12]怒りの矛先となった。記念像のかなりの割合が裁判所の構内にあり，したがって人種差別がいかに法と警察制度の中に[16]定着していると考えられているかの象徴であると認識している人もいる。

　研究によって，圧倒的多数の像は，南部の軍人たちの犠牲[17]に敬意を表することを意図した無害な記念像というよりも，戦争が終わって半世紀近く経った1900年代初期に建立されていることが示された。この時期には，黒人の公民権を抑圧することを意図した[18]包括的な法律が[19]制定されており，一部の人々には，像は黒人市民[21]を圧制するために意図的に建立された[20]威嚇的な象徴であるとみられている。何十体もの像が取り壊されたが，かなりの数が残っている。

トリビュートとオマージュ

tribute（敬意，賛辞）は，日本語「トリビュートアルバム」や「トリビュートコンサート」でおなじみ。芸術作品の中で先人やその作品への敬意を表することを意味する日本語には，フランス語 hommage に由来する「オマージュ」もある。対応する英語は homage だが，tribute と homage は，一般的な「敬意」の意味でも「オマージュ」の意味でも同様に用いられる。パッセージでは戦死者に敬意を表すという文脈で使われているように，どちらも死者を悼む場面でしばしば用いられる。

The Confederate Monument Controversy

---

1 ☐☐
commemoration
[kəmèmərèɪʃən]

▶ memorial, ceremony, remembrance
名 記念碑, 記念（式）
動 commemorate　形 commemorative

---

2 ☐☐
oppression
[əpréʃən]

▶ persecution, repression, suppression
名 圧制, 抑圧
動 oppress　形 oppressive　名 oppressor

---

3 ☐☐
bigotry
[bígətri]

▶ prejudice, bias
名（思想などの）頑迷さ, 偏狭
名 bigot（頑迷な人）　形 bigoted

---

4 ☐☐
perpetuate
[pərpétʃuèɪt]

動 を永続［固定］化する
形 perpetual　名 perpetuation, perpetuity
● immortalize（に不朽の名声を与える）とは区別される

---

5 ☐☐
subjugation
[sʌ̀bdʒugéɪʃən]

名 服従させること, 征服
動 subjugate

---

6 ☐☐
enslavement
[ɪnsléɪvmənt]

名 隷属させること, 奴隷化
動 enslave

---

7 ☐☐
in the wake of ～

▶ in the aftermath of, as a consequence of, as a result of
～の結果として

---

8 ☐☐
brutality
[bruːtǽləti]

▶ cruelty, ferocity, savagery
名 残虐行為, 残忍さ
形 brutal

---

9 ☐☐
homicide
[há(ː)mɪsàɪd]

▶ murder, killing
名 殺人
● 計画性のない殺人は manslaughter と言う

---

10 ☐☐
unjustified
[ʌ̀ndʒʌ́stɪfàɪd]

▶ unwarranted
形 不当な, 正当な理由のない
⇔ justified

---

11 ☐☐
spring up

▶ develop quickly, appear suddenly
急に起こる, 突然現れる

---

12 ☐☐ **ire** [áɪər]	▶ anger, rage, wrath **名**（激しい）怒り ● raise the ire of the public（大衆の怒りを買う）
13 ☐☐ **enforcement** [ɪnfɔ́ːrsmənt]	**名**（法の）執行，施行 **動** enforce ● law enforcement system は警察制度のこと
14 ☐☐ **trample** [trǽmpl]	**動** 踏みにじる〈on 他者の権利などを〉，を踏みにじる
15 ☐☐ **civil rights**	公民権，市民権
16 ☐☐ **entrenched** [ɪntréntʃt]	▶ fixed, ingrained, rooted **形** 定着した，根付いた〈in ～に〉 ● en-（～の中に）＋trench（塹壕）
17 ☐☐ **pay tribute to ～**	▶ honor （公式の場で）～に敬意を表する
18 ☐☐ **sweeping** [swíːpɪŋ]	▶ extensive, comprehensive, all-inclusive **形** 包括的な，全般的な ● sweeping trade agreement（包括的貿易協定）
19 ☐☐ **enact** [ɪnǽkt]	▶ establish, pass **動**（法律）を制定する **名** enactment
20 ☐☐ **menacing** [ménəsɪŋ]	▶ threatening **形** 威嚇的な，脅威を与える **名 動** menace
21 ☐☐ **tyrannize** [tírənàɪz]	**動** に暴政［暴虐］を行う **名** tyranny（暴虐），tyrant（暴君）

Nonhuman Rights

These days, more and more people have accepted the idea that intelligent animals should be recognized as possessing similar rights to the ones that humans have.

1   In the past, the idea that animals might have rights like those of humans was considered ¹**absurd**, and even the most ²**sadistic** acts of animal cruelty were ³**tried** as mere ⁴**misdemeanors** in the legal system. Today, however, recognition of animals' self-awareness, cognitive ability, and capacity for suffering has led to changes that make animal cruelty a ⁵**felony**. In fact, there is growing recognition that the similarities between humans and animals may be so ⁶**profound** that animals like chimps and elephants could possibly deserve legal recognition as "nonhuman persons."

10   Though this was once very much a fringe idea, groups such as the Nonhuman Rights Project are currently ⁷**litigating** on behalf of various animals to grant them the same rights that humans enjoy in the ⁸**judicial** system. Simultaneously, ⁹**grass-roots** political movements are ¹⁰**lobbying** ¹¹**legislatures** in various countries to pass bills that would recognize animals' rights.

    Currently, efforts to recognize animals as ¹²**sentient** beings with rights are focusing on higher animals, but some critics worry this could be a slippery slope. Should less sophisticated animals be granted rights, the ¹³**captivity** and ¹⁴**slaughter** involved in modern agriculture could mean that our food supply is contributing to an animal ¹⁵**holocaust**. However, animal activists say that whatever the implications of judicial ¹⁶**rulings** may be, higher mammals bearing the greatest similarity to humans must be protected.

(219 words)

ℓ.18 slippery slope：滑りやすい坂道（それ自体は悪いことでなくても，それをきっかけにどんど ん物事が悪い方に進んでいく危険性を含んでいるという意味）

人間以外の動物の権利

近ごろ，知能の高い動物は人間が持つ権利と同様の権利を保持していると認識されるべきだという考えを受け入れる人がますます増えている。

　かつては，動物は人間と同様の権利を持っているかもしれないという考えは[1]ばかばかしいと考えられたし，最も[2]加虐的な動物虐待行為も法制度においては単なる[4]軽犯罪として[3]裁かれた。しかしながら，今日では，動物の自己認識，認知能力，それに苦痛を感じる能力が認識され，動物虐待が[5]重罪とされるという変化につながった。実際，人間と動物との類似性は[6]非常に高いため，チンパンジーやゾウなどの動物は，「非人間人格」として法的な認知を受ける権利があるかもしれないという認識が深まりつつある。

　これはかつては非主流派の考えであったが，「非人間の権利プロジェクト」などのグループは，現在さまざまな動物に代わって，彼らに人間が[8]司法制度において享受しているのと同じ権利を与えるべく[7]訴訟を起こしている。同時に，[9]草の根の政治的運動が動物の権利を認めるような法案を通過させるようさまざまな国の[11]立法機関[10]にロビー活動をしている。

　現在，動物を権利を持った[12]感覚のある生き物として認知するための努力は高等動物に焦点を当てているが，一部の批評家たちは，これが「滑りやすい坂道」になりかねないと危惧している。もしより下等動物に権利が与えられるようなことがあれば，現代の農業で行われている[13]捕獲や[14]食肉処理は，我々の食料調達が動物の[15]大虐殺の一因であることを意味する可能性がある。しかしながら，動物活動家たちは，司法[16]判決の意味するところがどうであろうと，人類との類似性が最も高い高等ほ乳類は保護されるべきだと言っている。

動物の福祉と権利

animal welfare（動物福祉，アニマルウェルフェア）と animal rights（動物の権利）という 2 つの理念には，動物の ownership（所有）をどう考えるかという点に根本的な違いがある。動物福祉は，家畜やペットのように，人間と動物の interaction（関わり合い，交流）を必要なものと見なし，動物の suffering（苦しみ）を最小限にして quality of life（生活の質，QOL）を保証することを目指す。動物の権利を主張するグループは動物の所有を認めず，動物園のように wildlife（野生動物）が in captivity（飼育された）環境に置かれることも否定する。パッセージのように，動物に personhood（人格）を認めるべきだという考えもある。

Nonhuman Rights

1 ☐☐ **absurd** [əbsə́:rd]	▶ ridiculous, idiotic, preposterous 形 ばかげた，不条理な 名 absurdity
2 ☐☐ **sadistic** [sədístɪk]	形 加虐的な，サディスティックな 名 sadism, sadist ⇔ masochistic
3 ☐☐ **try** [traɪ]	▶ adjudicate, put ~ on trial 動 (事件) を審理する，(人) を裁判にかける 名 trial
4 ☐☐ **misdemeanor** [mìsdɪmí:nər]	名 軽犯罪
5 ☐☐ **felony** [féləni]	名 重罪 名 felon (重罪犯)　形 felonious
6 ☐☐ **profound** [prəfáund]	▶ extensive, major, significant 形 (程度が) 非常に大きい，深い 名 profundity
7 ☐☐ **litigate** [lítəgèɪt]	▶ sue, file a (law)suit 動 訴訟を起こす 名 litigation
8 ☐☐ **judicial** [dʒudíʃəl] ⓘ	形 司法の，裁判の ● 「立法の」は legislative，「行政の」は executive
9 ☐☐ **grass-roots** [grǽsrú:ts]	形 一般大衆の，草の根の ● the grass roots で「一般大衆，草の根」の意味
10 ☐☐ **lobby** [lá(:)bi]	動 (に) ロビー活動を行う 〈for ~を求めて〉 名 ロビー団体，陳情 [圧力] 団体 名 lobbyist
11 ☐☐ **legislature** [lédʒəslèɪtʃər]	▶ a body of people who have the power to make laws 名 立法機関

12 ☐☐ **sentient** [sénʃənt]	▶ capable of experiencing feelings and sensations 形 感覚を持った，知覚力のある ⇔ insentient
13 ☐☐ **captivity** [kæptívəti]	▶ confinement 名 捕獲された状態，捕らわれの身 形 captive
14 ☐☐ **slaughter** [slɔ́ːtər] ❶	▶ the killing of animals for food 名 畜殺，（家畜の）食肉処理
15 ☐☐ **holocaust** [hóʊləkɔ̀ːst]	名 大虐殺，ホロコースト
16 ☐☐ **ruling** [rúːlɪŋ]	▶ decision，judgment 名 判決，裁定 動 rule
☐☐ **mistreat** [mìstríːt]	▶ abuse，ill-treat，maltreat 動 を虐待する 名 mistreatment
☐☐ **emancipate** [ɪmǽnsɪpèɪt]	▶ free，liberate，release，set free 動 を解放する，を自由にする 名 emancipation
☐☐ **hubris** [hjúːbrɪs]	▶ arrogance，conceit 名 慢心，傲慢 ● human hubris（人間の傲慢さ）

政治・経済 **5**

Unpaid Labor and the Economy

Some economists argue that GDP statistics should include the economic contributions of people who do important but unpaid activities, like child raising and housework.

1   A nation's ¹**prosperity** is often measured in terms of its gross domestic product, or GDP, which is the ²**aggregate** value of all the goods and services produced in the country. While GDP ³**is intended to** provide a comprehensive measurement of the state of the nation's economy, some
5   economists contend that it excludes the contributions of women.

These economists argue that without ⁴**uncompensated** activities, such as child raising and domestic chores, which are often performed by women, the economic activities of male ⁵**breadwinners** would be impossible. This was demonstrated in 1975 when 90 percent of Icelandic
10   women refused to cook, clean, or look after children for a day, bringing the nation to a ⁶**standstill**. Of course, factoring unpaid labor into economic calculations is exceedingly difficult, but some say it is vital. According to one estimate, unpaid labor adds a ⁷**staggering** $10.9 trillion of value to the world economy.

15   Without a more comprehensive calculation that includes all ⁸**indicators** of economic activity, the government will lack critical ⁹**insights** into the true state of the nation. Since GDP is utilized when policymakers are ¹⁰**contemplating** crucial decisions about things like the ¹¹**allocation** of funds for economic ¹²**stimulus** ¹³**packages**, the
20   ¹⁴**redistribution** of wealth, and monetary policy, serious consideration should be given to a more comprehensive calculation of economic activity in the nation.   (216 words)

無償労働と経済

一部の経済学者たちは，GDP 統計に子育てや家事などの重要だが無償の活動をする人々の経済貢献を含むべきだと主張している。

　国家の ^{1}繁栄は，しばしば国内で生産されるすべての品物やサービスの ^{2}総額である国内総生産，すなわち GDP の観点から測られる。GDP が国家の経済状態の包括的な測定をする ^{3}ようにできている一方で，一部の経済学者たちはそこからは女性の貢献が除外されていると主張する。

　これらの経済学者たちは，しばしば女性たちが担っている子育てや家事などの ^{4}無償の働きなしでは，^{5}稼ぎ手としての男性の経済活動は不可能だと論じる。このことは1975 年にアイスランドの女性の 90％が料理，掃除，子育てを 1 日拒否した結果，国家が ^{6}完全に停止状態になったことで実証された。もちろん，無償労働を経済的算定の要素に入れることは非常に困難だが，それが必要不可欠だと言う人もいる。ある見積もりによると，無償労働は世界経済に ^{7}圧倒的な 10 兆 9 千億ドルもの価値を加えるという。

　すべての経済活動の ^{8}指標を加えた包括的な算定なしでは，政府は国家の実態に対する重大な ^{9}洞察を欠くことになる。GDP は政策立案者たちが経済 ^{12}刺激 ^{13}対策に対する資金の ^{11}割り当てや，富の ^{14}再分配，金融政策などに関する重大な決定 ^{10}について考慮するときに利用されるので，国家の経済活動のより包括的な算定に真剣な検討が必要である。

ねばねばの床

毎年発表される gender gap index（ジェンダーギャップ指数）は，経済・教育・保健・政治の 4 分野を基に世界各国の男女格差を数値化したもので，日本は世界 150 数カ国中 120 位前後が近年の定位置である。特に日本が遅れているのは女性の participation in politics（政治参加）と advancement in the workplace（職場進出）だと言われる。household chores（家事）や child rearing（育児）といった無償労働の主な担い手はいまだに女性であり，女性の workforce（労働人口）の半数以上は irregular employment（非正規雇用）である。昇進の可能性のない低賃金の仕事は sticky floor（ねばねばの床）と表現されることもある。

Unpaid Labor and the Economy

1 ☐☐ **prosperity** [prɑ(:)spérəti]	▶ affluence, wealth 名 繁栄, 裕福 動 prosper　形 prosperous
2 ☐☐ **aggregate** [ǽgrɪgət] ❶	▶ total 形 総計の　名 総計 名 aggregation
3 ☐☐ **be intended to _do_**	（事・物が）〜するために作られている
4 ☐☐ **uncompensated** [ʌnkɑ́(:)mpənsèɪtɪd]	▶ unpaid 形 補償されない, 無償の
5 ☐☐ **breadwinner** [brédwìnər]	▶ someone whose income supports their family 名 （家族の）稼ぎ手 ● 「パンを獲得する人」という意味
6 ☐☐ **standstill** [stǽndstìl]	▶ halt, stop 名 停止, 休止 ● be at a standstill（停止している）
7 ☐☐ **staggering** [stǽgərɪŋ]	▶ amazing, astounding, whopping 形 圧倒的な, 驚異的な 動 stagger　● 主に数量の大きさを強調する
8 ☐☐ **indicator** [índɪkèɪtər]	▶ sign, gauge, index, measure 名 指標, 尺度〈of 〜の〉 動 indicate　● economic indicator（経済指標）
9 ☐☐ **insight** [ínsàɪt] ❶	▶ understanding, comprehension 名 洞察（力）, 理解（力）〈into 〜への〉
10 ☐☐ **contemplate** [kɑ́(:)ntəmplèɪt] ❶	▶ consider, intend, think about [of] 動 を（しようかと）考える, を意図する 名 contemplation
11 ☐☐ **allocation** [æ̀ləkéɪʃən]	▶ allotment, assignment 名 割り当て, 配分 動 allocate

12 ☐☐ **stimulus** [stímjʊləs]	▶ spur, impetus, stimulant **名** 刺激 **動** stimulate ● 複数形は stimuli
13 ☐☐ **package** [pǽkɪdʒ] ❶	**名** 一括提案 ● financial aid package（学資援助パッケージ。複数の奨学金などを組み合わせたもの）
14 ☐☐ **redistribution** [rìːdɪstrɪbjúːʃən]	**名** 再配分 **動** redistribute
☐☐ **encompass** [ɪnkʌ́mpəs]	▶ cover, include, involve **動** を含む，を包含する ● all-encompassing（包括的な）
☐☐ **menial** [míːniəl]	▶ unskilled **形** 技術不要の，単純で退屈な ● menial work（単純労働）
☐☐ **devalue** [dìːvǽljuː]	▶ belittle, depreciate, undervalue **動** の価値を減じる，を低く評価する **名** devaluation

政治・経済 **6**

Compulsory Voting

This passage looks at the reasons that some countries have laws which say all adult citizens must vote in elections.

1   In countries including Australia, Brazil, and Turkey, voting in political elections is mandatory, and those who fail to [1]**cast ballots** are [2]**subject to** fines, and, in some cases, even [3]**imprisonment**. While there is a clear [4]**correlation** between countries with compulsory voting and high turnout

5   rates for elections, forcing people to vote is highly contentious.

[5]**Proponents** argue that compulsory voting provides a strong [6]**inducement** for politicians to make their policies clear to the entire electorate, rather than attempting to cater to certain [7]**segments** that are most likely to vote. Furthermore, [8]**dwindling** voter turnouts in recent

10   years have caused candidates and governments to [9]**expend** huge sums on campaigns encouraging people to [10]**go to the polls**, so compulsory voting would reduce this expense.

On the other hand, opponents maintain that compulsory voting infringes on people's freedom. Such [11]**coercion**, they argue, could lead to

15   people making uninformed decisions if they are only voting for the sake of [12]**evading** fines. They even claim that it could [13]**render** the electoral process meaningless if people began randomly marking ballots.

While voting is often considered both a [14]**civic** duty and an essential [15]**underpinning** of democracy, the question of whether it should be made

20   mandatory is a controversial one with strong arguments on both sides.

🏴 (206 words)

強制投票制度

この文章では，一部の国が成人の国民に投票を強制する法律を持っている理由を見ていく。

　オーストラリア，ブラジル，トルコを含む国々では，政治選挙における投票は義務であり，¹投票しない者は罰金か，場合によっては³収監²の対象となる。強制投票制度のある国と選挙の投票率の高さには，はっきりとした⁴相関関係があるが，人々に投票を強制することは大いに議論の余地がある。

　（制度の）⁵支持者たちは，強制投票制度は政治家に，投票する可能性の高い一部の⁷階層に迎合しようとするのではなく，全有権者に対して自分の政策をはっきりさせようという，強い⁶誘因を与えると主張する。さらに，近年の⁸低迷する投票率が原因で，候補者と政府は人々が¹⁰投票に行くように促すためのキャンペーンに，莫大なお金⁹を使うようになったので，強制投票制度はこのような費用の削減になるだろう。

　他方，反対派たちは，強制投票制度は人々の自由を侵害すると主張する。彼らによると，そのような¹¹強制は，もし人々が罰金¹²逃れのためだけに投票するのであれば，情報不足の状態で決断を下すことになりかねないと主張する。彼らは，人々が無作為に投票し始めたなら，それは選挙過程を無意味なもの¹³にするとさえ断言する。

　選挙制度は¹⁴市民としての義務であり，民主主義に欠かせない¹⁵土台であるとしばしば見なされるが，それが強制とされるべきかどうかという問題は，双方が強い主張を持った，賛否の分かれる問題である。

Compulsory Voting

1 ☐☐ **cast a ballot**	▶ cast a vote, vote 票を投じる
2 ☐☐ **subject to ～**	▶ under the control of （法律など）の支配下にあって，～に従属して ● be subject to tax（課税対象となる）
3 ☐☐ **imprisonment** [ɪmprízənmənt]	▶ incarceration **名** 投獄，禁固 **動** imprison ● life imprisonment（終身刑）
4 ☐☐ **correlation** [kɔ̀(:)rəléɪʃən]	▶ connection, relation **名** 相互関係，相関性〈between ～間の〉 **動** correlate **形** correlative
5 ☐☐ **proponent** [prəpóunənt]	▶ advocate, supporter, upholder **名** 支持者，擁護者 ⮀ opponent（反対者），critic（批判者）
6 ☐☐ **inducement** [ɪndjúːsmənt]	▶ incentive, motivation, motive **名** 誘因，動機〈to do ～する〉 **動** induce ● financial inducement（金銭的誘因）
7 ☐☐ **segment** [ségmənt]	▶ part, section, division, portion **名** 階層，部分，断片 **形** segmental ⮀ whole
8 ☐☐ **dwindle** [dwíndl]	▶ shrink **動** 次第に減少する，衰える ● dwindling population（先細りする人口）
9 ☐☐ **expend** [ɪkspénd]	▶ spend, use, lay out **動** を費やす，を使う〈on ～に〉 **名** expenditure, expense
10 ☐☐ **go to the polls**	投票に行く ● the polls は「投票所」の意味。The polls open at 7 a.m.（投票所は午前 7 時に開く）
11 ☐☐ **coercion** [kouə́ːrʃən]	▶ force, compulsion, pressure **名** 強制，威圧 **動** coerce **形** coercive

12 ☐☐ **evade** [ɪvéɪd]	▶ avoid, dodge, escape 動 (義務・責任など) を逃れる, を回避する 名 evasion 形 evasive
13 ☐☐ **render _A B_**	▶ make _A B_ A を B にする, A を B に変える ● 補語 B は形容詞
14 ☐☐ **civic** [sívɪk]	形 公民の, 市民としての ● 本来 civic は「市の, 町の」, civil は「(軍人・聖職者 に対して) 民間人の, 一般市民の」という意味
15 ☐☐ **underpinning** [ʌ́ndərpìnɪŋ]	▶ basis, foundation 名 基盤, 土台 動 underpin (を補強する)
☐☐ **statutory** [stǽtʃʊtɔ̀:ri]	▶ regulated or determined by law 形 法令の, 法定の 名 statute
☐☐ **mandate** [mǽndeɪt] ❶	▶ authority 名 (選挙を通じて与えられた) 権限 〈for ～の, to _do_ ～する〉
☐☐ **constituent** [kənstítʃuənt]	▶ voter, elector 名 (選挙区の) 有権者, 選挙人 名 constituency (選挙区)
☐☐ **nudge** [nʌdʒ]	▶ encourage, prompt 動 を促す, を後押しする 〈toward ～へと, into _doing_ ～するよう〉 ●「を肘でつつく」が本義

政治・経済 **7**

Economic Sanctions

Although economic sanctions are often used to pressure other countries into changing their policies, critics complain that they often do more harm than good.

In the face of human rights ¹**abuses** or ²**flagrant** violations of international treaties, various nations have turned to economic sanctions to pressure other countries into complying with the demands of the international community without resorting to military force. Sanctions and ³**blockades** can also reduce the threat of ⁴**rogue** nations acquiring weapons of mass destruction, hamper the activities of state-sponsored terrorist groups, and combat the illegal ⁵**narcotics** trade.

However, sanctions can have ⁶**unintended** consequences. Economic sanctions on Pakistan by the US, for example, are said to have increased its ⁷**reliance** on nuclear weapons, dangerously ⁸**escalating** tensions with India. Furthermore, sanctions can even bolster ⁹**authoritarian regimes** by creating scarcity. This permits governments to tighten controls on the distribution of goods and can ¹⁰**trigger** mass ¹¹**exoduses** of people that turn into refugee crises.

According to experts, for sanctions to be effective, they should generally not be imposed ¹²**unilaterally**, as targeted nations will likely just procure goods from another country instead. It is also believed that sanctions tend to be most effective when goals are ¹³**modest** and the countries involved have previously had an ¹⁴**amicable** relationship. Furthermore, sanctions are most effective when the target country is economically weak. While sanctions can be an effective tool, they should not be entered into ¹⁵**impetuously**.　　　　　　　　　(208 words)

経済制裁

経済制裁は他国が政策を変えるよう圧力をかけるために用いられることが多いが，批評家たちはそれらはしばしば有害無益であると不満を述べている。

人権 ¹侵害や ²言語道断な国際協定違反に直面して，さまざまな国は軍事力に訴えることなく他国が国際社会の要求に応じるよう圧力をかけるために，経済制裁に乗りだした。制裁と ³封鎖は，⁴ならずもの国家が大量破壊兵器を手に入れる脅威を減らし，国が資金を出しているテロリスト集団の活動を阻止し，違法な ⁵麻薬取引と戦うことをも可能にする。

しかし，制裁は ⁶意図していなかった結果を生む可能性がある。例えばアメリカによるパキスタンへの経済制裁が，彼らの核兵器 ⁷依存を高め，インドとの緊張を危険なほどに ⁸急激に高めたと言われている。さらに，制裁は物資不足を作り出すことによって，⁹権威主義体制を強化することすらある。このことは，政府が商品の流通に関する支配を強めることを許し，難民危機を生むような，人々の大規模な ¹¹国外脱出 ¹⁰のきっかけとなり得る。

専門家によると，対象国は代わりに他の国から商品を入手するだけだろうから，制裁を効果的にするには，一般的に言って，それらを ¹²一方的に課してはならない。また，制裁は目標が ¹³控えめで，関係する国々が以前は ¹⁴友好的な関係を持っていた場合に最も効果的になりやすいと信じられている。さらに，制裁は，対象国が経済的に弱い場合に最も効果的である。制裁は効果的な手段になり得るが，¹⁵性急に開始してはならない。

聖書由来の表現

exodus は聖書の Exodus（出エジプト記。モーセ率いるユダヤ人の大脱出）が普通名詞化した語。apocalypse（世界の終わり）や Armageddon（ハルマゲドン，最終戦争）のような特殊な語のみならず，scapegoat（スケープゴート，身代わり），broken heart（傷心），bite the dust（死ぬ，倒れる）といった日常的に用いる語やフレーズも聖書から来ている。You reap what you sow.（まいた種は自分で刈る，自業自得）など，聖書に起源を持つことわざも多い。Cast pearls before swine.（豚に真珠）も聖書の一節に由来する。

Economic Sanctions

1 ☐☐ **abuse** [əbjúːs] ❶	▶ maltreatment, mistreatment, violation 名 (権利の) 侵害, 虐待 形 abusive
2 ☐☐ **flagrant** [fléɪɡrənt]	▶ blatant, outrageous 形 言語道断の, 目に余る
3 ☐☐ **blockade** [blɑ(ː)kéɪd]	名 (港湾・道路などの) 封鎖　動 を封鎖する ● enforce a naval blockade (海軍による海上封鎖を実施する)
4 ☐☐ **rogue** [roʊɡ] ❶	形 (体制・基準から) はみ出した ● 名詞 rogue は「悪党, ならずもの」の意味
5 ☐☐ **narcotic** [nɑːrkɑ́(ː)t̬ɪk]	名 麻薬, 麻酔薬 形 麻薬の ● narcotics addict (麻薬常用者)
6 ☐☐ **unintended** [ʌ̀nɪnténdɪd]	▶ unintentional, accidental, inadvertent 形 意図的でない, 故意でない ⇄ intended
7 ☐☐ **reliance** [rɪláɪəns]	▶ dependence 名 依存 〈on, upon ～への〉 動 rely　形 reliant
8 ☐☐ **escalate** [éskəlèɪt] ❶	▶ increase, intensify, magnify 動 を増大させる, を激化させる 名 escalation
9 ☐☐ **authoritarian regime**	権威主義体制
10 ☐☐ **trigger** [tríɡər]	▶ cause, start, bring about, set off 動 のきっかけとなる, を引き起こす ●「引き金」が本義
11 ☐☐ **exodus** [éksədəs]	名 大量移動, 大量出国

12 ☐☐ **unilaterally** [jùːnilǽṭ̬ərəli]	副 一方的に 形 unilateral ⇄ bilaterally（双務的に）
13 ☐☐ **modest** [mά(ː)dəst]	▶ moderate, passable 形 （大きさ・程度などが）控えめな，適度の 名 modesty
14 ☐☐ **amicable** [ǽmɪkəbl]	▶ friendly, peaceful 形 （関係などが）友好的な，平和的な 名 amicability　副 amicably
15 ☐☐ **impetuously** [ɪmpétʃuəsli]	▶ impulsively, rashly 副 性急に，衝動的に 形 impetuous
☐☐ **freeze** [fríːz]	動 （資産など）を凍結する 名 （資産などの）凍結 ● have one's assets frozen（資産を凍結される）
☐☐ **pull out**	▶ withdraw, pull back 撤退する，手を引く〈of ～から〉 ● pull out of a project（プロジェクトから撤退する）
☐☐ **disrupt** [dɪsrʌ́pt]	▶ disturb, interrupt, obstruct 動 を混乱させる，を妨害する 名 disruption　形 disruptive
☐☐ **dissuade** [dɪswéɪd] ❶	▶ discourage 動 を説得して思いとどまらせる〈from ～を〉 ⇄ persuade
☐☐ **in coordination with ～**	▶ together with, in cooperation with ～と協調して，～と連携して

政治・経済 **8**

Election Promises

Despite politicians' reputation for being dishonest, research shows elected leaders actually keep a surprisingly high percentage of their election promises.

1　　Politicians are ¹**infamous** among the general public for making ²**grand** promises during election campaigns and then failing to ³**follow through** on them once ⁴**in office**. ⁵**Contrary to** ⁶**conventional wisdom** and common ⁷**portrayals** in the media, however, research shows that
5　political parties fulfill ⁸**the bulk of** their campaign ⁹**pledges**.

　　When surveyed on whether politicians were sincere when they made promises, fewer than a third of ¹⁰**respondents** agreed that politicians were actually ¹¹**striving** to keep their word. However, when researchers examined party ¹²**manifestos** for promises and then analyzed the party's
10　¹³**subsequent** actions, they found that in the UK, more than 85 percent of pledges had been at least partially enacted. The researchers did find, though, that political ¹⁴**expediency**, such as entering into coalitions, tended to greatly reduce the chances of a promise being kept, and that, unfortunately, the ¹⁵**odds** that a politician would ¹⁶**deliver on** promises
15　that voters felt were of the most consequence were much lower than for those considered less important.

　　The ¹⁷**striking** difference between public perceptions and the actual results of politicians' actions has been called the pledge ¹⁸**paradox**. One possible explanation for this is a so-called negativity bias that causes
20　voters to remember broken promises better than the ones they actually delivered on.　　　　　　　　　　　　　　🇬🇧 (205 words)

選挙公約

政治家は不誠実という世評にもかかわらず，研究によれば選出された指導者たちは実際，選挙公約を驚くべき高い割合で守っている。

政治家は選挙運動期間には ²壮大な約束をして，一旦 ⁴職に就くとそれらを ³守らないことで一般大衆に ¹悪評が高い。しかし，⁶社会通念やメディアのよくある ⁷描写 ⁵とは逆に，研究によると政党は選挙 ⁹公約 ⁸の大半を実行する。

政治家が公約をしたときに誠実であったかどうかを調査すると，政治家たちは実際に約束を守ろうと ¹¹努力しているということに賛成するのは，¹⁰回答者の3分の1以下であった。しかし，研究者たちが公約について党の ¹²マニフェストを調べた後，¹³それに続く党の行動を分析すると，英国では公約の85％以上が少なくとも部分的に実行されていた。研究者たちは，しかし，連立を組むなどの党の ¹⁴ご都合主義が，公約を果たす機会を大いに減少させる傾向にあり，また不幸にも，投票者たちが最も重大だと感じていた公約を政治家が ¹⁶実行する ¹⁵確率は，より重要性が低いと考えられる公約の確率よりもずっと低いということを確かに発見した。

政治家の行動に関する大衆の認識と実際の結果についての ¹⁷驚くべき相違が，公約の ¹⁸逆説と呼ばれてきた。このことについて考えられる説明の1つが，投票者たちは実際に実行された公約よりも，破られた公約の方を覚えているといういわゆるネガティビティバイアスである。

認知バイアス

人が情報を処理するとき無意識のうちに誤りを犯す現象を cognitive bias（認知バイアス）と言う。守られなかった公約のように記憶に残りやすいネガティブな情報によって生じる判断の偏りが，ネガティビティバイアスである。他に，予期しない事態に遭遇しても自分は大丈夫と楽観して判断を誤る normalcy bias（正常性バイアス），自分の先入観に合致する情報だけを集め都合の悪い情報は無視する confirmation bias（確証バイアス），すでに起こったことについて予測できていなかったことまで予測していたと勘違いする hindsight bias（後知恵バイアス）など，心理学者によってさまざまに分類されている。

Election Promises

1 ☐☐ **infamous** [ínfəməs] ❶	▶ notorious, disreputable 形 悪評の高い，悪名高い〈for 〜で〉 名 infamy
2 ☐☐ **grand** [grænd]	▶ grandiose, lofty, ostentatious 形 壮大な，遠大な 名 grandeur
3 ☐☐ **follow through**	▶ complete, finish やり遂げる，やり抜く〈on, with 約束・計画などを〉 ● follow through 〜（〜をやり抜く）という用法もある
4 ☐☐ **in office**	要職に就いて，在任して ⇔ out of office ● 官職・公職について用いる
5 ☐☐ **contrary to 〜**	▶ at odds with, in opposition to 〜と反対に，〜と違って
6 ☐☐ **conventional wisdom**	▶ commonly held and widely accepted views or beliefs 社会通念，一般通念
7 ☐☐ **portrayal** [pɔːrtréɪəl]	▶ depiction, description, account 名 描写，叙述 動 portray
8 ☐☐ **the bulk of 〜**	▶ most of, the major part of 〜の大半，〜の大部分
9 ☐☐ **pledge** [pledʒ]	▶ promise, commitment, undertaking 名 公約，約束 ● keep [break] a pledge（約束を守る［破る])
10 ☐☐ **respondent** [rɪspá(ː)ndənt]	名 （調査などの）回答者 動 respond ●「回答」は answer または reply
11 ☐☐ **strive** [straɪv]	▶ endeavor, labor, struggle 動 努力する，奮闘する〈to do 〜しようと〉 名 striving

12 ☐☐ **manifesto** [mǽnɪféstou] ❶	▶ platform, policy statement **名** (政党などの) 宣言 (書), マニフェスト
13 ☐☐ **subsequent** [sʌ́bsɪkwənt] ❶	▶ following, ensuing **形** それに続く, その後の **副** subsequently ⬌ previous
14 ☐☐ **expediency** [ɪkspí:diənsi]	▶ opportunism **名** ご都合主義, 便宜主義 **形** expedient
15 ☐☐ **odds** [ɑ(:)dz]	▶ chance, likelihood, probability **名** 見込み, 公算 ● have long odds ((成功などの) 見込みが小さい)
16 ☐☐ **deliver on ~**	▶ fulfill, keep, come through with (約束など) を果たす
17 ☐☐ **striking** [stráɪkɪŋ]	▶ remarkable, marked, noticeable **形** 著しい, 際立った **副** strikingly
18 ☐☐ **paradox** [pǽrədɑ̀(:)ks] ❶	**名** 逆説, パラドックス **形** paradoxical
☐☐ **out of sync**	一致しない, ずれて 〈with ~と〉 ⬌ in sync ● sync は synchronization (一致) の略
☐☐ **explicit** [ɪksplísɪt]	▶ clear, straightforward, unequivocal **形** (発言や文章の内容が) 明確な, 曖昧さのない **副** explicitly ⬌ implicit
☐☐ **consistent** [kənsístənt]	▶ steady, unswerving, unwavering **形** 首尾一貫した, 筋の通った **名** consistency ⬌ inconsistent

政治・経済 **9**

Fighting Corruption

This passage is a look at how things like education and an emphasis on traditional culture can be valuable in preventing corruption in business and government.

1　　The problem of corruption has ¹**plagued** mankind throughout human history, ²**impeding** both economic development and the ³**equitable** distribution of wealth. In societies where corruption has become deeply ⁴**embedded**, eradicating it can seem like a ⁵**futile** endeavor. However,

5　some societies have made successful efforts to reduce activities like ⁶**bribery**, ⁷**influence peddling**, and ⁸**embezzlement**.

　　Hong Kong, for instance, has developed a highly effective anti-corruption agency. Its success has been ⁹**attributed** not just **to** its proven ¹⁰**track record** of carrying out effective large-scale investigations, but also

10　to its emphasis on ¹¹**altering** public attitudes. It operates various public education programs to instill proper morals at all ages. For example, entertaining books and videos are provided to kindergartens that are filled with stories featuring cute cartoon characters facing ¹²**ethical** ¹³**dilemmas** in which the ¹⁴**morally** ¹⁵**upstanding** individual always wins.

15　　While corruption is often viewed as being rooted in culture and tradition, this is not always true. In fact, these very things are being used to fight corruption in Botswana. ¹⁶**Hierarchy** and ¹⁷**meritocracy** are an important part of the country's traditional tribal culture, and they have helped to make it possible to speedily remove ¹⁸**inept** or corrupt leaders.

20　These traditions have combined with effective accounting and ¹⁹**auditing** systems, whistle-blower protection laws, and ²⁰**oversight** agencies to make Botswana one of the least corrupt nations in Africa.　　　(218 words)

汚職と戦う

この文章は，教育や伝統文化に重点を置くことなどがいかにビジネスと政治における汚職を防ぐのに役立つかを示している。

　汚職の問題は，経済発展と ³公正な富の分配 ²を妨げることで，人間の歴史を通して人類 ¹を苦しめてきた。汚職が深く ⁴組み込まれてしまった社会においては，それを撲滅するのは ⁵無駄な努力のように見えてしまう。しかしながら，⁶贈収賄や ⁷あっ旋収賄，⁸横領などの活動を減少させる努力が成功した社会もある。

　例えば香港は，非常に効果的な汚職防止機関を発展させた。その成功は効果的な大規模調査を実施してきたという定評のある ¹⁰実績だけでなく，市民の態度 ¹¹を変えることに重点を置いた点にも ⁹起因すると考えられている。その機関は，あらゆる年代に正しい道徳を根付かせるようなさまざまな市民教育プログラムを実施している。例えば，幼稚園にはかわいいマンガのキャラクターが登場し，¹²倫理的な ¹³窮地に陥りながらも，必ず ¹⁴道徳的に ¹⁵正しい個人が勝利するという物語でいっぱいの面白い本やビデオを提供している。

　汚職はしばしば文化や伝統に根を下ろしていると見られるが，常にそうとは限らない。実際，まさにこれらがボツワナでの汚職との戦いに用いられているのだ。¹⁶階級制と ¹⁷能力主義はこの国の伝統的な部族文化の重要な部分であり，それらは ¹⁸無能な，あるいは腐敗した指導者たちを素早く排除することを可能にするのに役立ってきた。これらの伝統が効率的な会計および ¹⁹監査のシステム，告発者保護法，それに ²⁰監視機関と結びついて，ボツワナをアフリカで最も汚職の少ない国の1つにしたのである。

能力主義の功罪

meritocracy は merit（長所，功績）と接尾辞 -cracy（統治，支配）を組み合わせた語で，social mobility（社会的流動性）を阻害する要因，例えば social class（社会階級），nepotism（親族登用），cronyism（身びいき）などを排した，能力の高い者が上に立つ平等な競争社会に基づく統治制度を言う。一方，支配層が privileged class（特権階級）となることで富や地位が子孫に受け継がれる新たな hereditary system（世襲制）が固定し，equal opportunity（機会平等）という本来の理念が失われる可能性，また，empathy（共感力）や humility（謙遜）を欠いたエリートが統治する technocracy（技術官僚主義）が台頭する危険性も指摘されている。

Fighting Corruption

1 ☐☐
plague
[pleɪɡ] ⚠
▶ afflict, torment, torture
動 を絶えず苦しめる，を絶えず悩ます
● 「疫病」が本義。the plague は「ペスト」の意味

2 ☐☐
impede
[ɪmpíːd]
▶ block, hamper, hinder, obstruct
動 を妨げる，を邪魔する
名 impediment

3 ☐☐
equitable
[ékwətəbl]
▶ fair, just, impartial
形 公正な，公平な
名 equity **副** equitably **⇔** inequitable

4 ☐☐
embed
[ɪmbéd]
▶ plant, root
動 （考え方など）を刻み込む，を根付かせる
● 通例受身形で用いる

5 ☐☐
futile
[fjúːtl]
▶ pointless, useless, vain, worthless
形 無駄な，無益な
名 futility **⇔** worthwhile

6 ☐☐
bribery
[bráɪbəri]
名 贈収賄
動 名 bribe（を買収する；賄賂）

7 ☐☐
influence peddling
あっ旋収賄
● peddling は「（麻薬などの）密売」の意味

8 ☐☐
embezzlement
[ɪmbézlmənt]
▶ misappropriation
名 横領，着服
動 embezzle **名** embezzler

9 ☐☐
attribute A to B
▶ ascribe A to B
A を B に帰する，A を B の結果と見なす

10 ☐☐
track record
▶ achievement
実績，業績
● have a proven track record（確かな実績がある）

11 ☐☐
alter
[ɔ́ːltər] ⚠
▶ change, modify, vary, revamp
動 を変える
名 alteration

12 ☐☐ **ethical** [éθɪkəl]	▶ moral **形** 倫理上の，道徳の **名** ethics
13 ☐☐ **dilemma** [dɪlémə]	**名** ジレンマ，板挟み ● ethical dilemma は moral dilemma とも言う
14 ☐☐ **morally** [mɔ́(:)rəli]	▶ ethically **副** 道徳的に，道徳上 **形** **名** moral
15 ☐☐ **upstanding** [ʌ̀pstǽndɪŋ]	▶ honest, respectable, upright **形** 正直な，清廉な ● upstanding citizen（立派な市民）
16 ☐☐ **hierarchy** [háɪərɑ̀ːrki] ❶	**名** 階層［階級］制，ヒエラルキー **形** hierarchic(al) ● pecking order（（階級組織の）序列）という表現もある
17 ☐☐ **meritocracy** [mèrɪtá(:)krəsi]	**名** 能力［実力］主義（社会） **形** meritocratic
18 ☐☐ **inept** [ɪnépt]	▶ incompetent, unskillful **形** 無能な，力不足の **名** ineptitude ⇔ competent
19 ☐☐ **audit** [ɔ́ːdət]	**動** の会計監査をする **名** 会計監査 **名** auditor（会計監査人）
20 ☐☐ **oversight** [óʊvərsàɪt]	▶ supervision, superintendence, direction **名** 監視，監督 **動** oversee **名** overseer（監督者）

Referendums

···

Referendums, in which people vote directly on a single issue, are becoming increasingly common, but they have both advantages and disadvantages.

1   In democratic nations, the general public elects leaders to make political decisions for the country. However, on occasion, **[1]referendums**, in which the **[2]electorate** votes directly on a political issue, are held, particularly for matters such as decisions regarding whether a region will
5   **[3]secede** from a nation, or on constitutional matters.

[4]Advocates of this direct decision-making system say that in these days of voter apathy and **[5]disenchantment** with traditional elections, referendums engage voters in critical issues. Furthermore, referendums give clear mandates that add **[6]legitimacy** to government policies on
10   contentious issues, such as the reform of **[7]marijuana** laws, since it is clear that the electorate has spoken in favor of or against them.

[8]Detractors of referendums, however, argue that such votes are susceptible to **[9]deceitful** **[10]tactics**. For example, opposing **[11]camps** sometimes resort to **[12]distorting** the truth or even tell outright lies, and
15   this can be **[13]viciously** **[14]divisive**. Furthermore, some people also argue that average voters are not sufficiently well-informed to make decisions, and that since turnouts for referendums are often lower than those for elections, they are actually less democratic.

As referendums become more common, it seems that careful
20   consideration should be given to how and when they are used.

🏴 (198 words)

国民投票

国民投票，すなわち人々が1つの問題に対して直接投票することはますます一般的になっているが，これにはメリットとデメリットの両方がある。

　民主主義国家では，一般民衆が国の政治的決断をする指導者を選ぶ。しかし，時には1つの政治的問題，特にある地域が国から³離脱するかどうか決定するといった問題や，憲法問題について，²有権者が直接投票をする¹国民投票が行われる。

　この直接的な意思決定システムを⁴支持する人たちは，この従来の選挙に対する有権者たちの無関心と⁵幻滅の時代に，国民投票は重大な問題に有権者たちを参加させると言う。さらに，国民投票は，有権者たちが賛成や反対の意見を述べたことがはっきりしているので，例えば⁷大麻規制法の改正などの議論を呼びやすい問題についての政府の政策に⁶正当性を付け加えるような明確な権能を与える。

　しかしながら，国民投票の⁸反対者たちは，そのような投票は⁹人を欺く¹⁰戦術に影響されやすいと論じる。例えば，反対¹¹陣営は時には事実¹²を歪曲するという手段に訴えたり，まったくの嘘をついたりすることさえあり，これは¹³残虐に¹⁴分断を生む可能性がある。さらに，平均的な有権者たちは決定を下すのに十分な情報を得ておらず，国民投票の投票率はしばしば選挙よりも低いので，実はあまり民主的ではないと言う人もいる。

　国民投票がより一般的になるにしたがって，それらがどのように，いつ使用されるかについて注意深い考慮がなされなければならないと思われる。

Referendums

1 ☐☐
referendum
[rèfəréndəm]

▶ plebiscite, public vote
名 国民投票

---

2 ☐☐
electorate
[ɪléktərət]

▶ voters, electors
名 有権者
● 集合名詞

---

3 ☐☐
secede
[sɪsíːd]

▶ separate, become independent
動 離脱する, 独立する〈from 国などから〉
名 secession

---

4 ☐☐
advocate
[ǽdvəkət] ❶

▶ proponent, supporter, upholder
名（主義・政策などの）支持者, 主張者
名 advocacy ⇄ critic（批判者）

---

5 ☐☐
disenchantment
[dìsɪntʃǽntmənt]

▶ disillusionment
名 幻滅〈with 〜に対する〉
形 disenchanted

---

6 ☐☐
legitimacy
[lɪdʒítəməsi]

▶ legality, lawfulness
名 合法性, 適法性
形 legitimate ⇄ illegitimacy

---

7 ☐☐
marijuana
[mærɪhwáːnə] ❶

▶ cannabis, grass, weed
名 大麻, マリファナ

---

8 ☐☐
detractor
[dɪtrǽktər]

▶ critic
名 悪く言う人, 批判者

---

9 ☐☐
deceitful
[dɪsíːtfəl]

▶ dishonest, fraudulent
形 人を欺く, 詐欺の
動 deceive 名 deceit

---

10 ☐☐
tactic
[tǽktɪk]

▶ approach, method, strategy
名 策略, 方策
形 tactical 名 tactician（策略家）

---

11 ☐☐
camp
[kæmp]

▶ faction, group, side
名（政治的・思想的な）陣営
● the Democratic camp（民主党陣営）

12 ☐☐ **distort** [dɪstɔ́:rt]	▶ slant, twist, warp 動 (事実など) を歪曲する，をゆがめる 名 distortion
13 ☐☐ **viciously** [víʃəsli]	▶ savagely 副 残虐に，容赦なく 形 vicious
14 ☐☐ **divisive** [dɪváɪsɪv]	▶ disruptive 形 分断を生む，不和を生じる 動 divide 名 division
☐☐ **the status quo**	▶ the current situation 現状 ● maintain the status quo（現状を維持する）
☐☐ **unrest** [ʌnrést]	▶ disruption, disturbance, turmoil 名 騒乱，動乱 ● social unrest（社会不安）
☐☐ **credibility** [krèdəbíləti]	▶ reliability, trustworthiness 名 信頼性，信ぴょう性 形 credible ⬌ incredibility
☐☐ **shady** [ʃéɪdi]	▶ dubious, fishy 形 疑わしい，いかがわしい ●「日陰の」が本義

政治・経済 **11**

America's Gun Debate

Former president Barack Obama was unable to tighten America's gun legislation, partly due to opposition from a powerful lobby group's interpretation of the US Constitution.

1   Gun control is one of the most controversial topics in the US. It has become even more ¹**venomous** in the wake of mass shootings of innocents in public places. The Barack Obama administration hoped to pass stricter gun laws. Meanwhile, the National Rifle Association (NRA), a powerful
5   pro-gun lobby, was ²**gearing up to** fight the ³**imminent** legislation. They believed he wanted to ⁴**confiscate** automatic weapons and that it was ⁵**incumbent** on them to stand against anti-gun legislation at all costs, for it would ⁶**infringe** on the right of Americans to ⁷**bear** arms, as ⁸**enumerated** in the Constitution's Second Amendment.

10   In 2008, the Supreme Court basically agreed with the NRA. Their ruling in the court case *The District of Columbia versus Heller* determined that the amendment ⁹**endows** individuals with the right to bear arms. Their ¹⁰**verdict**, though, ¹¹**clashes** with earlier rulings, such as *The United States versus Cruikshank*, in which the Supreme Court ruled in 1875 that the
15   Second Amendment does not ¹²**grant** this right.

    Several Supreme Court Justices were ¹³**dissenters**, believing that the decision was based on false arguments and was therefore erroneous. In 1990, Chief Justice of the Supreme Court Warren Burger ¹⁴**decried** the NRA's interpretation of the Second Amendment as "¹⁵**fraud**" committed
20   by special ¹⁶**interest groups**. However, these arguments are now considered ¹⁷**moot** by legal experts and Americans continue to be legally ¹⁸**sanctioned** to own weapons.   (229 words)

アメリカの銃規制をめぐる議論

バラク・オバマ元大統領はアメリカの銃規制を強化することができなかったが，その一因は強力な
ロビー団体の合衆国憲法解釈による反対にあった。

　銃規制はアメリカで最も物議を醸す話題の１つである。何の罪もない人たちが公共
の場で大量に射殺された事件の結果，この銃規制の議論はさらにずっと [1]悪意に満ち
たものとなった。バラク・オバマ政権は，より厳しい銃規制の法律を通すことを望ん
だ。その一方で，強力な銃支持の圧力団体である全米ライフル協会（NRA）は，[3]差
し迫った立法措置に対抗[2]するための準備をしていた。彼（大統領）は自動小銃の [4]没
収を望んでおり，銃規制の法律に何としても反対することが自分たちに課された [5]義
務であると彼らは信じていた。それはそのような法律は憲法修正第２条で [8]挙げられ
ている，アメリカ人が武器 [7]を所持する権利を [6]侵害するものだからである。

　2008 年に，最高裁判所は NRA の主張に基本的に同意した。コロンビア特別区対ヘ
ラーの裁判における最高裁判所の裁定が，修正第２条は個人に武器を所持する権利を
[9]与えていると判断したのである。しかしこの [10]判断は，1875 年に最高裁判所が修正
第２条はこの権利 [12]を与えていないと裁定した合衆国対クルックシャンクの裁判など
の以前の裁定と [11]相反するものである。

　数名の最高裁判所判事はこの裁定は間違った論拠に基づいており，それゆえに誤っ
たものであると考え，[13]反対者の立場をとっていた。1990 年には，最高裁判所長官で
あったウォーレン・バーガーが NRA による修正第２条の解釈を特別 [16]利益団体によ
る「[15]欺瞞」だとして [14]公然と非難した。しかしながら，現在のところこれらの主張
は法律の専門家からは [17]考慮に値しないと考えられており，アメリカ人が武器を所持
することは引き続き法的に [18]認められている。

America's Gun Debate

1 ☐☐ **venomous** [vénəməs]	▶ vicious, spiteful, malevolent, malicious 形 悪意に満ちた，有害な，毒のある 名 venom（毒，悪意，恨み）
2 ☐☐ **gear up to** *do*	▶ prepare to *do* 〜するための準備をする
3 ☐☐ **imminent** [íminənt]	▶ impending 形 差し迫った，切迫した 名 imminence
4 ☐☐ **confiscate** [ká(:)nfiskèit]	▶ seize, expropriate, sequestrate 動 を没収する，を押収する 名 confiscation（没収，押収）
5 ☐☐ **incumbent** [inkámbənt]	▶ obligatory, compulsory, imperative 形 義務として当然の〈on 〜に課された〉 ● 政治家などについて「現職者，現職の」の意味もある
6 ☐☐ **infringe** [infrínd3]	▶ encroach, breach, violate 動 侵害する〈on 権利などを〉 名 infringement
7 ☐☐ **bear** [beər] ❶	▶ carry 動（武器など）を身に付ける，を帯びる ● bear arms で「武器を携帯［所有］する，武装する」
8 ☐☐ **enumerate** [injú:mərèit]	▶ list, name, specify, set out, spell out 動 を挙げる，を列挙する 名 enumeration
9 ☐☐ **endow** [indáu] ❶	▶ bestow, equip, provide, supply 動 に授ける〈with 〜を〉 名 endowment（才能，寄付（金））
10 ☐☐ **verdict** [vɔ́:rdikt]	▶ judgment, adjudication, ruling, decision 名 判断，審判
11 ☐☐ **clash** [klæʃ]	▶ disagree 動（意見などが）衝突する，相反する〈with 〜と〉 名 衝突，対立

12 ☐☐ **grant** [grǽnt]	▶ award, endow, bestow, allow, accord **動** を与える, を認める **名** 許可, 認可, 授与（されたもの）
13 ☐☐ **dissenter** [dɪséntər]	▶ dissident, dissentient, objector **名** 反対者, 異議を唱える者 **動 名** dissent（異議を唱える;（判決における）反対意見）
14 ☐☐ **decry** [dɪkráɪ]	▶ condemn, denounce, censure, criticize **動** を公然と非難する〈as ～だとして〉
15 ☐☐ **fraud** [frɔːd] ❶	▶ deception, trickery **名** 欺瞞, いんちき
16 ☐☐ **interest group**	利益団体, 利益集団
17 ☐☐ **moot** [muːt]	**形** 考慮に値しない
18 ☐☐ **sanction** [sǽŋkʃən]	▶ authorize, permit, approve, countenance **動** を認可する, を是認する **名** （法的）認可, 制裁

政治・経済

11

How Billionaires Back Out of Debt

Unlike ordinary citizens, billionaires are often not held responsible for their debts, causing investors, employees, and others to suffer when companies go bankrupt.

1　　When American consumers [1]**pile up** debts and can no longer [2]**keep up with** payments, they can always [3]**file for** [4]**bankruptcy**. Even then, some debt payments remain [5]**obligatory** under the bankruptcy law of 2005. Credit card debt and student loans are rarely [6]**remitted**. In addition,

5　if you have any ability to pay any of your debt from the point you file bankruptcy forward, you'll [7]**be on the hook for** it, according to Tamara Draut of Demos, a [8]**think tank**.

　　However, it is not so with corporate owners, who usually have several options, including [9]**shoring up** their company with personal funds, raising

10　new cash, or undergoing [10]**strategic default**. They often choose the last one. Instead of [11]**going all out to** [12]**salvage** their companies and save employee jobs, billionaires frequently and [13]**deliberately** choose to [14]**fall behind** or default on their obligations, even when they have [15]**assets** available elsewhere. They can, and often do, choose to [16]**walk away from**

15　a company [17]**in the red**. Moreover, they seldom suffer legally, socially, or even professionally by choosing not to [18]**bail out** their troubled companies. In such cases, [19]**shareholders**, bankers, vendors, and others [20]**are left holding the bag**. In 2011, 9,772 businesses filed for bankruptcy protection. While this may not be particularly harmful to the [21]**bottom**

20　**lines** of these billionaire owners, it is financially damaging for employees and the society as a whole.

🏴 (226 words)

億万長者の借金棒引き法

一般市民と違って億万長者は債務の責任を問われないことが多いことから，会社が倒産した際，投資家や従業員などが苦しむことになる。

　アメリカの消費者は借金 ¹を大量に抱え，もはや返済 ²を続けられなくなると，いつでも ⁴破産 ³申請をすることができる。破産申請をしても，2005 年に成立した破産法の下では一部の借金の返済は ⁵義務として残る。クレジットカードでの借金や学生ローンはめったに ⁶免除されない。加えて，デモスという ⁸シンクタンクのタマラ・ドラウトによれば，破産を申請した時点以降に借金を返済する能力が少しでもあれば，借金 ⁷の返済義務がある。

　しかし，法人のオーナーについてはその限りではなく，彼らには通常，個人の資金で会社 ⁹を支えたり，新たに資金を調達したり，¹⁰戦略的債務不履行を行ったりといったいくつかの選択肢がある。彼らはしばしば最後の選択肢を選ぶ。他に利用可能な ¹⁵資産があるときでさえ，¹¹全力を挙げて自分の会社 ¹²を救い，従業員の職を守る代わりに，億万長者はよく ¹³故意に ¹⁴滞納することや債務を履行しないことを選ぶ。彼らは ¹⁷赤字の会社 ¹⁶を放棄することができるし，しばしばそうする。さらに彼らは，問題を抱えた会社 ¹⁸を救わないことを選択しても，法的にも，社会的にも，さらに言えば職業的にも苦しむことはめったにない。その場合，¹⁹株主，銀行の役員，販売会社などが ²⁰全責任を負わされる。2011 年に 9,772 の事業が破産保護を申請した。このことは，億万長者であるオーナーの ²¹最終損益に特に害を及ぼさないが，従業員や社会全体には金銭的損害を与える。

保釈金

bail の本義は名詞「保釈（金）」，動詞「を保釈する」で，そこから bail out 〜「〜を（苦境から）救う」という意味が生じたが，今では「〜に資金援助をする」という意味で頻繁に使われている。bail out the country「その国に財政援助を行う」や，名詞 bailout を用いた give the bank a bailout「その銀行に資金援助をする」といった表現を覚えておきたい。

How Billionaires Back Out of Debt

1 □□ **pile up ~**	▶ collect, gather, heap up, accumulate ～を大量に抱え込む，～を蓄積する ● pile up debts [wealth]（借金［資産］をためる）
2 □□ **keep up with ~**	（支払いなど）をきちんと続ける，～に遅れない
3 □□ **file for ~**	▶ apply for ～を申請する
4 □□ **bankruptcy** [bǽŋkrʌptsi] ❶	▶ insolvency, failure, bust 图 破産，倒産 名 形 bankrupt（破産者；破産した）
5 □□ **obligatory** [əblígətɔ̀:ri]	▶ mandatory, compulsory 形 義務として負わされる，義務的な 動 oblige（を義務づける）
6 □□ **remit** [rɪmít]	▶ exempt, forgive 動 （借金など）を免除する
7 □□ **be on the hook for ~**	（お金）の返済義務がある，～の借金がある
8 □□ **think tank**	シンクタンク，研究所
9 □□ **shore up ~**	▶ support, reinforce, bolster （崩壊しそうな組織など）を支援する，～を補強する
10 □□ **strategic default**	戦略的債務不履行，返済能力があるのに債務を放棄すること ● default の動詞は「履行しない〈on 債務を〉」の意味
11 □□ **go all out to** *do*	▶ do *one's* utmost to *do*, strive to *do* 全力を挙げて～する

12 □□ **salvage** [sǽlvɪdʒ] ❶	▶ save, rescue **動** を救い出す，を救援する **名** 救助
13 □□ **deliberately** [dɪlíbərətli]	▶ intentionally, on purpose **副** 故意に **形** deliberate
14 □□ **fall behind**	▶ lag, be in arrears （支払いなどで）遅れる
15 □□ **asset** [ǽsèt]	▶ property, resources **名**（通例 -s）（破産者の，債務弁済に充てるべき）資産，財産
16 □□ **walk away from ～**	▶ shirk, elude （責任）を放棄する，～から逃れる
17 □□ **in the red**	▶ in deficit 赤字で
18 □□ **bail out ～**	▶ aid, rescue, relieve （経済的危機にある会社など）を救う ● 名詞 bail は「保釈金」の意味
19 □□ **shareholder** [ʃéərhòʊldər]	▶ stockholder, shareowner **名** 株主 ● share（株式）＋holder（持つ人）
20 □□ **be left holding the bag**	▶ be held responsible 責任を負わされる
21 □□ **bottom line**	最終損益

129

India's Coal Crisis

India has encountered various problems in attempting to build coal-burning power plants in order to meet its increasing energy needs.

1   India, with a population of 1.4 billion and a [1]**burgeoning** economy, struggles to meet its energy needs and continues to experience energy [2]**shortfalls**. In addition, hundreds of millions of Indians lack access to the [3]**power grid**. About 70 percent of India's energy comes from coal, and

5 until recently, there were plans to [4]**boost** its use of coal power.

    Tata, India's [5]**paramount** [6]**conglomerate** and private [7]**utility**, built a massive coal-powered plant called Tata Mundra. Other mega power plants were [8]**on the drawing board**, but have been canceled due to environmental concerns. India primarily uses [9]**domestically** [10]**mined** coal,

10 which, though environmentally [11]**filthy**, is relatively cheap. Unfortunately, Tata did not allow for the requirements of their new [12]**state-of-the-art** plant: Indian coal's quality was too low, so they had to [13]**resort to** importation.

    However, the demand for coal from India's main suppliers shot up,

15 [14]**driving up** prices. Tata claimed that Tata Mundra could not be financially viable without [15]**passing on** costs to utility users to [16]**offset** the costs of imported coal, [17]**unleashing** a [18]**barrage** of criticism. After all, the purpose of building the power plants was to provide cheap coal power to the public [19]**at the expense of** environmental pollution. However, that

20 [20]**trade-off** is no longer [21]**alluring**, since the new power plants rely on expensive imported coal, and awareness of coal's impact on the environment is increasing.   (223 words)

インドの石炭危機

インドは増加するエネルギー需要を満たすため石炭火力発電所を建設しようとしたが，その際，さまざまな問題に直面した。

14億の人口と[1]急成長する経済を抱えるインドはエネルギー需要を満たすことに苦慮し，エネルギー[2]不足を経験し続けている。加えて，インドでは何億ものインド人が[3]電力網を利用できない。インドではエネルギーの約70%が石炭によってもたらされており，最近まで石炭火力発電の使用[4]を増加させる計画があった。

インド[5]最大の[6]複合企業で民間の[7]公益企業であるタタは，タタ・ムンドゥラという巨大石炭火力発電所を建設した。他の巨大な発電所が[8]計画されていたが，環境に対する懸念のために中止された。インドでは[9]国内で[10]採掘され，環境を[11]汚染するが比較的安価な石炭が主に利用されている。不幸なことに，タタは新しい，[12]最先端技術の発電所の必要条件，すなわちインドの石炭の品質があまりにも低く，そのために輸入[13]に頼らなくてはならないことを考慮していなかったのだ。

しかしインドへの主たる供給国からの石炭需要は急上昇し，価格[14]を釣り上げている。タタは，タタ・ムンドゥラは電気の利用者に費用[15]を転嫁して輸入石炭にかかる費用[16]を相殺しなければ財政的にやっていけないと主張しており，これは非難の[18]集中砲火[17]を招いている。つまるところ，発電所を建設する目的は環境汚染[19]という犠牲を払って安価な石炭電力を一般の人々に供給することだったのだ。しかし，その[20]妥協は，新しい発電所が高価な輸入石炭に頼り，石炭が環境に及ぼす影響についての意識が高まっていることから，もはや[21]魅力的ではない。

India's Coal Crisis

1 ☐☐ **burgeoning** [bə́:rdʒənɪŋ]	▶ booming 形 急成長［発展］する，急増する，芽を出す
2 ☐☐ **shortfall** [ʃɔ́:rtfɔ:l]	▶ deficit, shortage, lack 名 不足（量）
3 ☐☐ **power grid**	▶ power network, transmission network 電力網，送電網
4 ☐☐ **boost** [bu:st]	▶ increase, advance, escalate, stimulate 動 を高める，を押し上げる ● boost demand（需要を高める）
5 ☐☐ **paramount** [pǽrəmàunt] ❶	▶ capital, chief, dominant 形 最大の，主要な
6 ☐☐ **conglomerate** [kənglá(:)mərət]	名 複合企業
7 ☐☐ **utility** [jutíləti]	名 （社会インフラを扱う）公益企業，公益事業，公益設備
8 ☐☐ **on the drawing board**	▶ being prepared, in the planning stage 計画中で
9 ☐☐ **domestically** [dəméstɪkəli]	▶ internally 副 国内で 形 domestic
10 ☐☐ **mine** [maɪn]	▶ excavate, dig up 動 （鉱石など）を採掘する 名 鉱山，鉱坑
11 ☐☐ **filthy** [fílθi]	▶ dirty, unclean, polluted 形 汚い，汚れた 名 filth（汚れ，汚染）

12 □□ **state-of-the-art** [stèɪtəvðɪáːrt]	▶ latest, newest, up-to-date 形 最先端技術を用いた，最新の
13 □□ **resort to 〜**	▶ look [turn] to, fall back on, have recourse to （手段など）に頼る
14 □□ **drive up 〜**	▶ inflate, raise, boost up （価格など）を釣り上げる，〜を跳ね上げる
15 □□ **pass on 〜**	▶ shift 〜を転嫁する，（費用など）を払わせる〈to 〜に〉
16 □□ **offset** [ɔ̀(ː)fsét] ❶	▶ counterbalance, compensate, balance out 動 （費用など）を相殺する，の埋め合わせをする
17 □□ **unleash** [ʌnlíːʃ]	▶ erupt, vent 動 （怒りなど）を引き起こす，を爆発させる ⇔ leash（を抑える）
18 □□ **barrage** [bərάːʒ]	▶ bombardment, onslaught 名 （質問・不平などの）集中砲火，噴出
19 □□ **at the expense of 〜**	▶ at the cost [sacrifice] of 〜という犠牲を払って，〜を犠牲にして
20 □□ **trade-off** [tréɪdɔ̀(ː)f]	▶ compromise, concession, give-and-take 名 （同時に手に入らないものの間でバランスをとる）妥協
21 □□ **alluring** [əlúərɪŋ]	▶ attractive, captivating, tempting 形 魅力的な 動 allure（を魅惑する）

Global Poverty

The number of people living in extreme poverty declined greatly in the early twenty-first century, thanks in large part to economic growth in China and various African nations.

1　　During the Great Recession of 2007–2009, many developed countries experienced a [1]**resurgence** of poverty. One would expect [2]**impoverished** citizens of developing countries to have [3]**fared** [4]**disproportionately** worse, yet during the economic crisis, data showed that the number of

5　people [5]**subsisting on** under $1.25 per day, then the [6]**benchmark** for absolute poverty, had not [7]**shot up**. In fact, statistics indicated that global poverty was only 50 percent of the level in 1990.

　　Half of the [8]**subsistence** level poverty was attributable to a single country — China, which had the world's highest [9]**incidence** of poverty in

10　the early 1980s, with 77 percent of its population [10]**bringing in** less than $1.25 a day. Roughly 660 million Chinese had [11]**climbed out of** poverty thanks to [12]**comprehensive** economic and social reforms, a remarkable feat in such a short time frame. Africa was another remarkable story. The number of [13]**destitute** individuals shot up between 1981 and 2005, but

15　then dropped by 12 million in 2008 and, for the first time, less than half the continent's population was living below the [14]**poverty line**. This [15]**turnaround**, too, was due to economic expansion and [16]**subventions** for [17]**beefed-up** social programs.

　　Unfortunately, however, in recent years, climate change, armed

20　conflict, and the [18]**outbreak** of COVID-19 have threatened to reverse some of the hard-won gains made previously.　　　　　　（214 words）

世界の貧困

極度の貧困下で生活している人々の数が 21 世紀初頭に大幅に減少した。これは主に中国やさまざまなアフリカ諸国の経済成長のおかげである。

2007 年から 2009 年の大不況の間，多くの先進国で貧困問題が [1]再発した。人々は発展途上国の [2]貧しい市民たちが [4]不相応なほどにいっそう悪い [3]暮らしをしていたと考えるだろうが，経済危機の間，当時の絶対貧困の [6]基準である日に 1.25 ドル未満 [5]で生活していた人の数は [7]急上昇していなかったことをデータは示している。それどころか，統計は，世界の貧困は 1990 年の水準のたった 50％だと示していた。

[8]ぎりぎりの生活レベルの貧困の半分はただ 1 つの国家——中国に起因していた。中国は 1980 年代初めに世界で貧困 [9]率が最も高く，総人口の 77％が 1 日に 1.25 ドルの [10]稼ぎもなかった。以来およそ 6 億 6 千万人の中国人が [12]包括的な経済社会改革により貧困 [11]から抜け出した。そのような短期間にしては顕著な功績である。アフリカは注目すべきもう 1 つの事例だ。[13]貧困者の数は 1981 年から 2005 年の間に急増したが，それから 2008 年に 1,200 万人減少し，[14]貧困線以下で生活している人の数が，初めてアフリカ大陸の総人口の半数を割った。この [15]転換も経済拡大と [17]強化された社会プログラムへの [16]補助金によるものである。

しかし，残念ながら近年では，気候変動や武力紛争，新型コロナウイルス感染症の [18]発生などにより，これまで苦労して成し遂げたいくつかの進歩が後退する恐れが出てきている。

貧困線

poverty line（貧困線）とは，最低限の生活をぎりぎり維持できる収入を指す。国によって事情が異なるため，国家間の貧困率を比較する共通の指標として，世界銀行が international poverty line（国際貧困線）を設定している。2008 年には 1.25 ドルと定められ，その後 2015 年に 1.9 ドルに変更された。国内の貧困率の指標としては，OECD（経済協力開発機構）による relative poverty（相対的貧困）が用いられることが多い。

Global Poverty

1 ☐☐
resurgence
[rɪsə́:rdʒəns]

▶ resurrection, return, revitalization
名 再燃, 再起
動 resurge (再び起こる)

2 ☐☐
impoverished
[ɪmpá(:)vərɪʃt]

▶ poor, needy, deprived
形 貧しい, 困窮状態の
動 impoverish (を貧しくする)

3 ☐☐
fare
[feər]

▶ do, get along, manage
動 生活する, やっていく, 食べる
● fare well [badly] (暮らし向きが良い [悪い])

4 ☐☐
disproportionately
[dìsprəpɔ́:rʃənətli]

▶ excessively, incommensurately
副 不相応 (なほど) に, 過剰に

5 ☐☐
subsist on ～

▶ live on
(金銭・資源・食料など) で生活する, ～で暮らす

6 ☐☐
benchmark
[béntʃmà:rk]

▶ criterion, gauge, standard
名 基準, 尺度

7 ☐☐
shoot up

▶ rise, skyrocket, sprout
急上昇 [急増] する

8 ☐☐
subsistence
[səbsístəns]

名 ぎりぎりの生活, 最低限の暮らし
動 subsist (どうにか生活する) ● live below (the) subsistence level (最低生活水準以下の生活をする)

9 ☐☐
incidence
[ínsɪdəns]

▶ frequency, degree of occurrence
名 (犯罪・病気などの) 発生率

10 ☐☐
bring in ～

▶ earn, profit, yield
(収入) を得る, ～を稼ぐ

11 ☐☐
climb out of ～

▶ pull oneself out of, surmount
(悪い状態) から抜け出す

12 ☐☐ **comprehensive** [kὰ(:)mprɪhénsɪv]	▶ all-inclusive, complete, full 形 包括的な，総合的な
13 ☐☐ **destitute** [déstɪtjùːt]	▶ extremely poor, dirt-poor, penniless 形 極貧の，貧窮した ● the destitute（極貧の人々）
14 ☐☐ **poverty line**	貧困線，最低限の生活に必要な収入基準 ● live below [at, on] the poverty line（最低限の生活水準以下で［で］暮らす）
15 ☐☐ **turnaround** [tə́ːrnəràund]	▶ turnabout, switch, transformation 名 転換
16 ☐☐ **subvention** [səbvénʃən]	▶ subsidy, financial support, grant, funding 名（政府などからの）補助金，助成金
17 ☐☐ **beefed-up** [bíːftʌp]	形 強化された 名 beef-up（強化）
18 ☐☐ **outbreak** [áutbrèɪk]	▶ epidemic, eruption 名（疫病などの）発生，突発 ● the outbreak of war（戦争の勃発）
☐☐ **solicit** [səlísət]	▶ beg, supplicate, seek 動（人）に求める，懇願する〈for 援助などを〉 名 solicitation
☐☐ **falter** [fɔ́ːltər]	▶ waver, stumble, stagger 動 勢いがなくなる，よろめく，口ごもる ● faltering economy（低迷している経済）
☐☐ **frugal** [frúːgəl]	▶ thrifty, sparing, prudent, economical 形 倹約的な，つつましい

Blaming the Bankers

After the Great Recession (2007–2009), some people argued that America's financial sector was too large and that salaries in the industry should be reduced.

1 　　American bankers have suffered a [1]**backlash** in recent years due to their role in the [2]**economic downturn**. The [3]**acrimony** is so intense that some people suggest they all be fired, which hardly seems to be a practical solution. Many economists do, however, recommend the financial [4]**sector**
5 be shrunk through [5]**stern** [6]**regulatory** policies. In the 1950s, a time of prosperity, the financial sector [7]**accounted for** just three percent of gross domestic product. However, as of 2018, that number has [8]**ballooned** to over seven percent, and the economy is in [9]**turmoil**.

　　A report prepared by three economists for the International
10 [10]**Monetary** Fund [11]**came up with** the same conclusion. They [12]**determined** that while countries with small financial sectors benefit from increased investment in that sector, the reverse is true once countries reach a certain [13]**threshold**. The US is clearly over that threshold.

　　Bankers have also received widespread [14]**condemnation** for their
15 [15]**remuneration**, which many people see as [16]**arbitrarily** [17]**inflated**. Thomas Philippon of the NYU Stern School of Business addressed that issue, saying that even though high salaries are necessary to [18]**lure** the best talent, they are now too high. He argues that employees in the financial industry are compensated too highly to be consistent with a
20 [19]**sustainable** labor market balance. Bankers are being paid anywhere from 30 to 50 percent more than their market value, and their salaries are being subsidized by the rest of society at a time of [20]**recession**.

■ (237 words)

銀行家の罪

大不況（2007〜2009年）の後，アメリカの金融部門は大き過ぎるので，金融業界の給与を下げるべきだと主張する人々がいた。

　近年アメリカの銀行の役員たちは，[2]経済沈滞で果たした役割のせいで[1]反発にあっている。その[3]辛辣さは非常に激しく，中には役員をみな解雇しろと言う人もいる。とても現実的な解決法ではないが。しかし，多くの経済学者が，[5]厳格な[6]規制政策による金融[4]部門の縮小を奨励している。繁栄の1950年代には，金融部門が国内総生産[7]に占める割合は3%にすぎなかった。ところが，2018年現在，その数値は7%を超えるまでに[8]急上昇し，経済は[9]混乱している。

　3人の経済学者が国際[10]通貨基金のために作成した報告書も同じ結論[11]に至った。彼らは金融部門が小規模な国はその部門への投資が増すことで利益を得るものの，一定の[13]閾値に達すると逆になる[12]と断定した。アメリカは明らかにその閾値を超えている。

　銀行の役員たちはまたその[15]報酬に対して広く[14]非難を受けてきた。多くの人がその報酬は[16]恣意的に[17]釣り上げられたと見ているのだ。ニューヨーク大学の経営大学院であるスターン・スクールのトーマス・フィリッポンはその問題に取り組み，最高の才能を持つ人材[18]を引きつけるには高額の給与が必要だが，今ではその給与は高額過ぎると言った。彼は金融業界の社員の報酬は高額過ぎて，[19]持続可能な労働市場の均衡と一致しないと主張する。銀行の役員たちは自分の市場価値より30〜50%も多い賃金を得ており，[20]不況時というのに彼らの給与は残りの社会から助成を受けていることになる。

持続可能性

sustainable（持続可能な），sustainability（持続可能性）という語はすっかり社会的に定着している。sustainable development（持続可能な開発），sustainable society（持続可能な社会），sustainable economic growth（持続可能な経済成長）などを覚えておきたい。

Blaming the Bankers

1 ☐☐
backlash
[bǽklæʃ]
▶ reaction, kickback, rebound
🔲 (人・政策などに対する) 反発, 反感

2 ☐☐
economic downturn
▶ economic stagnation [deterioration]
経済の落ち込み, 景気の悪化

3 ☐☐
acrimony
[ǽkrəmòuni]
▶ resentment, asperity, acerbity
🔲 激しい怒り, (言葉などの) 激しさ
🔲 acrimonious ((言葉・態度などが) 辛辣な)

4 ☐☐
sector
[séktər]
▶ department, division
🔲 (組織などの) 部門

5 ☐☐
stern
[stə:rn] ❶
▶ strict, severe, harsh
🔲 厳格な, 厳しい

6 ☐☐
regulatory
[régjulətò:ri]
▶ regulative
🔲 規制の, 取り締まる
🔲 regulate (を規制する) 🔲 regulation (規制)

7 ☐☐
account for 〜
▶ occupy, take up
(ある割合) を占める

8 ☐☐
balloon
[bəlú:n] ❶
▶ surge, spike, shoot up
🔲 (数値などが) 急上昇する, 急増する

9 ☐☐
turmoil
[tá:rmɔil]
▶ tumult, disturbance, confusion
🔲 混乱, 騒動, 動揺
● be in turmoil (混乱している, 騒動のさなかにある)

10 ☐☐
monetary
[má(:)nətèri]
▶ financial, fiscal
🔲 通貨の, 金銭の
● the International Monetary Fund (国際通貨基金)

11 ☐☐
come up with 〜
▶ think of, conceive
(解決策など) を提案する, (考えなど) を思いつく

12 ☐☐ **determine** [dɪtə́ːrmɪn] 🔈	▶ conclude, decide **動** と断定する，と結論を下す **名** determination
13 ☐☐ **threshold** [θréʃhoʊld]	**名** 閾値，限界水準
14 ☐☐ **condemnation** [kɑ̀(:)ndemnéɪʃən]	▶ accusation, disapproval, denunciation **名** 激しい非難 **動** condemn
15 ☐☐ **remuneration** [rɪmjùːnəréɪʃən]	▶ consideration, recompense, compensation **名** 報酬，給与
16 ☐☐ **arbitrarily** [ɑ̀ːrbətrérəli]	▶ absolutely, randomly **副** 恣意的に，独断的に **形** arbitrary
17 ☐☐ **inflated** [ɪnfléɪtɪd]	▶ skyrocketed **形**（金額などが）暴騰した，膨れ上がった
18 ☐☐ **lure** [ljʊər]	▶ allure, bait, decoy, entice **動** を誘惑する **名** 誘惑するもの，誘惑，おとり
19 ☐☐ **sustainable** [səstéɪnəbl]	▶ maintainable **形** 持続可能な **動** sustain（を維持する）
20 ☐☐ **recession** [rɪséʃən]	▶ depression, slump, slowdown **名**（一時的な）景気後退，不況
☐☐ **denounce** [dɪnáʊns]	▶ criticize, attack, scold **動** を公然と非難する〈as 〜として〉 **名** denunciation

Globalization's Changing Trends

Many call-center jobs in the tech industry were once outsourced, but the number is declining, probably due to the increasing complexity of the calls being received.

1　　As a result of international ¹**deregulation**, many American jobs have been ²**outsourced**, at the loss of American employment. The call-center industry is particularly ³**vilified** for taking away American jobs and hiring overseas, where wages are often lower. The industry responds that it all
5　⁴**boils down to** the bottom line: their survival ⁵**hinges on** cutting costs.

　　Now, there are ⁶**budding** signs that the trend is reversing. Mary Murcott, CEO of outsourcing firm Novo 1, estimated that, ⁷**at one time**, 30 percent of all call-center jobs for high-tech American companies were outsourced. Today, that number has dropped to 12 percent, which has been
10　⁸**conducive** to American employment. This is due mainly to the increasing ⁹**complexity** of calls that call-center employees must handle. In prior decades, many calls were about such simple tasks as resetting passwords. Now, many simple tasks are ¹⁰**automated**. In addition, more calls are "¹¹**context-sensitive**," which means that call-center employees have to
15　solve complex problems that ¹²**crop up**, which requires ¹³**expertise** as well as outstanding communication skills — in English, of course. These ¹⁴**attributes** are often easier to find in American employees.

　　Call-center jobs usually do not pay well, but they fit an important ¹⁵**niche** job market, since college graduation is not required. There are
20　now 2.1 million customer service jobs in the US, and that number is expected to grow, especially as the ¹⁶**momentum** in outsourcing ¹⁷**wanes**.

🇬🇧 (227 words)

国際化の波の変化

ハイテク産業の多くのコールセンターの仕事は，かつては外部委託されていたが，かかってくる電話の内容がますます複雑になっているためか，その数は減少している。

　国際的 ¹**規制緩和**の結果，アメリカの多くの仕事は ²**外部に委託され**，アメリカ人の雇用の損失となっている。アメリカ人の仕事を取り上げ，賃金がしばしばより安い海外で雇用していることでコールセンター事業は特に ³**そしられている**。事業者側は ⁴**つまるところ**事業が生き延びるのは経費削減 ⁵**にかかっている**というのが肝心な点なのだと返答する。

　今，その傾向が逆になる兆しが ⁶**見え始め**ている。外部委託業者ノヴォワンの最高経営責任者メアリー・マーコットは，⁷**かつては**アメリカのハイテク企業のコールセンターの仕事の 30％が海外で調達されていたと見積もっていた。今日ではその数値は 12％にまで下がり，アメリカ人の雇用に ⁸**貢献している**。これは主にコールセンターの従業員が扱わなければならない電話内容がより ⁹**複雑**になってきているためだ。過去数十年間は，多くの電話はパスワードのリセットなど単純作業に関するものだった。今では，多くの単純作業は ¹⁰**自動化されている**。加えて，より多くの電話は ¹¹**状況に大きく依存する**ものだ。つまり，コールセンターの従業員は ¹²**思いがけず生じる**複雑な問題を解決しなければならず，そのためには当然英語による卓越したコミュニケーション能力が必要で，同時に ¹³**専門知識**も必要とされる。こういった ¹⁴**属性**はアメリカ人従業員たちの中からの方がしばしば見つけやすい。

　コールセンターの仕事はたいていあまり収入が高くはないが，重要な ¹⁵**隙間的な求人市場**を埋めるにはぴったりだ。大学卒業は必要条件ではないからだ。今では合衆国には顧客サービスの仕事が 210 万件あり，とりわけ海外委託の ¹⁶**勢い**が ¹⁷**衰える**につれてその数字は今後さらに高くなると予想されている。

文脈依存

context-sensitive は本来は言語学用語で，「文脈依存の」と訳される。しかしこの英文では，sensitive は「感度の高い」という意味から考えた方がよい。photosensitive paper（感光紙）が光の作用に反応して印画される紙であるのと同様に，この context-sensitive は，文脈の微妙な変化を感じ取るということ。つまり，顧客との通話内容は会話の状況によってどのようにも変化し得る，という意味で用いられている。それに臨機応変に対応するためには，コミュニケーション能力と専門知識が必須なのである。

Globalization's Changing Trends

---

1 ☐☐
deregulation
[di:règjuléɪʃən]

▶ abolition of regulations
名 規制緩和，規制撤廃
動 deregulate ⇄ regulation（規制）

---

2 ☐☐
outsource
[áutsɔ̀:rs]

動 を外部に委託する，を外部調達する

---

3 ☐☐
vilify
[vílɪfàɪ]

▶ defame, libel, malign
動 をそしる，を中傷する

---

4 ☐☐
boil down to ～

▶ amount to, add up to
つまるところ～になる，～に帰着する

---

5 ☐☐
hinge on ～

▶ depend [rely] on, be subject to
～にかかっている，～次第である

---

6 ☐☐
budding
[bádɪŋ]

▶ developing, rising, nascent
形 現れかかっている
動 名 bud（芽を出す，発達の初期段階にある；つぼみ）

---

7 ☐☐
at one time

▶ formerly, in the past
かつては，以前は

---

8 ☐☐
conducive
[kəndjú:sɪv]

▶ contribute to
形 貢献する〈to ～に〉
動 conduce

---

9 ☐☐
complexity
[kəmpléksəti]

▶ complication, intricacy
名 複雑さ
形 complex

---

10 ☐☐
automate
[ɔ́:təmèɪt]

▶ automatize, robotize
動 を自動化する
名 automation

---

11 ☐☐
context-sensitive
[ká(:)ntekstsènsəṭɪv]

▶ vary with situation
形 状況に大きく依存する，状況によって異なる

---

12 ☐☐ **crop up**	▶ arise, emerge, pop [show, turn] up （問題などが）（思いがけなく）生じる
13 ☐☐ **expertise** [èkspə(:)rtíːz] ❶	▶ specialist knowledge 名 専門的知識，専門的技術
14 ☐☐ **attribute** [ǽtrɪbjùːt] ❶	▶ feature, quality, trait 名 属性，性質
15 ☐☐ **niche** [nɪtʃ] ❶	形 市場の隙間の，ニッチな
16 ☐☐ **momentum** [moʊméntəm] ❶	▶ impetus, drive, force 名 勢い，はずみ ● gain momentum（勢いづく）
17 ☐☐ **wane** [weɪn]	▶ decrease, fade, weaken 動 衰える，弱まる ⇔ wax（大きくなる，増大する）
☐☐ **tedious** [tíːdiəs] ❶	▶ boring, tiresome, humdrum 形 退屈な，冗長な ● a tedious job（退屈な仕事）
☐☐ **vertical integration**	垂直統合 ● 企業が部品の生産・組み立て・輸送・販売・サービス・研究開発などの事業に関わる側面で一体化すること
☐☐ **polarization** [pòʊlərəzéɪʃən]	名 二極化　動 polarize ● 経済・労働の分野では，オートメーションなどにより，専門的な上級職と単純労働の下級職に分かれること
☐☐ **downsizing** [dáʊnsàɪzɪŋ]	名 人員削減
☐☐ **offshore** [ɔ(ː)ffʃɔ́ːr]	形 （税制や法規制の有利な）外国で提供される，海外の ● offshore investments（海外投資）

政治・経済
確認テスト

1 次の日本語の意味の単語を下の **❶**～**⓰** の中から選んで書きなさい。

（1） 受益者	（ ：	）
（2） 骨の折れる，困難な	（ ：	）
（3） 踏みにじる	（ ：	）
（4） 畜殺，（家畜の）食肉処理	（ ：	）
（5） （家族の）稼ぎ手	（ ：	）
（6） 法令の，法定の	（ ：	）
（7） 一方的に	（ ：	）
（8） 公約，約束	（ ：	）
（9） 能力［実力］主義(社会)	（ ：	）
（10） 残虐に，容赦なく	（ ：	）
（11） 判断，審判	（ ：	）
（12） （借金など）を免除する	（ ：	）
（13） 汚い，汚れた	（ ：	）
（14） （疫病などの）発生，突発	（ ：	）
（15） 恣意的に，独断的に	（ ：	）
（16） をそしる，を中傷する	（ ：	）

❶ slaughter	❷ viciously	❸ beneficiary	❹ statutory
❺ vilify	❻ pledge	❼ filthy	❽ uphill
❾ outbreak	❿ meritocracy	⓫ verdict	⓬ trample
⓭ arbitrarily	⓮ remit	⓯ breadwinner	⓰ unilaterally

2 次の日本語の意味の単語を下の❶～⓬の中から選んで書きなさい。

（1）を宣言する　　　　　　　　　　（　　：　　　　　　　　　　　　　　）

（2）を浪費する，を無駄に使う　　　（　　：　　　　　　　　　　　　　　）

（3）（激しい）怒り　　　　　　　　（　　：　　　　　　　　　　　　　　）

（4）軽犯罪　　　　　　　　　　　　（　　：　　　　　　　　　　　　　　）

（5）次第に減少する，衰える　　　　（　　：　　　　　　　　　　　　　　）

（6）（関係などが）友好的な　　　　（　　：　　　　　　　　　　　　　　）

（7）を妨げる，を邪魔する　　　　　（　　：　　　　　　　　　　　　　　）

（8）策略，方策　　　　　　　　　　（　　：　　　　　　　　　　　　　　）

（9）最大の，主要な　　　　　　　　（　　：　　　　　　　　　　　　　　）

（10）極貧の，貧窮した　　　　　　（　　：　　　　　　　　　　　　　　）

（11）報酬，給与　　　　　　　　　（　　：　　　　　　　　　　　　　　）

（12）退屈な，冗長な　　　　　　　（　　：　　　　　　　　　　　　　　）

---

❶ paramount	❷ ire	❸ proclaim	❹ dwindle
❺ remuneration	❻ squander	❼ tactic	❽ impede
❾ misdemeanor	❿ tedious	⓫ destitute	⓬ amicable

解答

1 （1）❸ (→p. 84)　（2）❽ (→p. 88)　（3）⓬ (→p. 93)　（4）❶ (→p. 97)

（5）⓯ (→p. 100)　（6）❹ (→p. 105)　（7）⓰ (→p. 109)　（8）❻ (→p. 112)

（9）❿ (→p. 117)　（10）❷ (→p. 121)　（11）⓫ (→p. 124)　（12）⓮ (→p. 128)

（13）❼ (→p. 132)　（14）❾ (→p. 137)　（15）⓭ (→p. 141)　（16）❺ (→p. 144)

2 （1）❸ (→p. 85)　（2）❻ (→p. 88)　（3）❷ (→p. 93)　（4）❾ (→p. 96)

（5）❹ (→p. 104)　（6）⓬ (→p. 109)　（7）❽ (→p. 116)　（8）❼ (→p. 120)

（9）❶ (→p. 132)　（10）⓫ (→p. 137)　（11）❺ (→p. 141)　（12）❿ (→p. 145)

3 次の単語の意味に最も近いものをそれぞれ❶～❹の中から1つ選びなさい。

（1）colossal
- ❶ entrenched
- ❷ enormous
- ❸ deprived
- ❹ niche

（2）soar
- ❶ falter
- ❷ expend
- ❸ skyrocket
- ❹ establish

（3）bolster
- ❶ freeze
- ❷ endow
- ❸ reinforce
- ❹ offset

（4）oppression
- ❶ persecution
- ❷ legislature
- ❸ impetus
- ❹ constituent

（5）profound
- ❶ extensive
- ❷ moral
- ❸ monetary
- ❹ divisive

（6）mistreat
- ❶ divert
- ❷ nudge
- ❸ endeavor
- ❹ abuse

（7）aggregate
- ❶ total
- ❷ menacing
- ❸ astounding
- ❹ futile

（8）inducement
- ❶ electorate
- ❷ motivation
- ❸ faction
- ❹ reliance

（9）escalate
- ❶ dissuade
- ❷ conclude
- ❸ salvage
- ❹ intensify

（10）grand
- ❶ lofty
- ❷ frugal
- ❸ flagrant
- ❹ idiotic

（11）manifesto
- ❶ standstill
- ❷ platform
- ❸ connection
- ❹ embezzlement

（12）embed
- ❶ plant
- ❷ reap
- ❸ clash
- ❹ modify

(13) secede	❶ decry	❷ separate
	❸ evade	❹ erupt
(14) enumerate	❶ audit	❷ solicit
	❸ specify	❹ torment
(15) fraud	❶ logistics	❷ hubris
	❸ allotment	❹ deception
(16) shore up ～	❶ intrigue	❷ confiscate
	❸ bestow	❹ reinforce
(17) asset	❶ redistribution	❷ basis
	❸ property	❹ paradox
(18) drive up ～	❶ devalue	❷ mine
	❸ retain	❹ inflate
(19) benchmark	❶ criterion	❷ shortfall
	❸ complexity	❹ deregulation
(20) turmoil	❶ manifestation	❷ cruelty
	❸ disturbance	❹ coercion
(21) attribute	❶ feature	❷ dissenter
	❸ commitment	❹ trade-off
(22) momentum	❶ backlash	❷ impetus
	❸ combustion	❹ prejudice

政治・経済

確認テスト

解答

3 (1) ❷ (→p. 84) (2) ❸ (→p. 84) (3) ❸ (→p. 88) (4) ❶ (→p. 92)

(5) ❶ (→p. 96) (6) ❹ (→p. 97) (7) ❶ (→p. 100) (8) ❷ (→p. 104)

(9) ❹ (→p. 108) (10) ❶ (→p. 112) (11) ❷ (→p. 113) (12) ❶ (→p. 116)

(13) ❷ (→p. 120) (14) ❸ (→p. 124) (15) ❹ (→p. 125) (16) ❹ (→p. 128)

(17) ❸ (→p. 129) (18) ❹ (→p. 133) (19) ❶ (→p. 136) (20) ❸ (→p. 140)

(21) ❶ (→p. 145) (22) ❷ (→p. 145)

医学・テクノロジー

医学・テクノロジー

テーマを知る

　医学・テクノロジーは出題頻度が高く，内容は細胞や DNA，疾病の理由と対策，病原菌，情報技術，宇宙開発，その他の新技術や科学的知見，そしてこれらが人間の生活に与える影響や応用例についての説明が多い。特に新しい医学技術や医療問題などについてはかなり専門的な話が出題されることもあるため，日ごろからニュースなどに注目しておくことや，この分野で頻出の語彙を身に付けておくことが有効な対策となる。

注目用語

utilization of new technologies 新技術の活用

artificial intelligence（人工知能）や cloning technology（クローン技術）等，技術の進歩には大きな期待だけでなく，実社会での活用に関する議論や懸念が伴うこともしばしばである。本書では「医学・テクノロジー 1. AI in Hiring」や「医学・テクノロジー 4. Cloned Olympic Horses a Possibility」がその例と言えるだろう。

gene and genome 遺伝子とゲノム

gene（遺伝子）に関わる技術や研究は頻出トピックの 1 つ。gene は生物の設計図となるもので，そこに含まれるすべての情報を genome（ゲノム）と呼ぶ。DNA とは遺伝子を構成している物質である deoxyribonucleic acid（デオキシリボ核酸）の略称で double-helix structure（二重らせん構造）が特徴である。

キーワード・表現

AI in Hiring

Relying on artificial intelligence (AI) to help with hiring new employees offers benefits such as speed and efficiency. Critics, though, suggest that relying on AI can be harmful.

1   ¹**Sifting through** stacks of résumés in search of qualified candidates can be a ²**laborious** process for ³**human resources departments**. In recent years, therefore, many firms have ⁴**turned to** artificial intelligence (AI) for assistance in early ⁵**rounds** of the ⁶**screening** process.

5   Using complex ⁷**algorithms**, AI can scan applications to weed out individuals who lack suitable experience and find those whose skills best match the company's needs. There are even ⁸**claims** that it can ⁹**outdo** humans when it comes to formidable challenges like ¹⁰**assessing** a candidate's potential loyalty.

10   One of the biggest benefits of ¹¹**implementing** AI solutions to make hiring decisions should be that machines will not suffer from the prejudice and discrimination that can sometimes impact hiring decisions. Critics, though, ¹²**charge** that since machines are programmed by being fed enormous volumes of applications and hiring decisions made by people,

15 they may be ¹³**vulnerable** to, and even ¹⁴**amplify**, our biases. In fact, one tech giant has already scrapped a hiring tool because it was ¹⁵**discriminating** based on gender. Furthermore, there are ¹⁶**accusations** that since it is often unclear what ¹⁷**criteria** an AI's decisions are based on, there will be a lack of ¹⁸**transparency** in the hiring process. It seems

20 that while AI has the potential to make hiring more ¹⁹**impartial** and efficient, various ²⁰**bugs** need to be ²¹**worked out**, and its decisions must be closely ²²**scrutinized**.   📖 (224 words)

採用における AI

新入社員を採用する助けとして人工知能（AI）に頼ることには，スピードや効率などの利点がある。だが，AI に頼ることは害になる可能性があると言う批判的な人々もいる。

　適任の候補者を求めて山積みの履歴書 [1]をふるいにかけるのは [3]人事課にとっては [2]骨の折れる過程であろう。そのため，近年では多くの会社が [6]選抜作業の初期の [5]段階において人工知能（AI）の補助 [4]に頼るようになっている。

　複雑な [7]アルゴリズムを使って，AI は応募書類を読み取り，ふさわしい経験に欠ける個人を除外し，会社のニーズに最も合致する技能を持った人を見つけることができる。中には，応募者の潜在的な忠誠心 [10]を査定するなどの難しい課題となると AI が人間 [9]よりも優れているとする [8]主張すらある。

　雇用決定をするために AI による解決策 [11]を実行することの最も大きい利点の１つは，機械は人間が雇用を決定するときに影響しかねない偏見や差別に苦しまないということであろう。けれども，機械は膨大な量の応募書類と人間によってなされた雇用決定を入力することによってプログラムされているのだから，それらは我々の先入観に [13]影響を受けやすく，またそれどころか [14]増幅する可能性もある [12]と非難する批判的な人々もいる。実際，ある大手テクノロジー企業は雇用のツールが社会的性別に基づいた [15]差別をしているとしてそれを廃止した。さらに，AI の決定がどういう [17]基準に基づいているのかがはっきりしないことがしばしばあるため，採用過程の [18]透明性に欠けるという [16]非難もある。AI は雇用をより [19]公平で効率的にする可能性を持つとはいえ，多くの [20]不具合 [21]を解決し，その決定をていねいに [22]精査しなければならないようだ。

AI in Hiring

---

1 ☐☐
sift through ~

▶ go through, scrutinize
〜をふるいにかける，〜を精査する
● sift は「（小麦粉など）をふるう」という意味

---

2 ☐☐
laborious
[ləbɔ́:riəs] ❶

▶ difficult, arduous, strenuous
形 骨の折れる，困難な
⇄ easy, facile, effortless

---

3 ☐☐
human resources department

人事課，人事部
● 単に human resources とも言う。略語 HR

---

4 ☐☐
turn to ~

▶ consult, fall back on, resort to
〜に頼る，〜に求める〈for 支援・情報などを〉

---

5 ☐☐
round
[raʊnd]

▶ one of a series of related events
名 （関連する一連の出来事の）1 回，段階

---

6 ☐☐
screening
[skrí:nɪŋ]

▶ selection
名 選抜，ふるい分け
動 screen ● applicant screening（書類選考）

---

7 ☐☐
algorithm
[ǽlgərìðm]

▶ a series of mathematical steps that must be followed to solve a particular problem
名 アルゴリズム

---

8 ☐☐
claim
[kleɪm]

▶ assertion, contention, insistence
名 主張 動 を［と］主張する

---

9 ☐☐
outdo
[àʊtdú:]

▶ beat, excel, surpass, outstrip
動 より優れている，に勝る

---

10 ☐☐
assess
[əsés]

▶ appraise, judge, estimate, evaluate
動 を査定する，を評価する
名 assessment

---

11 ☐☐
implement
[ímplɪmènt] ❶

▶ carry out, execute
動 を実行する，を遂行する
名 implementation

---

12 ☐☐ **charge** [tʃɑːrdʒ]	▶ accuse, criticize, reproach, decry 動 を［と］非難する 名 非難
13 ☐☐ **vulnerable** [vʌ́lnərəbl]	▶ susceptible, liable 形 傷つきやすい，受けやすい〈to 攻撃・非難などを〉 名 vulnerability ⇔ invulnerable
14 ☐☐ **amplify** [ǽmplɪfài]	▶ boost, intensify, magnify, strengthen 動 を増幅する，を増強する 名 amplification（増幅），amplifier（増幅器）
15 ☐☐ **discriminate** [dɪskrímɪnèɪt]	▶ treat someone unfairly because of who they are 動 差別する，差別待遇をする 名 discrimination 形 discriminatory
16 ☐☐ **accusation** [æ̀kjuzéɪʃən]	▶ censure, condemnation, reproach 名 非難 動 accuse 形 accusatory
17 ☐☐ **criterion** [kraɪtíəriən] ❶	▶ standard, benchmark, yardstick 名 基準，尺度 ● 複数形は criteria
18 ☐☐ **transparency** [trænspǽrənsi]	▶ clarity 名 透明性，透明さ 形 transparent ⇔ opacity（不明瞭さ）
19 ☐☐ **impartial** [ɪmpáːrʃəl]	▶ fair, unbiased 形 公平な，偏見のない 名 impartiality ⇔ partial, biased
20 ☐☐ **bug** [bʌg]	▶ glitch 名 （システムなどの）不具合，バグ ● debug は「のバグを取り除く」という動詞
21 ☐☐ **work out ～**	▶ solve, resolve, figure out （問題）を解決する
22 ☐☐ **scrutinize** [skrúːtənàɪz]	▶ examine carefully, pore over, sift 動 を精査する，を注意深く調べる 名 scrutiny

The Internet as Social Revolution

One of the Internet's most notable effects has been the democratization of the media, reducing the control that government and businesses used to enjoy over it.

1   In the early 1990s, technology experts predicted the Internet would become a social milestone, changing the course of history. Their [1]**premonitions** were [2]**borne out** but not in the way that was envisioned. The Internet has indeed become an advanced tool for communication,
5   research, and entertainment [3]**embraced** by all. However, in addition, the Internet adds up to a system of information exchange that is powered by individuals rather than governments.

Before the Internet, people were mostly dependent on broadcast media, which were [4]**more often than not** [5]**overseen** by [6]**top-down**
10   **hierarchies** that could [7]**dictate** messages to shape the public's views. Today, however, Internet users have [8]**a vast array of** information sources [9]**at their fingertips**, which is uncontrollable by any overall authority. [10]**Breaking news** reaches the public [11]**swiftly**, before governments can [12]**come out with** their own [13]**spin** on [14]**developments**. Corporations and
15   small businesses alike are challenged by a surprisingly [15]**savvy** public. For instance, consumers can instantly research quality, prices, and other concerns about potential purchases thanks to easily accessible apps and websites.

Governments have learned that mobile phone applications and [16]**social**
20   **networking sites** provide communication tools for [17]**rebels** and protestors. Officials in some countries have [18]**censored** the Internet and even [19]**shut** it **down**, but it has become so integral to economic interests that [20]**interfering with** it can be [21]**precarious** to the governments themselves.   🏴 (220 words)

世の中を変えるインターネット

インターネットの最も注目されるべき影響の1つはメディアの民主化で，政府や企業がかつて享受していたメディアに対する支配力を低下させている。

　1990年代初期，科学技術の専門家たちはインターネットが歴史の進路を変える社会の節目となると予測した。彼らの ¹予感は ²実証されたが，想像していたようにではなかった。確かにインターネットはコミュニケーション，研究，娯楽のための先進的ツールとなり，あらゆる人に ³受け入れられた。しかし，それだけでなく，インターネットは，政府よりも個人が影響力を持つ情報交換システムになっている。

　インターネット以前，人々は放送メディアにほぼ頼りきりで，このメディアは ⁴たいてい大衆の考えを方向づけるメッセージ ⁷を押しつけることのできる ⁶上意下達式の支配層によって ⁵監視されていた。しかし今日，インターネット利用者は，⁹すぐに利用できる ⁸莫大な情報源を手にしている。それはいかなる絶対権力でも制御不能なものだ。¹⁰ニュース速報は，政府が ¹⁴事件について ¹³政府見解 ¹²を発表する前に，¹¹素早く大衆に届く。大企業も中小企業も一様に驚くほど ¹⁵知恵のある大衆の挑戦を受けている。例えば，消費者は簡単にアクセスできるアプリやウェブサイトのおかげで，買う可能性のあるものの品質や価格，その他気になることをすぐに調べることができる。

　政府は携帯アプリや ¹⁶交流サイトが，¹⁷反乱者や抗議者にコミュニケーションツールを提供することがわかってきた。中には当局がインターネット ¹⁸を検閲し，¹⁹閉鎖にまで至った国もある。しかし，インターネットは経済的利益に欠かせなくなったので，それ ²⁰に干渉することはかえって政府にとって ²¹危険になりかねない。

The Internet as Social Revolution

1 ☐☐ **premonition** [prèməníʃən]	▶ presentiment, foreboding 名 予感, 前兆, 予告 形 premonitory（予告の, 前兆の）
2 ☐☐ **bear out 〜**	▶ confirm, justify, prove （仮説など）を実証する
3 ☐☐ **embrace** [ɪmbréɪs]	▶ accept, adopt 動 （新しい考えなど）を受け入れる, （機会など）を利用する
4 ☐☐ **more often than not**	▶ frequently, generally, regularly たいてい, しばしば
5 ☐☐ **oversee** [òʊvərsíː]	▶ supervise, administer, superintend 動 を監視する, を取り締まる
6 ☐☐ **top-down hierarchy**	上意下達式の支配［権力］層
7 ☐☐ **dictate** [díkteɪt] ❶	▶ command, demand, order 動 （条件・方針など）を押しつける, を命じる 名 dictation
8 ☐☐ **a vast array of 〜**	▶ a huge number of, an enormous amount of 莫大な〜 ● array は「並んだもの, ひと並び」
9 ☐☐ **at *one's* fingertips**	▶ accessible, at hand, handy すぐに利用できるところに, すぐに手に入れられる状態で　● fingertip は「指先」
10 ☐☐ **breaking news**	▶ newsflash, flash news, bulletin ニュース速報
11 ☐☐ **swiftly** [swíftli]	▶ promptly, rapidly 副 速やかに, 迅速に

12 ☐☐ **come out with 〜**	▶ issue, pronounce, make public 〜を発表する，〜を公表する
13 ☐☐ **spin** [spɪn]	▶ official view, government perspective 名（政府などによる）独自の解釈，政府見解，情報操作
14 ☐☐ **development** [dɪvéləpmənt]	▶ turn of events, incident, circumstance 名 事件，（新）事実，事態の進展
15 ☐☐ **savvy** [sǽvi]	▶ shrewd, experienced, in the know 形 知恵［経験］のある，抜け目のない 名 実際の知識［能力］
16 ☐☐ **social networking site**	▶ social networking service （インターネット上の）交流サイト，SNS
17 ☐☐ **rebel** [rébəl]	▶ insurgent, defier 名 反乱者，反抗者　動 反抗する　形 反逆の 名 rebellion（反抗）　形 rebellious
18 ☐☐ **censor** [sénsər]	▶ inspect, review 動 を検閲する　名 検閲官 名 censorship（検閲）
19 ☐☐ **shut down 〜**	▶ cease, close down （システム・ネットワークなど）を閉鎖する，〜を止める
20 ☐☐ **interfere with 〜**	▶ meddle with, horn in on, intervene in 〜に干渉する
21 ☐☐ **precarious** [prɪkéəriəs]	▶ risky, uncertain, unstable 形 危険な，不安定な
☐☐ **Jasmine Revolution**	ジャスミン革命 ● 2010 年から 2011 年にチュニジアで起こった民主化運動・革命。インターネットが大きな役割を果たした

Technological Innovator Idris Ayodeji Bello

Idris Ayodeji Bello is attempting to use technical solutions, such as mobile phones and the Internet, to improve healthcare and education for people in Africa.

1   Idris Ayodeji Bello is a man on a [1]**mission** to bring technology to both his native Nigeria and other parts of Africa where there is now a [2]**void**. He is part of a new wave of young, highly educated Africans who [3]**excel** at technology and are passionate about the [4]**prospects** that technological
5   innovations promise. Bello has worked for [5]**multinational corporations** abroad, and is involved in several startups.

   Bello is the [6]**founder** of Wennovation Hub, a technology space that invites ambitious entrepreneurs to come and work together, which [7]**spurs** them to innovate. He has also used his technological skills to move both
10 education and health forward. He co-founded AfyaZima, a company that [8]**leveraged** mobile phones and other [9]**accessible** technologies to provide people in [10]**isolated** areas with access to health information. The company created an [11]**inexpensive** device that monitored blood pressure and [12]**transmitted** medical data by mobile phone. The device also allowed
15 doctors to remotely send [13]**diagnoses** and remedies to patients.

   Bello has also been involved in a project to bring offline wireless service to Africans who lack Internet access, which [14]**impairs** their economic prospects. The technology enables users to access cloud computing services even when a regular Internet connection is
20 unavailable. He aims to provide online courses and other educational tools to a wider [15]**audience**. He hopes that by providing broader technological opportunities, more Africans can [16]**tap into** their creativity to innovate solutions.

⬛ (232 words)

ℓ.16 offline wireless service：ここで言及されているシステムは，無線のアクセスポイントにな
るサーバーに一度インターネットからデータをダウンロードすれば，以降はインターネット
に接続できない場所に持っていっても，すでにダウンロードしたデータを無線で各端末に配
信できるというもの。

技術革新者　イドゥリス・アヨダジー・ベリョ

イドゥリス・アヨダジー・ベリョは携帯電話やインターネットなどの技術的解決法を使ってアフリカの人々の医療と教育の改善を試みている。

イドゥリス・アヨダジー・ベリョは，現在技術の ²行き渡っていない彼の母国であるナイジェリアとアフリカの他の地域の両方に科学技術をもたらす ¹使命を帯びている人物だ。彼は，技術に ³長け，技術革新が約束する ⁴可能性に情熱をかける，高学歴の若きアフリカ人たちの新たなうねりを担う一員である。ベリョは海外で ⁵多国籍企業に勤めた経験があり，スタートアップ企業にもいくつか関わっている。

ベリョは意欲的な起業家たちを招き，ともに働くことで革新 ⁷を促す技術の場であるウェノベーション・ハブの ⁶創設者である。また，彼は教育と健康を推進するために自分の科学技術の腕を利用してきた。彼は携帯電話やその他の ⁹利用可能な技術 ⁸を活用して，¹⁰孤立した地域に住む人々が医療情報を入手できるようにする会社として，アフヤズィーマを共同で設立した。その会社は血圧を測定したり，携帯電話で医療データ ¹²を送信したりする ¹¹安価な装置を作り出した。その装置はまた，医師が離れた場所から患者に ¹³診断や治療法を送ることを可能にした。

ベリョはインターネットにアクセスできないために，経済的展望 ¹⁴を失っているアフリカ人たちにオフラインの無線サービスを提供するプロジェクトにも関わってきた。その技術によって，通常のインターネット接続ができないときでも利用者はクラウドコンピューティングサービスにアクセスすることができる。彼はオンラインの講座やその他の教育手段をより多くの ¹⁵人たちに提供することを目指している。より幅広い技術的な機会を提供することによって，より多くのアフリカ人が自分たちの創造力 ¹⁶を使って，解決策を新しく導入できるようになることを彼は望んでいる。

3

Technological Innovator Idris Ayodeji Bello

1 ☐☐ **mission** [míʃən]	▶ assignment, role, task 名 使命, 任務 〈to do ～するという〉 ● on a mission（使命を帯びて）
2 ☐☐ **void** [vɔɪd]	▶ emptiness, vacuity 名 何もないこと, 無 形 ない, 空っぽの
3 ☐☐ **excel** [ɪksél] ❶	▶ be excellent, be talented, stand out 動 秀で（てい）る 名 excellence
4 ☐☐ **prospect** [prá(:)spekt]	▶ anticipation, expectation, outlook 名 期待, 見通し 形 prospective（予想される, 将来の）
5 ☐☐ **multinational corporation**	▶ multinational enterprise, transnational company 多国籍企業
6 ☐☐ **founder** [fáʊndər]	▶ originator, initiator 名 創設者, 設立者 動 found 名 foundation（創設）
7 ☐☐ **spur** [spəːr] ❶	▶ urge, stimulate, encourage 動 (人) を鼓舞する, を刺激する 〈to do ～するよう〉
8 ☐☐ **leverage** [lévərɪdʒ]	▶ utilize, exploit 動 (資源など) を最大限利用する 名 効力, 影響力
9 ☐☐ **accessible** [əksésəbl]	▶ available, obtainable, usable 形 利用可能な, 利用しやすい
10 ☐☐ **isolated** [áɪsəlèɪt̬ɪd]	▶ remote, secluded, lonesome 形 孤立した 動 isolate 名 isolation
11 ☐☐ **inexpensive** [ìnɪkspénsɪv]	▶ low-priced, affordable, cheap 形 安価な ⇄ expensive

12 □□ **transmit** [trænsmít] ❗	▶ send, convey, pass on **動** (信号・データ) を送る
13 □□ **diagnosis** [dàɪəgnóʊsɪs]	**名** 診断 **動** diagnose ● 複数形は diagnoses
14 □□ **impair** [ɪmpéər]	▶ injure, deteriorate, debilitate **動** を損なう, を害する **名** impairment (損傷)
15 □□ **audience** [ɔ́:diəns]	▶ viewer, spectator, listener **名** 聴衆, 観衆, 読者 ● 情報の受け手となる人々を指す
16 □□ **tap into ～**	▶ utilize, make use of (知識・経験など) を利用する, ～を活用する
□□ **watershed** [wɔ́:tərʃèd]	▶ landmark, milepost, milestone **名** 転換点, 分水嶺
□□ **telemedicine** [téləmèdsən]	**名** 遠隔医療
□□ **distance learning**	遠隔学習, 通信教育

Cloned Olympic Horses a Possibility

An equestrian organization has lifted a ban on cloned horses in competitions, opening up the possibility that such horses will soon appear in the Olympics.

1　　The first successfully [1]**cloned** horse was born in 2003. Only a few hundred horses have been cloned mainly for [2]**breeding**, since it costs over a hundred thousand dollars to clone a single animal. Racing [3]**associations** and the Olympics [4]**banned** cloned horses from competitions, reasoning
5　that [5]**duplicating** champions constitutes an unfair advantage. In July, 2012, however, the Fédération Equestre Internationale (FEI), the [6]**authoritative** body for Olympic [7]**equestrian** events, [8]**amended** its earlier [9]**prohibition** and decided to allow clones to compete in future Olympics. The reversal [10]**pivoted on** the realization that cloned offspring
10　are not really [11]**identical** copies: their [12]**genes** vary by about two percent. Moreover, environment, including such things as diet, training, and relationships with the rider, has an [13]**immeasurable** impact on a horse's performance.

　　Not everyone agrees with the decision. Cloning of champions is still
15　[14]**controversial** and several racing associations [15]**disallow** them. Some critics say that cloning removes the intrigue of horse racing, along with other enjoyable elements of the sport. One racehorse farm owner says of cloning, "Where's the fun?"

　　The FEI [16]**decreed** that cloning is now considered just one of several
20　breeding techniques. However, they [17]**underscore** that they will never allow [18]**genetically modified** horses that have been made into superhorses.　　　　　　　　　　　　　　　　　　　🏴󠁧󠁢󠁥󠁮󠁧󠁿 (201 words)

クローン馬がオリンピックに出場する可能性

馬術団体がクローン馬の試合出場の禁止を解除したことで，そのような馬が近いうちにオリンピックに登場する可能性が出てきた。

　　初めて[1]**クローンを作る**ことに成功した馬は 2003 年に生まれた。1 頭の動物のクローンを作るには 10 万ドル以上の費用がかかるため，主に[2]**繁殖**を目的とした数百頭の馬しかこれまでクローンが作られていない。競馬[3]**協会**とオリンピック大会は，チャンピオン[5]**を複製する**ことは不当に有利になるとして，クローンの馬が試合に出場すること[4]**を禁止した**。しかし，2012 年 7 月，オリンピックの[7]**馬術競技**の[6]**権威ある**団体，国際馬術連盟（FEI）は初期の[9]**禁止事項**[8]**を改訂し**，将来オリンピックでクローンが競技に出場することを許可する決定をした。逆の決定は，クローンの子孫は[11]**そっくりそのままの**コピーではないという認識[10]**によって決まった**のだった。クローンらの[12]**遺伝子**は約 2％異なる。さらに食事，訓練，騎手との関係といった環境も馬の成績に[13]**計り知れない**影響を及ぼす。

　　全員がその決定に同意しているわけではない。チャンピオン馬のクローン作成はいまだに[14]**物議を醸しており**，[15]**許可しない**競馬協会もいくつかある。批評家の中には，クローン技術は競技のその他の楽しみとともに競馬の醍醐味も奪うと言う人もいる。ある競走馬の牧場主はクローン技術について「どこに面白みがあるのか」と言う。

　　FEI は，クローン技術は今では単にいくつかある繁殖技術の 1 つだ[16]**と定めた**。しかし，スーパーホースに変えられた[18]**遺伝子組み換えによる**馬は決して認めないということは[17]**強調している**。

iPS 細胞

クローン技術を含む life science（生命科学）の分野で大きく注目されているのが，iPS 細胞である。正式には induced pluripotent stem cell（人工多能性幹細胞）と言う。pluripotent は，接頭辞 pluri- が plural「複数の」，potent が「力のある」で，「多能性の」と訳されるように，身体を構成するさまざまな臓器や組織の細胞に分化する能力を持つ，という意味である。iPS 細胞は，失われた身体の部位を再生させる技術である regenerative medicine（再生医療）の切り札と期待され，実用化への取り組みが進んでいる。

Cloned Olympic Horses a Possibility

1 ☐☐ **clone** [kloʊn]	▶ copy, duplicate, reproduce 動 のクローンを作る 名 クローン
2 ☐☐ **breeding** [bríːdɪŋ]	▶ procreation, multiplication, reproduction 名 繁殖, 生殖 動 breed
3 ☐☐ **association** [əsòʊsiéɪʃən]	▶ alliance, consortium, federation 名 協会, 組合, 連盟 動 associate
4 ☐☐ **ban** [bæn]	▶ prohibit, forbid, bar 動 を禁止する, を閉め出す〈from ～から〉 名 禁止
5 ☐☐ **duplicate** [djúːplɪkèɪt]	▶ copy, reproduce 動 を複製する 名 duplication
6 ☐☐ **authoritative** [əθɔ́ːrətèɪtɪv]	▶ authorized, commanding, magisterial 形 権威のある, 権力を持った 名 authority（権威, 権力）
7 ☐☐ **equestrian** [ɪkwéstriən]	形 馬術の, 乗馬の
8 ☐☐ **amend** [əménd]	▶ revise, rectify, modify 動（法律など）を修正する, を改正する 名 amendment
9 ☐☐ **prohibition** [pròʊhəbíʃən]	▶ ban, embargo 名 禁止 動 prohibit
10 ☐☐ **pivot on ～**	▶ depend on, be decided on （議論などが）～によって決まる ● pivot は「軸」の意味
11 ☐☐ **identical** [aɪdén̬ɪkəl]	▶ equal, equivalent, the same 形（完全に）同一の

12 ☐☐ **gene** [dʒiːn]	名 遺伝子 形 genetic
13 ☐☐ **immeasurable** [ɪméʒərəbl]	▶ immense, measureless, infinite 形 計り知れないほど（大きい）
14 ☐☐ **controversial** [kà(ː)ntrəvə́ːrʃəl]	▶ questionable, arguable, debatable 形 物議を醸す，論争となるような 名 controversy（論争，議論）
15 ☐☐ **disallow** [dìsəláʊ]	▶ reject, deny, disclaim 動 を許さない，を認めない 名 disallowance ⇔ allow（を許可する）
16 ☐☐ **decree** [dɪkríː]	▶ proclaim, declare 動 を定める，を宣言する，を布告する 名 布告
17 ☐☐ **underscore** [ʌ̀ndərskɔ́ːr]	▶ emphasize, accentuate, underline 動 を強調する，に（強調のために）下線を引く
18 ☐☐ **genetically modified**	▶ genetically engineered 遺伝子が組み換えられた，遺伝子操作によって作られた
☐☐ **living modified organism**	遺伝子組み換え生物

Messages from across the Universe

Some scientists suggest that the best way to search for alien life is to look for messages in particles called neutrinos.

1   Scientists have been sending codes out into space since the 1960s in hopes that intelligent life forms will find them. They first utilized radios, and more recently, lasers, to send out their messages. However, two scientists, John Learned of the University of Hawaii and Anthony Zee of
5   the University of California, offer what they believe to be a better [1]**telecommunications** alternative. [2]**Radio waves** and [3]**light waves**, ideal for telecommunications on Earth, consist of [4]**photons**, which are absorbed and [5]**scattered** by gas and [6]**debris** in space. The scientists are promoting [7]**neutrinos** as new alien communications tools, since they pass directly
10   through [8]**obstructions**: [9]**matter** in space would no longer be [10]**impediments**. In addition, neutrinos are detectable by neutrino telescopes on Earth.

   Neutrinos are abundant in the universe, second only in [11]**abundance** to photons. However, they are difficult to observe, because they rarely
15   [12]**interact with** other forms of matter. Detecting artificial neutrinos sent by aliens would require [13]**filtering out** the natural neutrino [14]**background noise**, but the scientists believe that would likely not be a major impediment, for artificial neutrinos would likely have much higher energy levels than the low-level background noise of natural neutrinos. If aliens
20   sent [15]**beams** of neutrinos that were a billion times more energetic than the neutrinos [16]**emanating** from stars, background noise would be [17]**virtually** unnoticeable.   ▉≡ (216 words)

宇宙のかなたからのメッセージ

科学者の中には，地球外生命体を探す最良の方法は，ニュートリノと呼ばれる粒子の中にメッセージを探すことだと示唆する者もいる。

　科学者たちは，知的生命体が見つけてくれることを願って，1960年代から宇宙空間にメッセージを送り続けている。彼らはメッセージを発信するために当初は電波を使い，最近になってはレーザーを利用している。しかし，ハワイ大学のジョン・ラーニッドとカリフォルニア大学のアンソニー・ズィーの2人の科学者が，¹遠距離通信のより良い代替手段と信じる方法を提案している。²電波も³光波も地球上では申し分ない遠距離通信の手段だが，⁴光子で構成されているため，宇宙空間ではガスや⁶デブリによって吸収されたり⁵拡散されたりしてしまう。科学者たちは⁷ニュートリノを宇宙人との新しい通信手段として奨励している。ニュートリノは⁸障害物をまっすぐに通り抜けるからだ。宇宙の⁹物質はもはや¹⁰障害にはならないだろう。加えて，ニュートリノはニュートリノ望遠鏡で地上から検知可能だ。

　ニュートリノは宇宙に大量にあり，¹¹存在量は光子に次いで2番目だ。しかし，他の物質にめったに¹²反応しないため，ニュートリノを観測するのは難しい。宇宙人によって送られる人工ニュートリノを検知するには自然のニュートリノの¹⁴背景雑音信号¹³をろ過して取り除く必要がある。しかし科学者たちはおそらくそれは重大な障害にはならないと信じている。というのも人工ニュートリノは低レベルの自然のニュートリノの背景雑音信号よりおそらくはるかに高いエネルギーレベルを持つからだ。宇宙人が，星から¹⁶発生するニュートリノより10億倍のエネルギーのニュートリノの¹⁵ビームを送れば，背景雑音信号は¹⁷事実上気づかない程度のものとなるだろう。

Messages from across the Universe

1 ☐☐ **telecommunication** [tèləkəmjùːnɪkéɪʃən]	名 (通例 -s) 遠距離通信, 電気通信
2 ☐☐ **radio wave**	▶ electrical wave 電波
3 ☐☐ **light wave**	▶ optical wave 光波
4 ☐☐ **photon** [fóʊtɑ(ː)n]	名 光子
5 ☐☐ **scatter** [skǽtər]	▶ disperse, sprinkle, spread 動 を拡散させる
6 ☐☐ **debris** [dəbríː] ❶	▶ remains, rubble, rubbish 名 デブリ, (壊れたものの) 破片
7 ☐☐ **neutrino** [njutríːnoʊ]	名 ニュートリノ, 中性微子
8 ☐☐ **obstruction** [əbstrʌ́kʃən]	▶ blockage, hindrance, obstacle 名 障害物 動 obstruct
9 ☐☐ **matter** [mǽtər]	▶ material, stuff, substance 名 物質, 物体
10 ☐☐ **impediment** [ɪmpédɪmənt]	▶ obstacle, obstruction, hurdle 名 障害, 妨害物 動 impede
11 ☐☐ **abundance** [əbʌ́ndəns]	▶ copiousness, heap, profusion 名 (物質の) 存在量, 豊富

12 ☐☐ **interact with ～**	▶ react to ～に反応する，～と相互に作用する 名 interaction（相互作用）
13 ☐☐ **filter out ～**	▶ leach，comb out ～を（ろ過して）取り除く
14 ☐☐ **background noise**	背景雑音（信号）
15 ☐☐ **beam** [bi:m]	▶ ray，stream 名（光・粒子などの）一直線の流れ
16 ☐☐ **emanate** [émənèɪt]	▶ emit，give off，radiate 動 発する，発散する，放射する 名 emanation
17 ☐☐ **virtually** [vɔ́ːrtʃuəli]	▶ in fact，substantially，practically 副 事実上，実質的に 形 virtual
☐☐ **extraterrestrial** [èkstrətəréstriəl]	形 地球外の，宇宙の 名 地球外生物 ● extra-（～外の）＋terrestri-（地球の）＋-al（形容詞語尾）
☐☐ **sound wave**	▶ sonic wave 音波 ● ultrasonic [supersonic] wave（超音波）
☐☐ **dwarf planet**	準惑星
☐☐ **asteroid** [æstərɔ̀ɪd]	名 小惑星

Intelligent Skyscrapers

This passage is about how advances in technology and design are allowing skyscrapers to be both more functional and more sustainable.

1   Architects must keep many issues in mind when designing a particularly tall ¹**skyscraper**. They must ²**factor in** ³**gravity**, high wind speeds, extreme weather, and ⁴**occupant** safety, which has become a major ⁵**liability** after the terrorist attacks of September 11. Architects must
5 also consider such things as ⁶**compliance** with local building ⁷**codes**, ⁸**amenity** expectations of owners, and such environmental considerations as ⁹**conserving** fuel and water. This makes skyscraper design inherently more daunting than smaller projects, and requires technological know-how to enable buildings to reach their full potential.

10   Today's architects ¹⁰**are obliged to** be flexible. Technology is progressing so rapidly that skyscrapers must be designed for future ¹¹**contingencies**. Designers often must consider the local environment as well. Take Adrian Smith, architect for the 700-meter-tall Burj Khalifa in Dubai, for example, who designed exterior walls in order to ¹²**shield**
15 interior spaces from the hot desert sun. The exterior walls reflect 82 percent of the solar heat and sun-shading devices capture much of the remaining heat, which is then ¹³**extracted**. Smith also designed the building to take advantage of the country's extreme humidity. ¹⁴**Condensation** that builds up from the humid air coming into contact
20 with the building's cooling system is collected and stored. Nearly 15 million gallons of water is ¹⁵**accumulated** in this way per year, enough to fill up 20 Olympic-sized pools. Advances in technology allow buildings to be ever more functional as well as sustainable.

(233 words)

自動制御が可能な高層ビル

この文章は，高層ビルが技術と設計の進歩により，いかにより機能的で，より持続可能なものになっているかについてのものである。

　特に高い¹高層ビルを設計する際には，建築家たちは多くの問題を考えに入れなければならない。³重力，高風速，過酷な天候，そして９月11日のテロ攻撃以降主要な⁵責務となった⁴入居者の安全²を考慮に入れなければならないのだ。建築家たちはまた，現地の建築⁷規約の⁶順守，所有者の⁸快適さへの期待，燃料や水⁹を節約するなど環境への配慮についても考慮しなければならない。このことによって高層ビルの設計は小規模の計画よりも本質的により困難なものとなり，建築物がその潜在力を最大に発揮できるようにするための技術的ノウハウを必要とする。

　今日の建築家たちは柔軟であること¹⁰を余儀なくされている。科学技術はあまりにも急速に進歩しているため，高層ビルは将来の¹¹不測の事態にも備えて設計されなければならない。設計者たちはしばしば現地の環境も同様に考慮しなければならない。ドバイにある高さ700メートルのブルジュ・ハリーファの設計者エイドリアン・スミスを例に挙げよう。彼は砂漠の熱い太陽から内部の空間¹²を保護するために外部の壁を設計した。その外部の壁は太陽熱の82％を反射し，残りの熱の多くを遮光装置に取り込み，そこで熱が¹³取り出される。スミスはその国の極度に高い湿度をも利用できるように建物を設計した。湿った空気がその建物の冷却装置に接触することによって増える¹⁴結露は回収され，貯蔵される。この方法で年に1,500万ガロン近くの水が¹⁵貯まる。これはオリンピック規格のプール20個分を満たすのに十分な量である。技術の進歩は建物を持続可能にすると同時にかつてないほど機能的なものにしている。

補償責任

liability は「責任」と訳されるが，responsibility と異なるのは，「金銭を支払う責任」という意味合いが含まれることである。例えば，Product Liability Law（製造物責任法）は，欠陥のある製品により損害が生じた場合の賠償責任を定めている。
2001年９月11日のテロ攻撃の犠牲者に対する補償は米国政府が創設した基金などで支払われているが，通常の事故であればビルの側が補償責任を問われることになる。

Intelligent Skyscrapers

1 ☐☐ **skyscraper** [skáɪskrèɪpər]	▶ high-rise building, tall building 名 超高層ビル, 摩天楼 ● sky（空）+ scraper（こするもの）
2 ☐☐ **factor in ~**	▶ count in, consider, take ~ into account [consideration] ～を考慮に入れる, ～を計算に入れる
3 ☐☐ **gravity** [grǽvəti]	名 重力 名 gravitation（重力（作用）） 形 gravitational（重力の）
4 ☐☐ **occupant** [á(:)kjʊpənt]	▶ inhabitant, resident 名（ある時点である場所に）いる人, 入居者 動 occupy（を占有する, に居住する）
5 ☐☐ **liability** [làɪəbíləti]	▶ responsibility, obligation, duty 名 責任, 義務 形 liable
6 ☐☐ **compliance** [kəmpláɪəns]	▶ conformity, obedience, observance 名 順守〈with 法令などの〉 動 comply（従う）
7 ☐☐ **code** [koʊd]	▶ regulation, ordinance 名 規約, 条例
8 ☐☐ **amenity** [əmíːnəti]	▶ pleasantness, comfort 名（建物・場所などの）快適さ
9 ☐☐ **conserve** [kənsə́ːrv]	▶ save, preserve 動（資源など）を節約する, を大切に使う
10 ☐☐ **be obliged to _do_**	▶ be liable to _do_, have an obligation to _do_ 余儀なく～する, ～する義務がある
11 ☐☐ **contingency** [kəntíndʒənsi]	▶ accident, incident, fortuity 名 不測の事態, 偶発的事件 形 contingent

12 □□ **shield** [ʃiːld]	▶ protect, defend, shelter 🔵 を保護する，を守る〈from ～から〉 🔴 保護する物
13 □□ **extract** [ɪkstrǽkt] ❶	▶ pull out, take out, remove 🔵 を取り出す，を抜き取る 🔴 extraction
14 □□ **condensation** [kɑ̀(ː)ndenséɪʃən]	▶ dewdrop, bedewing 🔴 結露，凝縮［液化］したもの 🔵 condense（凝結する）
15 □□ **accumulate** [əkjúːmjulèɪt]	▶ amass, garner 🔵 を貯める，を蓄積する 🔴 accumulation
□□ **inaugurate** [ɪnɔ́ːgjərèɪt]	🔵（建物・施設など）の使用を開始する，の落成式を行う 🔴 inauguration
□□ **refurbish** [riːfə́ːrbɪʃ]	▶ renew, renovate, recondition 🔵 を改装［リフォーム］する，を一新する
□□ **refrigerant** [rɪfrídʒərənt]	▶ a substance used for cooling something 🔴 冷媒，冷却剤　🔶 冷却する 🔵 refrigerate

A Breakthrough in the Microwave Laser

An old paper by a Japanese researcher has led to a major advance in a type of laser that uses microwaves instead of light.

1   Before the invention of lasers, scientists had developed [1]**microwave** lasers, or masers. Lasers, which rely on the same [2]**principles** of [3]**physics** as masers, are based on [4]**optical** light rather than microwaves, and are much more powerful and useful for applications. After the invention of
5   lasers, [5]**funding** for maser research [6]**dried up**.

Physicist Mark Oxborrow of the UK National Physical Laboratory [7]**stumbled upon** a [8]**dated** publication by a Japanese researcher that [9]**hypothesized** that when shooting a laser through a crystal containing an organic molecule known as pentacene, the electrons in the pentacene
10   would become [10]**excited** and create a powerful maser. To test the [11]**validity** of the hypothesis, Oxborrow, who [12]**collaborated** with two other colleagues, obtained a laser and a few chemicals and created the crystal as the publication had suggested. Everything seemed [13]**straightforward**, but Oxborrow ran into an obstacle — himself. As he
15   was so nervous that the experiment would fail, he [14]**procrastinated** for several days. When he finally did carry out the experiment, the outcome was [15]**nothing short of** astonishing: the signal was roughly a hundred million times bigger than any existing maser. Oxborrow is optimistic he can [16]**coax out** an even bigger maser the next time, since his first crystal
20   was [17]**coarsely** made.

The findings could [18]**wind up** [19]**ushering in** a new age of masers, and the powerful masers, once [20]**harnessed**, could lead to advancements in communications and space exploration.   ▦ (230 words)

マイクロ波レーザーの飛躍的進展

日本の研究者による古い論文は，光の代わりにマイクロ波を使う種類のレーザーの大きな進歩につながった。

レーザーが発明される前に，科学者たちは [1]マイクロ波のレーザー，つまりメーザーを開発した。メーザーと同じ[3]物理[2]原理に依存するレーザーはマイクロ波ではなく[4]可視光に基づいており，メーザーより強力で応用しやすい。レーザーが発明された後，メーザー研究の[5]資金は[6]枯渇した。

イギリス国立物理学研究所の物理学者マーク・オクスボローはある日本人研究者による[8]古い論文[7]を偶然見つけた。その論文は，ペンタセンとして知られる有機分子を含む結晶体を通してレーザーを放射するとペンタセンの中の電子は[10]刺激されて強力なメーザーを作り出す[9]という仮説を立てた。仮説の[11]妥当性を検証するために，オクスボローは2人の同僚と[12]共同研究し，レーザーと数種の化学薬品を入手し，論文が提案する通りに結晶体を作った。すべてが[13]単純に見えたが，オクスボローは，自分自身という壁にぶつかった。彼は実験が失敗することを恐れてとても神経質になっていたので，数日[14]先延ばしにした。彼がついに実験を行ったとき，その結果は[15]まったくもって驚くべきものであった。その信号は存在するあらゆるメーザーと比べて，大ざっぱに見ても1億倍以上の大きなものだった。オクスボローは彼の最初の結晶体は[17]雑に作られたものだったため，次回はさらに大きなメーザー[16]を首尾よく引き出せるだろうと楽観している。

その発見は[18]結局はメーザーの新たな時代[19]の到来を告げるものとなるかもしれず，その強力なメーザーがひとたび[20]利用されれば，情報伝達や宇宙開発の進歩につながるかもしれない。

明日に延ばす

procrastinate は難しそうな語に見えるが，まったくの日常語である。「するべきことをせずに先延ばしにする」という意味で，単に「延期する」の postpone や put off とはニュアンスが違う。procrastinate の語源は，ラテン語で put off until tomorrow という意味。この物理学者は実験を行うのを数日延ばしにしていたのだから，その状況を表す語としては postpone や put off よりも procrastinate がふさわしい。宿題をサボることから政治課題への対処を怠ることまで，procrastination の対象は幅広い。

A Breakthrough in the Microwave Laser

1 ☐☐ **microwave** [máɪkrəwèɪv]	名 マイクロ波，電子レンジ 動 を電子レンジで加熱する
2 ☐☐ **principle** [prínsəpəl]	▶ basis, doctrine, fundamental 名 原理
3 ☐☐ **physics** [fízɪks] ●	名 物理学 名 physicist（物理学者） 形 physical（物理学の，物理的な）
4 ☐☐ **optical** [á(:)ptɪkəl]	▶ visible 形 可視（光線）の
5 ☐☐ **funding** [fʌ́ndɪŋ]	▶ treasury, monetary resources, financial backing 名 財源，財政的支援
6 ☐☐ **dry up**	▶ be exhausted, drain out （資金・ものの供給などが）なくなる，途絶える
7 ☐☐ **stumble upon ～**	～を偶然見つける
8 ☐☐ **dated** [déɪt̬ɪd]	▶ old-fashioned, obsolete, out-of-date 形 古い，過去の
9 ☐☐ **hypothesize** [haɪpá(:)θəsàɪz]	▶ speculate, presuppose, presume 動 を仮定する 名 hypothesis（仮説，仮定）
10 ☐☐ **excite** [ɪksáɪt] ●	▶ stimulate, stir up, arouse 動 （分子・原子など）を励起する，を刺激する
11 ☐☐ **validity** [vəlídət̬i]	▶ adequacy, reasonability, lawfulness 名 妥当性，正当性 動 validate（の正当性を証明する）　形 valid

12 ☐☐ **collaborate** [kəlǽbərèɪt]	▶ cooperate, coproduce, team up 動 共同研究する 名 collaboration 形 collaborative
13 ☐☐ **straightforward** [strèɪtfɔ́:rwərd] ❶	▶ easy, simple, uncomplicated 形 単純な
14 ☐☐ **procrastinate** [prəkrǽstɪnèɪt]	▶ put off, postpone, delay 動 先延ばしにする，ぐずぐずする 名 procrastination
15 ☐☐ **nothing short of** 〜	▶ none other than まったく〜である，まさに〜にほかならない
16 ☐☐ **coax out 〜**	▶ wheedle, cajole, beguile 〜をうまく引き出す
17 ☐☐ **coarsely** [kɔ́:rsli]	▶ roughly, crudely 副 雑に，粗く
18 ☐☐ **wind up *doing***	▶ end up *doing*, come down to *doing*, turn out to *do* 最終的に〜することになる
19 ☐☐ **usher in 〜**	▶ herald （時代）の到来を告げる
20 ☐☐ **harness** [hɑ́:rnɪs]	▶ use, utilize, employ 動 （自然の力など）を利用する
☐☐ **frequency** [frí:kwənsi] ❶	名 周波数 ● high [low] frequency（高［低］周波）

Sugar Floating in Outer Space

The discovery of a type of sugar molecule called glycolaldehyde in outer space increases the possibility that life exists in places other than Earth.

1   Astronomer Jes Jorgensen of Copenhagen University in Denmark and his team of scientists discovered simple sugar [1]**molecules** floating in a [2]**gaseous** mass near a young star 400 light years from Earth. They use the term "sugar" [3]**in a broad sense**, referring to [4]**organic** molecules called
5   carbohydrates, composed of carbon, [5]**hydrogen**, and oxygen. This discovery [6]**stands out**, since it is the first time sugar has been [7]**located** near a star similar to our own. The simple sugar, called glycolaldehyde, is also found on Earth, normally appearing as an [8]**odorless** white powder. This type of sugar is believed to be a catalyst for a [9]**chemical reaction** in
10   the synthesis of ribonucleic acid (RNA), a vital molecule [10]**manifest** in the cells of every living [11]**organism**. [12]**Consequently**, astronomers [13]**were keyed up** to locate this sugar floating in space. Scientists are not yet sure how the sugar is created, but they suspect it is formed on icy dust particles floating in [14]**frigid** molecular clouds.

15   Though the discovery is not [15]**outright** evidence of alien life, it does make the existence of life on other planets more [16]**plausible**, since such simple sugar molecules are known as the [17]**building blocks** of life. Jorgensen says the results give astronomers motivation to look for other, possibly more complex, molecules in regions where stars and planets are
20   forming.   (217 words)

宇宙に漂う糖

宇宙空間でのグリコールアルデヒドと呼ばれる糖分子の一種の発見は，地球外に生命体が存在する可能性を高める。

　デンマークにあるコペンハーゲン大学の天文学者，イェス・ヨルゲンセンと科学者たちの研究チームは，地球から400光年離れた若い恒星近くの²**ガス**の塊の中に単糖類¹**分子**が浮遊しているのを発見した。彼らは炭素，⁵**水素**，酸素から構成される炭水化物と呼ばれる⁴**有機**分子を指して，³**広い意味**で「糖」という語を用いている。糖が私たちの太陽に似た恒星近くで⁷**見つけられた**のは初めてであるため，この発見は⁶**際立っている**。グリコールアルデヒドと呼ばれる単糖は，地球上でも見つかるもので，通常は⁸**無臭の**白い粉末だ。この種の糖はすべての¹¹**生物**の細胞に¹⁰**存在することが明らかな**重要な分子であるリボ核酸（RNA）を合成する⁹**化学反応**の触媒と考えられている。¹²**したがって**，天文学者たちは宇宙を漂うこの糖を見つけたことに¹³**興奮していた**。科学者たちはその糖がどのように作られるのかまだわかっていないが，¹⁴**極寒の**分子雲の中を漂う氷に覆われた塵粒子上で形成されるのではないかと考えている。

　この発見は地球外生命の¹⁵**明白な**証拠ではないが，他の惑星での生命の存在をより¹⁶**信ぴょう性のある**ものとする。なぜならそのような単糖分子は生命の¹⁷**基礎単位**として知られるからだ。今回の結果は天文学者に，他の，おそらくより複雑な分子を恒星や惑星の形成領域で探そうとする動機を提供してくれるとヨルゲンセンは言う。

Sugar Floating in Outer Space

1 ⬜⬜ **molecule** [má(ː)lɪkjùːl] ❶	名 分子 形 molecular
2 ⬜⬜ **gaseous** [ɡǽsiəs]	▶ aeriform 形 ガス状の，気体の
3 ⬜⬜ **in a broad sense**	▶ in the general meaning, as a rule of thumb 広い意味で，大ざっぱに ⬌ in a narrow sense（狭い意味で，厳密に）
4 ⬜⬜ **organic** [ɔːrɡǽnɪk] ❶	▶ biotic, living 形 有機（体）の ⬌ inorganic（無機の）
5 ⬜⬜ **hydrogen** [háɪdrədʒən]	名 水素
6 ⬜⬜ **stand out**	▶ be conspicuous, be distinct [striking], stick out 際立つ，傑出している
7 ⬜⬜ **locate** [lóʊkeɪt] ❶	▶ detect, discover, track down 動 を探し出す，のありかを突き止める 名 location（場所）
8 ⬜⬜ **odorless** [óʊdərləs]	▶ odor-free, scentless 形 無臭の，匂いのない ● odor（匂い）＋ -less（がない）
9 ⬜⬜ **chemical reaction**	化学反応
10 ⬜⬜ **manifest** [mǽnɪfèst] ❶	▶ clear, obvious, apparent 形 （存在などが）明らかな
11 ⬜⬜ **organism** [ɔ́ːrɡənìzm]	▶ living thing, being, creature 名 生物，有機体

12 ☐☐ **consequently** [ká(:)nsəkwèntli] ❶	▶ therefore, as a result, accordingly **副** したがって，結果として **名** consequence **形** consequent
13 ☐☐ **be keyed up**	▶ excited 興奮する，緊張する
14 ☐☐ **frigid** [frídʒɪd]	▶ extremely cold, arctic, gelid **形** 極寒の，非常に温度の低い
15 ☐☐ **outright** [áʊtràɪt]	▶ clear, obvious, explicit **形** 明白な，無条件の
16 ☐☐ **plausible** [plɔ́ːzəbl]	▶ possible, probable, conceivable **形** あり得る，もっともらしい **名** plausibility（もっともらしさ）**⇔** implausible
17 ☐☐ **building block**	▶ component, constituent, elementary unit 基本的な構成要素
☐☐ **ammunition** [æ̀mjuníʃən]	**名**（主張を証明するためなどの）材料，手段 ● 本義は「武器」
☐☐ **stellar** [stélər]	▶ relating to the stars **形** 星の ● stellar cluster（星団）
☐☐ **meteorite** [míːṭiəràɪt] ❶	▶ a piece of rock from outer space that hits the Earth's surface **名** 隕石
☐☐ **comet** [ká(:)mɪt]	**名** 彗星 ● Halley's Comet（ハレー彗星）

医学・テクノロジー **9**

Copying Nature's Designs

Inventors sometimes use biomimicry, or copying designs from nature, to create new technologies, such as a system that maintains a stable temperature naturally in a building.

1   Some ¹**resourceful** inventors derive their inspiration by ²**sizing up** and ³**emulating** nature's designs. By studying the innate ⁴**properties** of life forms, they seek to solve problems and create new innovations in engineering, material science, medicine, and other fields. Their rationale
5 is simple: through evolution, nature has ⁵**consummated** life's designs based on ⁶**rigorous** ⁷**trial and error** over a span of 3.6 billion years. ⁸**Dissecting** and copying nature's designs for practical applications is a field called ⁹**biomimicry**, a ¹⁰**branch** of engineering. Though the term is relatively new, people have been copying nature's designs for centuries.
10 Leonardo da Vinci observed birds in flight and took copious notes in the hope that man would someday fly. The Wright brothers' airplane, the first to fly, was inspired by observations of pigeons in flight. Swiss chemist George de Mestral got the idea for creating Velcro in 1948 by ¹¹**pondering** over why a type of ¹²**bur** ¹³**clung** so stubbornly to his dog's coat.
15   A modern example of biomimicry started with scientists researching why the interior temperatures of termite mounds in Africa could keep a stable temperature when those on the outside ¹⁴**fluctuated** within 1.5 to 40 degrees ¹⁵**Celsius**. Their observations inspired the design of a ¹⁶**phenomenally** ¹⁷**eco-friendly** office complex in Zimbabwe, Africa,
20 which remains cool without air conditioning and has reduced energy consumption to just 10 percent of what a similarly sized complex normally uses.   (228 words)

自然の意匠を手本に

発明家は時に生体模倣技術，すなわち自然の意匠を模倣する技術を使って，自然に建物内で気温を一定に保つシステムなどの新しい技術を創り出す。

　[1]工夫に富む発明家の中には自然の意匠[2]を評価し，[3]まねることによって着想を得る人もいる。生き物が生まれ持った[4]特性を研究することで，彼らは工学，材料科学，医学やその他の分野で問題を解決し，新機軸を創造しようとする。彼らの論理的根拠は単純だ。進化の過程で，自然は36億年にわたる[6]厳しい[7]試行錯誤を基に生物の意匠[5]を完成してきた。実用化のために自然の意匠[8]を分析し模倣することは，[9]生体模倣技術と呼ばれる工学の一[10]分野である。この用語は比較的新しいが，人類は何世紀にもわたって自然の意匠を模倣してきた。レオナルド・ダ・ヴィンチは飛翔する鳥を観察し，いつか人類も飛べるであろうことを願って多くのメモを取った。最初に飛行したライト兄弟の飛行機は，飛翔するハトの観察から発想を得た。スイスの化学者ジョルジュ・デ・メストラルは，ある種の[12]いがが彼の犬の毛になぜ執拗に[13]くっついて離れないのかを[11]熟考し，1948年にマジックテープを生み出す着想を得た。

　現代の生体模倣技術の1つの例は，科学者がなぜアフリカのシロアリ塚の内部が，外部の気温が[15]摂氏1.5度から40度の範囲で[14]変動したときに，気温を一定に保つことができるのかを研究することから始まった。彼らの観察結果はアフリカのジンバブエの[16]驚くほど[17]環境に優しいオフィスビルの設計にひらめきを与えた。そのビルはエアコンがなくても涼しいままで，エネルギー消費量を同じような大きさの建物が通常使う量のわずか10%まで削減している。

商標起源の語

eponymという名詞がある。固有名詞を起源とする語のことで，トランプ好きのサンドイッチ伯爵が片手で食べられるからと作らせたsandwichが一例である。商標がeponymとなることも多く，この英文で挙がっているVelcro（マジックテープ）もその1つ。英語でも日本語でも一般化している語には，Band-Aid，Sellotape，Tupperwareなどがある。Jell-O（ゼリー），Kleenex（ティッシュペーパー），Q-tips（綿棒）なども英語では普通名詞として用いられている。escalatorやzipperも以前は商標だった。「ゼロックスする」という日本語はほとんど死語だが，英語ではXeroxは名詞・動詞ともに「コピー（を取る）」の意味で使われることもある。

Copying Nature's Designs

1 ☐☐
resourceful
[rɪsɔ́ːrsfəl]
▶ creative, imaginative, talented
形 工夫に富んだ
名 resource（機知，機転）

2 ☐☐
size up ～
▶ evaluate, measure, gauge
～を（よく見て）評価する，～の大きさを測る

3 ☐☐
emulate
[émjulèɪt]
▶ imitate, copy, mimic
動 をまねる
名 emulation

4 ☐☐
property
[prá(:)pərti]
▶ characteristic, feature, trait
名 特質，特性

5 ☐☐
consummate
[ká(:)nsəmèɪt]
▶ complete, perfect, fulfill
動 を完成する，を達成する
名 consummation（完成）

6 ☐☐
rigorous
[rígərəs]
▶ challenging, demanding, severe
形 厳しい，過酷な
名 rigor

7 ☐☐
trial and error
試行錯誤

8 ☐☐
dissect
[dɪsékt]
▶ analyze
動 を分析する，を解剖する
名 dissection

9 ☐☐
biomimicry
[bàɪoʊmímɪkri]
名 生体模倣技術

10 ☐☐
branch
[bræntʃ]
▶ category, division, section
名 部門，分科

11 ☐☐
ponder
[pá(:)ndər]
▶ cogitate, consider, contemplate
動 熟考する，じっくり考える〈over, on, about ～
について〉

12 ☐☐ **bur** [bəːr]	▶ prickle, thorn **名**（植物の）いが
13 ☐☐ **cling** [klɪŋ]	▶ adhere, stick, attach **動** くっついて離れない，ぴったりくっつく〈to ～に〉
14 ☐☐ **fluctuate** [flʌ́ktʃuèɪt]	▶ go up and down, undulate, vacillate **動**（不規則に）変動する，揺れる **名** fluctuation
15 ☐☐ **Celsius** [sélsiəs]	▶ centigrade **形** 摂氏の ● 温度の後に置いて用いる。「華氏」は Fahrenheit
16 ☐☐ **phenomenally** [fəná(ː)mɪnəli]	▶ remarkably, outstandingly, extraordinarily **副** 驚くほど，驚異的に **名** phenomenon（並外れたもの，現象）
17 ☐☐ **eco-friendly** [ìːkoʊfréndli]	▶ environmentally-friendly, green **形** 環境に優しい

The Temptation of Fatty Foods

Researchers suggest that a "second brain" called the enteric nervous system in our guts may be a factor in making it difficult to resist the temptation of fatty foods.

1   Why are we so tempted by junk food? Pizzas, sausages, ice cream, and other fatty foods can ¹**entice** us when we feel stressed or down. Our brain may ²**admonish** us to ³**abstain from** fatty foods and warn us to stay away from fat, especially ⁴**saturated** fat, which often gets a ⁵**bum rap** for
5   its unhealthy properties. So why do we often ⁶**succumb to** these ⁷**urges**? There is actually a "second brain" that ⁸**resides** in our ⁹**gastrointestinal system** that ¹⁰**subverts** the sensible voice of our mind. Though made up of only one-thousandth of the number of ¹¹**neurons** of the brain, the ¹²**enteric** nervous system (ENS) sends us powerful messages independent
10   of the brain. Those impulses can often ¹³**prevail over** good sense.

Michael Gershon, a professor at Columbia University, says the gut can function as a second brain, working independently of the body's primary brain. The ENS manufactures ¹⁴**serotonin**, which helps control mood, especially pleasure. Researchers found that a meal ¹⁵**loaded with** fat can
15   release serotonin and help people fight depression. Participants in a study were given either a ¹⁶**saline solution** or an ¹⁷**infusion** of ¹⁸**fatty acids** when listening to melancholic music. Those given the fats had substantially reduced feelings of sadness. So the next time you feel enticed to eat a piece of pizza, you should not necessarily see it as a
20   ¹⁹**setback** if you give in. It is just your enteric nervous system ²⁰**overriding** your brain.   ⬛ (236 words)

脂肪分の多い食べ物の誘惑

研究者たちは，私たちの胃腸にある腸管神経系と呼ばれる「第二の脳」が脂肪分の多い食べ物の誘惑に抵抗するのを難しくしている要因かもしれないと示唆する。

　私たちはなぜジャンクフードにこれほど誘惑されるのだろうか。ピザ，ソーセージ，アイスクリーム，その他の脂肪分の多い食べ物は，ストレスを感じたり，気が滅入ったりしているときに私たち [1]を誘惑する。脳は私たちに脂肪分の多い食べ物 [3]を控えるよう [2]忠告し，しばしば健康に良くないという [5]不当な非難を浴びる脂肪，特に [4]飽和脂肪を避けるように警告する。それでは，なぜ私たちは頻繁にこういった [7]衝動 [6]に屈してしまうのだろうか。実は [9]消化器系には分別のある心の声 [10]を覆してしまう「第二の脳」が [8]存在するからだ。[12]腸管神経系（ENS）は脳のわずか 1,000 分の 1 の数の [11]ニューロンから成っているとはいえ，脳とは無関係に強力なメッセージを私たちに送る。それらの衝動はしばしば分別 [13]に勝ることがある。

　コロンビア大学のマイケル・ガーション教授は，胃腸は第二の脳として機能し，体の第一の脳とは無関係に活動できると言う。ENS は [14]セロトニンを生成し，それは心的状態，特に喜びの感情をつかさどるのを助ける。研究者たちは，脂肪分 [15]をたくさん含む食事がセロトニンを放出し，憂うつな気分に立ち向かう助けとなることを発見した。ある研究では被験者たちは物悲しい音楽を聴きながら，[16]食塩水または [18]脂肪酸を [17]混ぜた液体を与えられた。脂肪分を与えられた被験者たちは悲しい気分をかなり減少させることができた。だから今度あなたがピザを食べたいという誘惑に駆られたら，その欲求に屈してしまっても，必ずしもそれを [19]挫折だと考えることもない。腸管神経系が脳 [20]に勝っているだけなのだ。

脂肪酸

脂肪酸には，saturated fat（飽和脂肪）と unsaturated fat（不飽和脂肪）の 2 種類がある。飽和脂肪は肉・乳製品に多く含まれ，摂り過ぎると血中コレステロール値を高める。一方，不飽和脂肪の一種である trans fat（トランス脂肪）も健康に悪影響を及ぼす恐れがあるものとして知られており，アメリカでは州や自治体によっては使用に規制がある。

The Temptation of Fatty Foods

1 ☐☐ **entice** [ɪntáɪs]	▶ seduce, tempt, lure **動** を誘惑する **名** enticement
2 ☐☐ **admonish** [ədmá(:)nɪʃ]	▶ counsel, advise **動** (人) に忠告する，を諭す 〈to do ～するように〉 **名** admonishment, admonition (忠告)
3 ☐☐ **abstain from ～**	▶ abjure, withhold, refrain from ～を控える，～をやめる
4 ☐☐ **saturated** [sǽtʃərèɪtɪd]	▶ pervaded **形** (化学的に) 飽和した，飽和状態の **名** saturation (飽和 (状態))
5 ☐☐ **bum rap**	不当な非難，濡れ衣 ● get a bum rap (不当な非難を受ける) 　give ～ a bum rap (～を不当に非難する)
6 ☐☐ **succumb to ～**	▶ bow to, cave in to, surrender to (誘惑など) に屈する，～に負ける
7 ☐☐ **urge** [əːrdʒ] ❶	▶ impulse, compulsion, drive **名** 衝動 **動** を駆り立てる，をせき立てる
8 ☐☐ **reside** [rɪzáɪd] ❶	▶ be located, dwell, abide **動** (ある場所に) 存在する
9 ☐☐ **gastrointestinal system**	消化器系 ● gastrointestinal は「胃腸の」。gastro- (胃 (の)) + intestinal (腸の)
10 ☐☐ **subvert** [səbvə́ːrt]	▶ destroy, overthrow, overturn **動** を覆す，を打倒する **名** subversion (転覆，破壊)　**形** subversive
11 ☐☐ **neuron** [njúərɑ(:)n]	▶ nerve cell **名** ニューロン，神経単位 **形** neuronic

12 ☐☐ **enteric** [entérɪk]	▶ intestinal **形** 腸（内）の
13 ☐☐ **prevail over ～**	▶ defeat, overpower ～に勝る，～に打ち勝つ
14 ☐☐ **serotonin** [sìərətóunən]	**名** セロトニン，神経伝達物質
15 ☐☐ **be loaded with ～**	▶ be packed with, be full with ～をたくさん含む，～でいっぱいの
16 ☐☐ **saline solution**	（生理）食塩水 ● saline は salt の形容詞形の 1 つで，発音は [séɪliːn]。 solution は「溶液」
17 ☐☐ **infusion** [ɪnfjúːʒən]	▶ injection, instillation **名** 混和物，注入，点滴 **動** infuse（を注入する）
18 ☐☐ **fatty acid**	脂肪酸
19 ☐☐ **setback** [sétbæk]	▶ discomfiture, defeat **名** 挫折，敗北
20 ☐☐ **override** [òuvərráɪd]	▶ outweigh, supersede **動** に勝る，に優先する
☐☐ **diabetes** [dàɪəbíːtəs]	**名** 糖尿病

医学・テクノロジー **11**

Ebola, a Mysterious Disease

Scientists are trying to discover which animals are hosts to a deadly disease called Ebola that first appeared in the 1970s.

1　　Ebola is one of the most ¹**contagious** and ²**deadliest** diseases known to man. It has a ³**mortality** rate of up to 90 percent. Its early ⁴**symptoms** can appear ⁵**deceptively** ⁶**benign** — hiccups, stomach pains, red eyes, and vomiting — but its later onset is ⁷**exceedingly** uncomfortable, with
5　internal and sometimes ⁸**external** bleeding. Those few who do ⁹**pull through** are often ¹⁰**discriminated against**: many people wrongly assume that Ebola is a ¹¹**chronic** disease, like HIV, and they fear the contagion may spread to them.

　　The first outbreak was diagnosed in the Democratic Republic of the
10　Congo in 1976, and there have been several ¹²**epidemics** in Africa since then. During a recent outbreak, the president of Uganda asked his people not to shake hands since, he explained, the disease is transmitted by sweat. However, medical experts ¹³**dispelled** this rumor by showing that spreading Ebola through touching is a ¹⁴**misconception**.

15　　Medical investigators are trying to determine which animals ¹⁵**host** the disease. Previously, some researchers suspected that the disease originally came from birds, since the virus's protein structure shares characteristics ¹⁶**corresponding with** viruses found in birds. This theory is no longer in fashion though, and bats are thought to be the current hosts, with various
20　findings ¹⁷**backing** the idea **up**. One researcher ¹⁸**injected** bats with the Ebola virus and they survived, showing that they had built up immunity to the disease. Currently, researchers are searching for vaccines or treatments for this deadly illness.　　　　　　　　　　　　(237 words)

謎の病気，エボラ

科学者たちは，どの動物が 1970 年代に初めて現れたエボラと呼ばれる致命的な病気の宿主であるかを発見しようとしている。

エボラは知られている中で最も [1]伝染力が強く最も [2]致命的な病気の１つである。[3]死亡率は最大 90％にものぼる。初期の [4]症状は，しゃっくり，腹痛，目の充血，嘔吐で，[5]一見 [6]危険のないもののように見える。しかし，その後の症状は内出血，時には [8]外出血があり，[7]非常に不快なものだ。病気を [9]切り抜けた少数の人は往々にして [10]差別される。多くの人がエボラは HIV のような [11]慢性疾患だと誤って思い込んでおり，伝染が自分に及ぶことを恐れるからだ。

最初の発症は 1976 年にコンゴ民主共和国で診断された。以来，アフリカ大陸では数回の [12]流行があった。近年発生したとき，ウガンダ大統領は国民に，病気は汗で感染すると説明し，握手をしないよう呼びかけた。しかし医療専門家は，エボラが接触感染するというのは [14]誤解だと示し，その噂 [13]を打ち消した。

医学研究者はどの動物がエボラ [15]の宿主かを確定しようとしている。過去には，研究者の中にその病気がもとは鳥から発生したと考える者もいた。ウイルスのタンパク質構造が鳥で見つかるウイルス [16]と共通する特徴を持っているからだ。しかし，この学説はもう主流ではなく，コウモリが最新の宿主だと考えられており，さまざまな研究報告がそれ [17]を裏づけている。ある研究者がエボラウイルスをコウモリ [18]に注射したところ，コウモリは生き延びた。つまりコウモリはエボラに対する免疫をつけていたのだ。現在，研究者たちはこの致命的な病気に対するワクチンや治療法を探している。

---

epidemic と pandemic

epidemic と pandemic はともに，死をもたらす可能性のある（lethal）流行病について用いられる語だが，違いは病気が流行している地域の広さにある。epidemic は限定された地域でのみ流行している病気だが，それが世界的・大陸的に拡大したものが pandemic である。例えば，毎年冬になるとインフルエンザ流行のニュースが流れるが，日本全国に広がった程度では epidemic でしかない。しかし，Hong Kong flu（香港風邪）や Spanish flu（スペイン風邪）のように世界中で犠牲者を出すようなインフルエンザは pandemic と呼ばれる。エボラ出血熱の epidemics があった，ということは，流行がアフリカ大陸の一部にとどまったことを意味している。アフリカ全土に拡大したなら，pandemic と呼ばれることになる。

Ebola, a Mysterious Disease

1 ☐☐ **contagious** [kəntéɪdʒəs]	▶ transmittable, infectious, epidemic 形 (病気が) 感染性の, 伝染性の 名 contagion
2 ☐☐ **deadly** [dédli]	▶ fatal, lethal, mortal 形 致命的な, 致死の
3 ☐☐ **mortality** [mɔːrtǽləṭi]	▶ death rate, fatality rate 名 死亡率 形 mortal (死ぬ運命にある, 致命的な)
4 ☐☐ **symptom** [símptəm]	▶ sign, indication, signal 名 症状, (病気の) 兆候
5 ☐☐ **deceptively** [dɪséptɪvli]	▶ fallaciously, misleadingly, ambiguously 副 一見, 人を欺くように 動 deceive (を欺く)　形 deceptive
6 ☐☐ **benign** [bənáɪn] ❶	▶ harmless, curable, remediable 形 (病気が) 良性の, 害のない ⇔ malignant (悪性の)
7 ☐☐ **exceedingly** [ɪksíːdɪŋli]	▶ exceptionally, extremely, greatly 副 非常に, 極めて 動 exceed ((限度など) を超える)
8 ☐☐ **external** [ɪkstɔ́ːrnəl]	▶ outside, outer, extrinsic 形 外部の, 外面の ⇔ internal (内部の)
9 ☐☐ **pull through**	▶ recover, survive, get over (病気などを) 切り抜ける, 乗り切る
10 ☐☐ **discriminate** **against** ～	▶ disfavor, persecute, treat as inferior ～を差別する, ～を冷遇する
11 ☐☐ **chronic** [krá(ː)nɪk]	▶ lingering, confirmed, deep-rooted 形 (病気が) 慢性の ⇔ acute　● chronic condition (慢性症状)

12 ☐☐ **epidemic** [èpɪdémɪk]	▶ pandemic, spread **名**（伝染病の）流行 **形** 伝染性の, 流行の
13 ☐☐ **dispel** [dɪspél]	▶ drive away, disperse, dissipate **動**（恐れ・疑念など）を払拭する ● dispel the fears of ~（~の不安を一掃する）
14 ☐☐ **misconception** [mìskənsépʃən]	▶ delusion, misunderstanding, fallacy **名** 誤解, 誤った考え **動** misconceive（を誤解する）
15 ☐☐ **host** [hoʊst] ❶	**動**（病気・寄生動植物など）の宿主となる **名** 宿主
16 ☐☐ **correspond with** **~**	▶ accord with, be consistent with, conform with ~と一致する
17 ☐☐ **back up ~**	▶ support, corroborate, bear out ~を支持する, ~を裏打ちする
18 ☐☐ **inject** [ɪndʒékt]	▶ shoot, vaccinate, inoculate **動** に注射［注入］する〈with ~を〉 **名** injection
☐☐ **stamp out ~**	▶ extinguish, eradicate, put an end to （犯罪・病気など）を撲滅する

New Breakthrough in DNA Research

Human genome research has led to the discovery that so-called junk DNA appears to play a role in disease, and may be a promising area of research for treatments.

1   Scientists were ¹**elated** when the outline for the human genome was ²**decoded** in 2000. They believed that the ³**culmination** of the effort to ⁴**plot** the genome would allow them to pinpoint various diseases that could be ⁵**hereditary**, such as cancer and ⁶**autism**, by identifying

5   alterations in the genes, specifically the genes that create ⁷**proteins**. However, in the ⁸**ensuing** years, the genome map pointed to only a few uncommon diseases. Research by the pharmaceutical industry ⁹**delving into** the genome was largely ¹⁰**aborted**, as it was seen to be a ¹¹**dead end**. John Stamatoyannopoulos, a genome scientist of the University of

10 Washington School of Medicine, reports that about 95 percent of the information from the studies points to regions of the genome that do not make proteins.

    However, it is these "other regions," located between the protein-producing genes, that are now exciting researchers. Scientists had earlier

15 concluded these regions held "junk DNA" that made them ¹²**inconsequential** to disease research. Hundreds of scientists have ¹³**teamed up** to decipher the unusual language of the junk DNA. They discovered it was not junk at all, but served as switches that ¹⁴**activate** and deactivate genes as well as control protein making. Researchers are now

20 taking a more ¹⁵**holistic** view of the human genome, realizing they have to incorporate new findings and complexity in their search to link the genome to a variety of diseases.   (228 words)

DNA 研究の新しい突破口

ヒトゲノムの研究は，いわゆるジャンク DNA が病気（の発生）に役割を果たすようだという発見につながっており，治療に関する有望な研究分野かもしれない。

　2000 年にヒトゲノムの概要が ^{2}解読されたとき，科学者たちは ^{1}意気が上がった。ゲノム ^{4}の見取り図を作る努力の ^{3}結果，遺伝子，特に ^{7}タンパク質を作る遺伝子の変異を特定することによって，がんや ^{6}自閉症といった ^{5}遺伝性である可能性のあるさまざまな病気の原因を突き止められると彼らは考えた。しかし，^{8}その後の数年間で，ゲノムマップが示したのはごくわずかのまれな病気だけだった。製薬業界によるゲノム ^{9}の徹底した研究は，^{11}将来性がないと見なされて大部分が ^{10}中止された。ワシントン大学医学部のゲノム科学者であるジョン・スタマトヤノポロスは，これらの研究から得られた情報の 95％近くはタンパク質を作らないゲノム領域を示していると報告している。

　しかし今，研究者たちを興奮させているのは，タンパク質を作る遺伝子間にあるこれらの「他の領域」である。以前，科学者たちはこれらの領域にあるのは「ジャンク DNA」なので，病気の研究には ^{12}重要でないと結論づけていた。何百人もの科学者が，ジャンク DNA の独特な言語の解読に ^{13}共同した。彼らはそれがジャンク（がらくた）どころか，タンパク質生成の制御をするとともに，遺伝子 ^{14}を活性化，不活性化するスイッチの役割をしていることを発見した。研究者たちは，ゲノムとさまざまな病気とを結びつけるためには，新しい発見と複雑さを自分たちの研究に組み入れなければならないことに気づいて，これまでよりヒトゲノムを ^{15}全体的な視点でとらえている。

全体論

holism（全体論）は，「全体」（whole）を意味する接頭辞 hol(o)- に ism を加えて 20 世紀に作られた比較的新しい語で，holistic はその形容詞である。本来は哲学的概念だが，holistic がよく使われるのは医学の分野で，過度に専門的に分化した近代医療を批判する立場から，心身を一体と考えて患者を治療する holistic medicine（全人的医療）が唱えられている。スピリチュアルなものが好まれる米国では，holistic medicine は alternative medicine（代替医療）の 1 つとして幅広く実践されている。ただし，holistic は「全体的な視野からの」の意味で一般的に用いられることも多く，この英文では，ゲノムには重要でない（inconsequential）部分などなく全体が重要だ，という考え方を意味している。

New Breakthrough in DNA Research

1 ☐☐ **elate** [ɪléɪt]	▶ cheer, uplift, exhilarate **動** を高揚させる，を得意がらせる，を興奮させる
2 ☐☐ **decode** [dì:kóʊd]	▶ decipher, decrypt, crack **動** (暗号など) を解読する ⇔ encode, code (を暗号化する，を符号化する)
3 ☐☐ **culmination** [kʌlmɪnéɪʃən]	▶ consequence, conclusion, progeny **名** (努力の) 結果，最高点 **動** culminate (結果としてなる〈in, with ～に〉)
4 ☐☐ **plot** [plɑ(:)t]	▶ draft, chart, map **動** の図面を作る，の地図を描く
5 ☐☐ **hereditary** [hərédətèri]	▶ genetic, inherited **形** 遺伝性の，遺伝的な **名** heredity ● hereditary disease (遺伝性疾患)
6 ☐☐ **autism** [ɔ́:tìzm]	**名** 自閉症 **形** autistic
7 ☐☐ **protein** [próʊti:n] ❶	**名** タンパク質
8 ☐☐ **ensuing** [ensjú:ɪŋ]	▶ following, subsequent, consequent **形** その後の，次の，続く **動** ensue (続いて起こる)
9 ☐☐ **delve into ～**	▶ look into, investigate, dig ～を徹底的に調べる
10 ☐☐ **abort** [əbɔ́:rt]	▶ stop, abandon, call off **動** (計画など) を中止する，を中絶する **名** abortion **形** abortive
11 ☐☐ **dead end**	▶ deadlock, impasse, stalemate 行き詰まり，それ以上進む余地のない状態

12 ☐☐ **inconsequential** [ɪnkà(ː)nsɪkwénʃəl]	▶ trivial, insignificant, negligible 形 重要でない，取るに足らない ⇔ consequential（結果として起こる，重大な）
13 ☐☐ **team up**	▶ cooperate, collaborate, work together 共同する，協力する，組む
14 ☐☐ **activate** [ǽktɪvèɪt]	▶ stimulate, animate, rejuvenate 動 を活性化する，を活動状態にする 名 activation（活性化），activator（活性剤，触媒）
15 ☐☐ **holistic** [hoʊlístɪk]	▶ comprehensive, integrated 形 全体的視野からの，全体論的な 名 holism（全体論）
☐☐ **gene therapy**	▶ gene treatment 遺伝子療法
☐☐ **congenital** [kəndʒénəṭəl]	▶ inborn, innate 形 （病気などが）先天性の ⇔ acquired（後天性の）
☐☐ **syndrome** [síndroʊm]	名 症候群，シンドローム ● acquired immune deficiency syndrome（後天性免疫不全症候群，AIDS）
☐☐ **tumor** [tjúːmər]	▶ growth, lump, swelling 名 腫瘍 ● benign [malignant] tumor（良性［悪性］腫瘍）

Big Bonuses from Bilingualism

Although being bilingual has disadvantages in terms of vocabulary, it also has numerous benefits, including improving concentration and helping to prevent diseases of the brain.

1   Bilingual education has always stirred controversy in the US. While many people argue that the ¹**privilege** of having American citizenship should come with a ²**commitment** to use English, bilinguals have a few disadvantages. They often have smaller English vocabularies than ³**monolinguals**, though they tend to have larger combined vocabularies. Many bilinguals have also been shown to experience ⁴**momentary** hesitation during word selection.

However, numerous research studies suggest bilingualism offers significant ⁵**neurological** benefits. The ability to use two languages may ⁶**rewire** the brain to function differently. Basically, the benefits are derived from the ⁷**incessant** demands of listening to and interpreting two languages, stimulating neurons and neural connections. Bilinguals are shown to be superior to monolinguals at concentration, ⁸**multitasking**, and even empathizing with other people.

Bilingualism also makes for better health. It helps ⁹**stave off** ¹⁰**dementia** and ¹¹**Alzheimer's** by keeping the brain ¹²**vibrant**. The longer people speak two or more languages, the bigger the cognitive effect. However, it is never too late to reap rewards. Studies show there are positive cognitive benefits for older monolinguals who ¹³**take up** a second language.

Based on these findings, some believe that it would be ¹⁴**prudent** to reflect on the positive role of bilingualism.   (198 words)

二言語使用能力の大きな特典

バイリンガルであることは，語彙力の点では不利だが，集中力の向上や脳の病気の予防に役立つなど，数多くの利点もある。

　二言語使用教育は米国で常に論争を引き起こしてきた。多くの人はアメリカの市民権を持つという [1]特権には当然英語を使う [2]義務が付いてくるべきだと主張するが，二言語の話者はいくつかの不利な点も持つ。2 つの言語を合わせた語彙数は [3]単一言語の話者よりも多い傾向があるのだが，英語の語彙数で言えば少ない。また多くの二言語話者は語を選ぶときに，[4]一瞬のためらいを経験することが明らかになっている。

　ところが，数多くの研究により二言語使用が [5]神経学的に大きな利点をもたらすことが示されている。二言語を使用する能力は脳 [6]を配線し直して機能のしかたを変えるのかもしれない。基本的には，2 つの言語を聞き取り，解釈する必要が [7]絶えず生じているため，ニューロンと神経系の連結を刺激することから利益が得られるのだ。二言語話者は，集中力や [8]複数のことを同時に処理したり，他の人に共感したりすることも，単一言語の話者に比べて優れていることが明らかになっている。

　二言語を使用すると健康にも良い。脳の働きを [12]活発にさせ続けることで [10]認知症や [11]アルツハイマー病の進行 [9]を食い止めるのに役立つのである。2 つかそれ以上の言語を話す期間が長ければ長いほど，認知能力への効果は高まる。けれども，恩恵を得るのに遅過ぎるということはない。比較的年を取ってから第二言語 [13]を学び始める一言語話者にも認知能力へのプラスの作用があることを複数の研究が示している。

　このような調査結果から，二言語使用のプラスの役割について検討してみるのが [14]賢明だと考える人もいる。

マルチなタスク

本来 multitasking は，コンピュータが同時に複数の task（処理）を実行できることを指す専門用語だが，そこから，人が「複数の作業を同時に行うこと」という意味で広く用いられるようになった。パソコンで作業しながら電話に出る，複数のプロジェクトを並行して担当するなど仕事のやり方について用いられることが多いが，食事をしながら携帯でメールを打つことも multitasking と言われている。仕事・育児・家事をこなす母親を multitasking mom と言うこともある。

Big Bonuses from Bilingualism

1 ☐☐
privilege
[prívəlɪdʒ] ❶
▶ perquisite, prerogative, advantage
名 特権　動 に特権を与える
形 privileged

2 ☐☐
commitment
[kəmítmənt]
▶ responsibility, duty, engagement
名 義務，約束〈to do ～するという〉
動 commit

3 ☐☐
monolingual
[mà(:)nəlíŋgwəl]
名 一言語話者，1つの言語しか話さない人
形 1つの言語を用いる

4 ☐☐
momentary
[móʊməntèri] ❶
▶ brief, fleeting, instantaneous
形 瞬間的な，ほんの一瞬の
名 moment

5 ☐☐
neurological
[njʊ̀ərəlá(:)dʒɪkəl]
形 神経（学）の
名 neurology

6 ☐☐
rewire
[rì:wáɪər]
動 を配線し直す，の配線を変える

7 ☐☐
incessant
[ɪnsésənt]
▶ constant, continuous, ceaseless
形 絶え間ない，ひっきりなしの
名 incessancy

8 ☐☐
multitasking
[mʌltitǽskɪŋ]
▶ performing several activities simultaneously
名 複数の作業を同時に行うこと

9 ☐☐
stave off ～
▶ hold off, keep ～ at bay, impede
～を（一時的に）食い止める，～を遅らせる

10 ☐☐
dementia
[dɪménʃə]
▶ Alzheimer's disease, mental deterioration
名 認知症，痴呆

11 ☐☐
Alzheimer's
[á(:)ltshaɪmərz]
▶ dementia, mental deterioration
名 アルツハイマー病
● Alzheimer's disease の略

13

12 ☐☐ **vibrant** [váɪbrənt]	▶ lively, vivacious, spirited 形 活発な，活力のある
13 ☐☐ **take up ～**	▶ adopt, start, embark on （趣味・仕事など）を始める，～を習慣的に用いる［行う］ようになる
14 ☐☐ **prudent** [prúːdənt]	▶ wise, sensible, reasonable 形 賢明な，分別のある 名 prudence
☐☐ **linguist** [líŋgwɪst]	▶ multilingual speaker 名 複数言語を話せる人，言語学者
☐☐ **code switching**	▶ the practice of changing between languages when you are speaking （話をしている最中の）使用言語の切り替え
☐☐ **multilingualism** [mʌ̀ltilíŋgwəlìzm]	▶ the use of many languages 名 多言語使用

A New Cure with Old Roots

Since various bacteria species have gained increased immunity to antibiotics, some researchers suggest using phage viruses, which may be an effective alternative.

1 ¹**Antibiotics** are often ²**overprescribed** and misused. Moreover, pharmaceutical companies have turned away from the development of effective new antibiotics towards more lucrative ³**concerns**. As a result, strains of ⁴**vicious** new bacteria called "superbugs" have ⁵**materialized**
5 which are ⁶**impervious to** antibiotics and other commonly used ⁷**medical interventions**.

Since antibiotics have become a dead end for many patients, some medical experts are ⁸**banking on** an ⁹**alternative treatment** for infections, once offered in the US in the 1940s. The treatment utilizes
10 phage viruses, which attack harmful bacteria. The viruses are ¹⁰**parasites** that attach themselves to the walls of bacteria and inject their DNA inside. The injected DNA particles act as ¹¹**stealth** reproductive agents, for they hijack the bacteria's reproductive system and use it to create more phage viruses. The viruses then ¹²**break out of** the bacteria's cell and attack
15 other bacteria. The viruses ¹³**stem** the increase of bacteria, giving the human body a way to ¹⁴**fend off** superbugs. While many physicians are ¹⁵**receptive** to the treatment, others are not. Viruses ¹⁶**mingle** their DNA with the host bacteria's. This sometimes creates new ¹⁷**hybrids**, including such deadly ¹⁸**pathogens** as ¹⁹**E. coli** O157.

20 Treatments with phage viruses can also be time-consuming. Unlike antibiotics, which are effective against a variety of bacteria, each type of phage virus attacks limited types. This means ²⁰**microbiologists** must spend up to weeks identifying the infecting bacteria and then selecting and ²¹**incubating** the appropriate phage viruses to eradicate them.

⚒ (238 words)

昔からあった新しい治療法

さまざまなバクテリアが抗生物質に対する免疫力を高めていることから，ファージ・ウイルスの利用を提案する研究者もおり，このことは効果的な代替法になる可能性がある。

¹抗生物質はしばしば ²過剰に処方されて，誤用されている。さらに，製薬会社は効用のある新しい抗生物質を開発することから，より利益を生む ³商売へと転換を図っている。その結果，抗生物質やその他の一般に用いられている ⁷治療処置 ⁶が効かない「スーパーバグ」と呼ばれる新しい型の ⁴悪性のバクテリアが ⁵現れた。

多くの患者にとって抗生物質は効果のないものとなっているので，医療専門家の中には，かつて 1940 年代にアメリカで提供された感染症に対する ⁹代替療法 ⁸を頼みとしている者もいる。その治療法は有害なバクテリアを攻撃するファージ・ウイルスを利用する。そのウイルスはバクテリアの壁に付着し自らのDNAを内部に注入する ¹⁰寄生菌である。注入されたDNAの粒子は ¹¹こっそり増殖を行う主体として機能する。それらはバクテリアの再生系を乗っ取り，それをより多くのファージ・ウイルスを作り出すために利用するのだ。それからウイルスはバクテリアの細胞 ¹²から抜け出し，他のバクテリアを攻撃する。ウイルスはバクテリアの増殖 ¹³を阻止し，人の身体にスーパーバグ ¹⁴を寄せつけない手段を与える。多くの医者がその治療法を ¹⁵容認しているがそうでない医者もいる。ウイルスは自分のDNAと宿主のバクテリアのDNA ¹⁶を混ぜてしまう。これは，時に ¹⁹大腸菌 O157 のような致命的な ¹⁸病原菌を含む新しい ¹⁷雑種を作り出してしまう。

ファージ・ウイルスによる治療法はまた時間もかかる。さまざまなバクテリアに効き目のある抗生物質と違って，ファージ・ウイルスはその種類ごとに限られた種類のバクテリアを攻撃する。これは，²⁰微生物学者が何週間もかけて感染しているバクテリアを特定し，それらを根絶するための適切なファージ・ウイルスを選び出して ²¹培養しなくてはならないことを意味する。

バクテリアを食べる

phage はギリシャ語で eater（食べる人）を意味する語に由来する。この英文で描写されているようなバクテリアへの攻撃方法が，あたかもバクテリアを食べてしまうように見えることから付けられた名前である。ウイルスではなく，phagocyte（食細胞）の一種に macrophage（マクロファージ）がある。macro + phage = big eater という意味で，「大食細胞」とも訳される。マクロファージは重要な immune cell（免疫細胞）の1つで，炎症が起きた箇所に集まり，バクテリアを攻撃し「食べる」ことで，感染から体を守る働きをしている。

医学・テクノロジー

14

207

A New Cure with Old Roots

1 ☐☐ **antibiotic** [æ̀ntibaɪá(ː)tɪk]	名 抗生物質 形 抗生物質の ● anti-（反）＋biotic（生物の）
2 ☐☐ **overprescribe** [òʊvərprɪskráɪb]	動 （薬剤）を過剰に処方する 名 overprescription
3 ☐☐ **concern** [kənsə́ːrn]	▶ affair, business, transaction 名 商売，事業，営業
4 ☐☐ **vicious** [víʃəs] ❶	▶ malicious, ferocious, malignant 形 悪い，どう猛な 名 vice（悪，悪癖，悪行）
5 ☐☐ **materialize** [mətíəriəlàɪz]	▶ appear, emerge, come into being 動 現れる，実体化する 形 material
6 ☐☐ **impervious to ～**	▶ immune to, invulnerable to ～に影響されない，～に耐える
7 ☐☐ **medical intervention**	▶ medical practice, remedial treatment 治療処置，内科治療
8 ☐☐ **bank on ～**	▶ depend on, rely on, count on ～を頼り［当て］にする
9 ☐☐ **alternative treatment**	▶ alternative therapy 代替療法
10 ☐☐ **parasite** [pǽrəsàɪt]	▶ parasitic animal 名 寄生体［生物］ 形 parasitic
11 ☐☐ **stealth** [stelθ] ❶	▶ sneaking, surreptitious, in secret 形 こっそり行われる　名 こっそり行うこと 動 steal（そっと動く）

12 ☐☐ **break out of ~** [brek]	▶ get out of, get away from, escape ～から抜け出す，～から脱出する
13 ☐☐ **stem** [stem]	▶ stop, curb, quell 動 を阻止する，を抑える
14 ☐☐ **fend off ~**	▶ avert, parry, ward off ～を寄せつけない，～をかわす
15 ☐☐ **receptive** [rɪséptɪv]	▶ amenable, open-minded 形 受け入れる〈to ～を〉，理解を示す〈to ～に〉 動 receive 名 reception
16 ☐☐ **mingle** [míŋgl]	▶ mix, blend, compound 動 を混ぜる〈with ～と〉
17 ☐☐ **hybrid** [háɪbrɪd]	▶ composite, cross, half-breed 名 雑種，交配種 形 雑種の
18 ☐☐ **pathogen** [pǽθədʒən]	▶ germ, contagion, microbe 名 病原菌，病原体 形 pathogenic（病原性の）
19 ☐☐ **E. coli**	大腸菌 ● Escherichia coli の略
20 ☐☐ **microbiologist** [màɪkroʊbaɪá(:)lədʒɪst]	▶ bacteriologist 名 微生物学者，細菌学者 名 microbiology（微生物学）
21 ☐☐ **incubate** [íŋkjubèɪt]	▶ culture, grow, breed 動 を培養する 名 incubation
☐☐ **chemotherapy** [kì:moʊθérəpi]	▶ the treatment of disease, especially cancer, with the use of chemical substances 名 （特にがんに対する）化学療法

The Significance of Sunburn

Researchers who looked into what happens to skin cells when they experience sunburn have found that the ultraviolet light affects their RNA.

1   Researchers recently discovered why our skin sunburns and the role RNA plays in its recovery. Richard Gallo, chief of ¹**dermatology** at the University of California, San Diego, and his colleagues aimed to add to the ²**dearth** of knowledge about sunburn. They gave human cells a
5   ³**dosage** of ultraviolet light that is ⁴**equivalent** to up to a 30-minute ⁵**duration** of bright sunlight, enough to cause sunburn. They observed that one kind of RNA within cells breaks apart when ⁶**overexposed** to ultraviolet light, effectively killing the cells. ⁷**Receptor** molecules in nearby healthy cells detect the broken RNA and send messages that tell
10   other cells surrounding the dead cell to become ⁸**inflamed**, causing sunburn.

     RNA usually serves as ⁹**cellular** messengers by "coding" our DNA, which they are able to do since they share the same ¹⁰**double-helix structure** as DNA. However, the RNA that sets off sunburn is known as
15   non-coding RNA. Instead of transmitting genetic information, it controls our genes. To confirm their findings, the researchers exposed ¹¹**rodents** who lacked the RNA-detecting receptor to ultraviolet light. ¹²**As anticipated**, the rodents had less inflammation.

     Sunburn ¹³**facilitates** healthy skin in several ways. First, it removes
20   cells killed by ultraviolet light, which enables skin to ¹⁴**recuperate**. Second, ridding our bodies of cells with genetic damage also prevents cancer from ¹⁵**setting in**. Finally, the ¹⁶**sting** of sunburn teaches us not to stay in the sun too long, saving our skin from unnecessary ¹⁷**wear and tear**.   (238 words)

ℓ.2   RNA：ribonucleic acid の略で「リボ核酸」。全細胞に存在し，タンパク質の合成に関与する。

日焼けの重要性

日焼けをしたときに皮膚細胞に何が起こるかを調べた研究者たちは，紫外線が RNA に影響を与えることを発見した。

　研究者たちは最近，私たちの皮膚が日焼けする原因と RNA が回復に果たす役割を発見した。カリフォルニア大学サンディエゴ校の ¹皮膚科長であるリチャード・ガロと同僚たちは日焼けについての知識の ²欠如を補うことを目指した。彼らは人の細胞に，明るい日光の下で 30 分 ⁵間さらされるという日焼けを引き起こすのに十分な量と ⁴同量の紫外線 ³量を与えた。彼らは紫外線に ⁶過度にさらされると細胞内のある種の RNA が破壊され，事実上その細胞を殺してしまうことを観察した。近くにある健康な細胞の ⁷受容体分子は破壊された RNA を感知し，その死んだ細胞を囲む他の細胞に ⁸炎症を起こすように伝え，日焼けを引き起こす。

　通常，RNA は私たちの DNA を「コード化する」ことで ⁹細胞の伝達子として働くが，それは DNA と同じ ¹⁰二重らせん構造を持つため，そのようにできるのだ。しかし，日焼けを引き起こす RNA はコード化していない RNA として知られている。遺伝子情報を伝達する代わりにそれは私たちの遺伝子を制御する。こういった研究結果を確かめるため，研究者たちは RNA を感知する受容体を持たない ¹¹げっ歯動物を紫外線にさらした。¹²予想通り，そのげっ歯動物はそれほど炎症を起こさなかった。

　日焼けはいくつかの方法で健康な皮膚 ¹³の手助けをする。第一に，紫外線によって殺された細胞を取り除き，皮膚が ¹⁴回復するのを可能にする。第二に，遺伝的損傷のある細胞を体から取り除くことでがんが ¹⁵発病するのを防ぐ。そして最後に，日焼けの ¹⁶痛みは私たちに太陽の下にあまり長くとどまるべきではないと教え，皮膚を不要な ¹⁷消耗から守ってくれる。

The Significance of Sunburn

1 □□ **dermatology** [dəːrmətá(ː)lədʒi]	名 皮膚科学
2 □□ **dearth** [dəːrθ]	▶ lack, deficiency 名 不足, 欠乏 〈of ～の〉 ● a dearth of information（情報不足）
3 □□ **dosage** [dóʊsɪdʒ]	▶ amount of dose 名（薬剤・放射線などの）1 回分の投与量 名 動 dose（1 回の服用量；に投薬する）
4 □□ **equivalent** [ɪkwívələnt] ❶	▶ equal, comparable, corresponding 形 相当する 〈to ～に〉 名 equivalence, equivalency
5 □□ **duration** [djuəréɪʃən]	▶ continuance, period, span 名 継続時間 ［期間］
6 □□ **overexpose** [òʊvərɪkspóʊz]	動 を露出させ過ぎる 〈to ～に〉
7 □□ **receptor** [rɪséptər]	▶ acceptor 名 受容体
8 □□ **inflamed** [ɪnfléɪmd]	▶ irritated 形 炎症を起こした 名 inflammation 形 inflammatory（炎症性の）
9 □□ **cellular** [séljʊlər]	形 細胞の 名 cell
10 □□ **double-helix structure**	二重らせん構造
11 □□ **rodent** [róʊdənt]	名 げっ歯動物

12 ☐☐ **as anticipated**	▶ predictably, as expected, sure enough 予想［期待］通りに，案の定
13 ☐☐ **facilitate** [fəsílətèɪt]	▶ expedite, further, promote **動** を促進［助長］する **名** facilitation
14 ☐☐ **recuperate** [rɪkjúːpərèɪt]	▶ recover, heal, get well **動** 回復する，健康を取り戻す **名** recuperation
15 ☐☐ **set in**	▶ begin, start, break out （好ましくない状態が）始まる
16 ☐☐ **sting** [stɪŋ]	▶ prickle, stab **名** 刺すような痛み **動** （昆虫の針などが）刺す
17 ☐☐ **wear and tear**	▶ abrasion, attrition 消耗，摩耗
☐☐ **breakdown** [bréɪkdàʊn]	▶ failure, collapse, languishment **名** （心身の）衰弱，（機械の）故障 ● nervous breakdown（神経衰弱）
☐☐ **infrared light**	赤外線 ● infra-（の下）＋red（赤）

15

Generating New Organs and Body Parts

Scientists are making progress in designing special printers that will be able to grow human organs.

1 ¹**Regenerative medicine** has ²**taken off**, thanks to the ³**cumulative** efforts of the US military, academic laboratories, and biotechnology companies. Scientists have already produced different organs, introduced ⁴**spray-on** skin, ⁵**transplanted** lab-grown muscle, and given sight to the
5 blind. Many other breakthroughs are ⁶**right around the corner**. Researchers predict that in coming years, it will be common to grow organs for patients using "bioprinters." According to Dr. Anthony Atala of Wake Forest University, it is currently only possible to create organs, such as new ears, one by one. However, bioprinting will make it possible to
10 scale the process up.

Several ⁷**concurrent** projects are testing spray-on skin which, to avoid ⁸**rejection** issues, utilizes a patient's own skin. Skin ⁹**grafts** have been the technique of choice for mending ¹⁰**grievous** skin burns or closing traumatic wounds, but this process leaves scars. One spray-on product
15 uses a ¹¹**plug** of the patient's skin, which is broken down by ¹²**enzymes** and then sprayed over injured areas. Cells multiply to form a smooth layer of natural-looking skin — all within days.

Recently, scientists used human ¹³**embryonic** ¹⁴**stem cells** to restore partial vision to two blind patients. The stem cells were incubated and,
20 through the use of specialized chemicals, transformed into ¹⁵**retinal** cells, which were introduced into their eyes.

The ¹⁶**prognosis** for the future is now brighter for ¹⁷**amputees**, for those suffering from ¹⁸**paralysis**, and for many other patients. Scientists are now collaborating to ¹⁹**take on** more demanding tasks, such as ²⁰**self-**
25 **generation** of fingers and even entire ²¹**limbs**.　　　　(247 words)

214

新しい臓器と身体部位を作り出す

科学者たちは，人間の臓器を培養することができる特別なプリンターの設計を進めている。

[1]再生医療は，米国の軍と大学の実験室とバイオテクノロジー企業の努力の[3]積み重ねのおかげで，[2]うまく進み始めた。科学者たちはすでにいろいろな器官を作り出し，[4]スプレー式の皮膚を導入し，研究室で培養した筋肉[5]を移植し，目の見えない人々を見えるようにしてきた。他にも飛躍的な進歩が数多く[6]すぐそこまで来ている。これから数年のうちに，「バイオプリンター」を使って患者のための器官を培養することが一般的になるであろうと研究者たちは予測している。ウェイク・フォレスト大学のアンソニー・アタラ博士によると，現在は新しい耳などの器官を1つずつ作り出すことしかできないそうだ。しかし，バイオプリンティングはこのプロセスの規模を拡大することを可能にする。

いくつかの[7]共同事業計画でスプレー式の皮膚（の再生）を検証しているが，[8]拒絶反応を防ぐために，患者自身の皮膚を用いている。皮膚[9]移植が，皮膚の[10]重度のやけどを治療したり，外傷性の傷を閉じたりする最上の手段であったが，この方法では跡が残る。あるスプレー式の製品は患者の皮膚でできた[11]詰め物を使い，それを[12]酵素によって分解し，その後傷を負った部位に吹きかける。すると細胞が増殖し，自然に見える滑らかな皮膚の層を形成し，しかもすべてが数日内にできる。

最近では，科学者たちは人間の[13]胚性[14]幹細胞を使って，目の見えない2人の患者の視力を部分的に回復させた。その幹細胞は培養され，特殊な化学薬品を使用して[15]網膜細胞へ変化させ，眼球に移植された。

[17]切断手術を受けた人々や，[18]麻痺に苦しむ人々，また他にも多くの患者にとって今や[16]予後はさらに明るいものである。現在，科学者たちは共同研究で，指やさらには[21]手足の全体が[20]自己生成するといった，いっそう難しい仕事[19]に取り組んでいる。

倫理上の問題

embryonic stem cell（胚性幹細胞）は，略して ES 細胞と呼ばれる。ES 細胞は，受精卵が分裂を始めた embryo（胚）を体内から取り出して操作することで作られるため，人に応用した場合に bioethics（生命倫理）に抵触するのではないかと議論されている。胚は成長すれば人となるのだから，ES 細胞を作ることは生命を奪う行為だというのが反対派の論点で，ES 細胞の人への応用を認めるかどうかは国によって対応が分かれている。一方 iPS 細胞は受精卵を用いず，皮膚細胞から作ることが可能なので，こうした倫理的問題を回避できる。これが，iPS 細胞に大きな期待が集まっている理由の1つである。

Generating New Organs and Body Parts

1 ☐☐ **regenerative medicine**	再生医療［医学］ ● regeneration は「（器官・組織などの）再生」
2 ☐☐ **take off**	▶ get under way うまく進み始める
3 ☐☐ **cumulative** [kjúːmjʊlətɪv]	▶ accumulated, amassed 形 累積による，蓄積された 動 cumulate　名 cumulation
4 ☐☐ **spray-on** [spréɪɑ̀(ː)n]	形 スプレー式の，吹きつけ式の
5 ☐☐ **transplant** [trænsplǽnt]	▶ graft, replant 動 （臓器）を移植する
6 ☐☐ **right around the corner**	▶ close at hand, close by, near at hand すぐそこまで来ている，間近である
7 ☐☐ **concurrent** [kənkɔ́ːrənt]	▶ conjoint, cooperating, joint 形 共同の，同時に起こる 名 concurrence
8 ☐☐ **rejection** [rɪdʒékʃən]	▶ refusal, denial, rebuff 名 （移植臓器などの）拒絶（反応），拒否（反応） 動 reject
9 ☐☐ **graft** [grǽft]	▶ transplant, implant 名 移植，接ぎ木 動 （皮膚など）を移植する
10 ☐☐ **grievous** [gríːvəs]	▶ very severe or very painful 形 ひどい，耐え難い
11 ☐☐ **plug** [plʌg]	名 （穴・管などをふさぐ）詰め物，栓

12 ☐☐ **enzyme** [énzaɪm]	名 酵素 形 enzymatic, enzymic
13 ☐☐ **embryonic** [èmbriá(:)nɪk]	▶ germinal, immature 形 胚の，初期の，未発達の 名 embryo
14 ☐☐ **stem cell**	幹細胞
15 ☐☐ **retinal** [rétənəl]	形 網膜の 名 retina
16 ☐☐ **prognosis** [prɑ(:)gnóʊsəs]	▶ prospect, forecast, projection 名 (病気の）予後，予測
17 ☐☐ **amputee** [æ̀mpjʊtíː]	名 切断手術を受けた人 動 amputate（（手足など）を手術で切断する） 名 amputation（（手足などの）切断手術）
18 ☐☐ **paralysis** [pərǽləsɪs]	▶ paresis, immobility, torpor 名 麻痺 形 paralytic, paralyzed
19 ☐☐ **take on ～**	▶ accept, undertake, take over （仕事など）の責任を引き受ける
20 ☐☐ **self-generation** [sèlfdʒènəréɪʃən]	▶ spontaneous generation, autogenesis 名 自己生成，自然発生
21 ☐☐ **limb** [lɪm] 🔈	▶ an arm or a leg 名 手足のうちの１本

1 次の日本語の意味の単語を下の❶～⓰の中から選んで書きなさい。

（1）傷つきやすい，受けやすい　　　（　　：　　　　　　　　　　　）

（2）知恵［経験］のある　　　　　　（　　：　　　　　　　　　　　）

（3）（人）を鼓舞する，を刺激する　（　　：　　　　　　　　　　　）

（4）を複製する　　　　　　　　　　（　　：　　　　　　　　　　　）

（5）光子　　　　　　　　　　　　　（　　：　　　　　　　　　　　）

（6）重力　　　　　　　　　　　　　（　　：　　　　　　　　　　　）

（7）単純な　　　　　　　　　　　　（　　：　　　　　　　　　　　）

（8）あり得る，もっともらしい　　　（　　：　　　　　　　　　　　）

（9）熟考する，じっくり考える　　　（　　：　　　　　　　　　　　）

（10）（ある場所に）存在する　　　　（　　：　　　　　　　　　　　）

（11）誤解，誤った考え　　　　　　　（　　：　　　　　　　　　　　）

（12）全体的視野からの，全体論的な（　　：　　　　　　　　　　　）

（13）絶え間ない，ひっきりなしの　（　　：　　　　　　　　　　　）

（14）悪い，どう猛な　　　　　　　　（　　：　　　　　　　　　　　）

（15）げっ歯動物　　　　　　　　　　（　　：　　　　　　　　　　　）

（16）網膜の　　　　　　　　　　　　（　　：　　　　　　　　　　　）

❶ ponder	❷ vicious	❸ vulnerable	❹ photon
❺ misconception	❻ retinal	❼ savvy	❽ straightforward
❾ holistic	❿ gravity	⓫ incessant	⓬ spur
⓭ rodent	⓮ plausible	⓯ reside	⓰ duplicate

2 次の日本語の意味の単語を下の❶〜⓬の中から選んで書きなさい。

（1）を実行する，を遂行する　　　（　：　　　　　　　　　　　）

（2）危険な，不安定な　　　　　　（　：　　　　　　　　　　　）

（3）繁殖，生殖　　　　　　　　　（　：　　　　　　　　　　　）

（4）超高層ビル，摩天楼　　　　　（　：　　　　　　　　　　　）

（5）妥当性，正当性　　　　　　　（　：　　　　　　　　　　　）

（6）したがって，結果として　　　（　：　　　　　　　　　　　）

（7）を分析する，を解剖する　　　（　：　　　　　　　　　　　）

（8）一見，人を欺くように　　　　（　：　　　　　　　　　　　）

（9）腫瘍　　　　　　　　　　　　（　：　　　　　　　　　　　）

（10）認知症，痴呆　　　　　　　　（　：　　　　　　　　　　　）

（11）こっそり行われる　　　　　　（　：　　　　　　　　　　　）

（12）共同の，同時に起こる　　　　（　：　　　　　　　　　　　）

医学・テクノロジー

確認テスト

❶ breeding	❷ skyscraper	❸ precarious	❹ tumor
❺ stealth	❻ consequently	❼ deceptively	❽ implement
❾ dissect	❿ concurrent	⓫ dementia	⓬ validity

解答

1　（1）❸（→p. 157）（2）❼（→p. 161）（3）⓬（→p. 164）（4）⓰（→p. 168）

　　（5）❹（→p. 172）（6）❿（→p. 176）（7）❽（→p. 181）（8）⓮（→p. 185）

　　（9）❶（→p. 188）（10）⓯（→p. 192）（11）❺（→p. 197）（12）❾（→p. 201）

　　（13）⓫（→p. 204）（14）❷（→p. 208）（15）⓭（→p. 212）（16）❻（→p. 217）

2　（1）❽（→p. 156）（2）❸（→p. 161）（3）❶（→p. 168）（4）❷（→p. 176）

　　（5）⓬（→p. 180）（6）❻（→p. 185）（7）❾（→p. 188）（8）❼（→p. 196）

　　（9）❹（→p. 201）（10）⓫（→p. 204）（11）❺（→p. 208）（12）❿（→p. 216）

3 次の単語の意味に最も近いものをそれぞれ❶～❹の中から1つ選びなさい。

(1) outdo
- ❶ emulate
- ❷ plot
- ❸ beat
- ❹ exploit

(2) dictate
- ❶ command
- ❷ mingle
- ❸ hypothesize
- ❹ accuse

(3) isolated
- ❶ frigid
- ❷ remote
- ❸ vibrant
- ❹ trivial

(4) amend
- ❶ transmit
- ❷ dispel
- ❸ revise
- ❹ emerge

(5) prohibition
- ❶ embargo
- ❷ obstruction
- ❸ ammunition
- ❹ impulse

(6) impediment
- ❶ mission
- ❷ obstacle
- ❸ abundance
- ❹ alliance

(7) amenity
- ❶ watershed
- ❷ pleasantness
- ❸ meteorite
- ❹ injection

(8) accumulate
- ❶ elate
- ❷ censor
- ❸ disperse
- ❹ amass

(9) usher in ～
- ❶ emit
- ❷ inject
- ❸ herald
- ❹ cooperate

(10) organic
- ❶ biotic
- ❷ optical
- ❸ laborious
- ❹ intestinal

(11) manifest
- ❶ obvious
- ❷ inflamed
- ❸ contagious
- ❹ grievous

(12) rigorous
- ❶ challenging
- ❷ hereditary
- ❸ authoritative
- ❹ composite

(13) entice   ❶ amplify   ❷ seduce
               ❸ detect   ❹ refurbish
(14) subvert   ❶ inaugurate   ❷ fluctuate
               ❸ overthrow   ❹ recover
(15) benign   ❶ identical   ❷ risky
               ❸ harmless   ❹ congenital
(16) culmination ❶ beam   ❷ consequence
               ❸ compliance   ❹ doctrine
(17) privilege ❶ infusion   ❷ antibiotic
               ❸ inhabitant   ❹ perquisite
(18) momentary ❶ equivalent   ❷ brief
               ❸ ensuing   ❹ fatal
(19) pathogen ❶ hydrogen   ❷ paralysis
               ❸ parasite   ❹ germ
(20) duration ❶ accusation   ❷ prospect
               ❸ continuance   ❹ liability
(21) facilitate ❶ expedite   ❷ impair
               ❸ scrutinize   ❹ shelter
(22) embryonic ❶ germinal   ❷ comparable
               ❸ enteric   ❹ chronic

解答

3 (1) ❸ (→p. 156) (2) ❶ (→p. 160) (3) ❷ (→p. 164) (4) ❸ (→p. 168)
(5) ❶ (→p. 168) (6) ❷ (→p. 172) (7) ❷ (→p. 176) (8) ❹ (→p. 177)
(9) ❸ (→p. 181) (10) ❶ (→p. 184) (11) ❶ (→p. 184) (12) ❶ (→p. 188)
(13) ❷ (→p. 192) (14) ❸ (→p. 192) (15) ❸ (→p. 196) (16) ❷ (→p. 200)
(17) ❹ (→p. 204) (18) ❷ (→p. 204) (19) ❹ (→p. 209) (20) ❸ (→p. 212)
(21) ❶ (→p. 213) (22) ❶ (→p. 217)

自然・環境

自然・環境

テーマを知る

　自然・環境では，身近な自然環境や食料品の問題から生物の生態，地球規模の問題まで，幅広い内容が扱われる。具体的には，生態系，外来種，自然破壊，廃棄物が自然に与える影響，気候変動の影響，環境への意識の高まり，環境保護運動，食料生産方法，興味深い生態を持つ生物などの話題が取り上げられる。環境問題については，日ごろから問題意識を持っていることが重要である。

注目用語

sustainability 持続可能性

2015 年に国連総会で採択された Sustainable Development Goals（持続可能な開発目標，SDGs）で sustainability（持続可能性）は注目を集めた。各国政府だけでなく企業も，現在だけでなく未来の社会や環境について配慮した経営を行うことが corporate social responsibility（企業の社会的責任，CSR）だとする考え方もあり，持続可能性は国家，企業，個人とさまざまな視点の高さでとらえることができる。

the theory of evolution 進化論

生物は不変ではなく，natural selection（自然選択・自然淘汰）や mutation（突然変異）を経て生存に優位な trait（特性）を descendants（子孫）に残しながら進化するという説。1859 年にチャールズ・ダーウィンが *On the Origin of Species*（『種の起源』）において科学的に確立した。生物学的および宗教的な観点からしばしば議論の的になり，特に creationism（創造論）を信じる多くの人々からはいまだに否定されている。

キーワード・表現

自然・環境

American Mustangs

This passage discusses the debate over the US government's policy regarding the management of wild horses known as mustangs.

1   Imported from Europe centuries ago, the mustang is an [1]**iconic** symbol of the American West. Huge numbers of these wild horses still [2]**roam** the plains today, but their management has become highly controversial, with critics claiming that the government agency responsible for their welfare

5   has been failing to act in the best interests of these [3]**majestic** animals.

As of 2021, approximately 80,000 mustangs inhabit government wilderness [4]**preserves** in the US, but each year, thousands are [5]**rounded up** and confined to [6]**holding pens** and [7]**pastures**, while [8]**fertility**-control [9]**injections** are [10]**administered** to others. This is because, with no natural

10   predators, their [11]**booming** populations have [12]**degraded** ecosystems that were already [13]**deteriorating** due to droughts. The situation has also [14]**outraged** livestock ranchers who feel that the [15]**grazing** mustangs are [16]**depriving** their own animals **of** feed.

Activists claim that had fertility-control programs [17]**commenced** long

15   ago, the current population crisis would not have arisen and are demanding that they be greatly expanded. These critics claim the roundups themselves, as well as life in captivity where they are separated from their [18]**kin**, are highly [19]**traumatic** for the animals. The government agency, however, argues that there are [20]**feasibility** issues preventing increased fertilization

20   control. Currently, research is being carried out and various interest groups are being consulted in the hope that a solution can be found soon.

(218 words)

ℓ.14 had fertility-control programs commenced long ago = if fertility-control programs had commenced long ago：if を省略し，倒置にすることで条件を表した仮定法の文。

アメリカ・マスタング

この文章は，マスタングとして知られている野生の馬の管理に関する米国政府の政策をめぐる議論について述べたものである。

何世紀も前にヨーロッパから持ち込まれたマスタングは，アメリカ西部の[1]偶像的な象徴である。今日，いまだに膨大な数のこれらの野生の馬が平原[2]を歩き回っているが，彼らの管理については大いに物議を醸しており，批判的な人々は，それらの保護を担当する政府機関がこの[3]堂々たる動物の最大の利益のために行動していないと主張している。

2021年現在，アメリカの国立の野生[4]保護地区にはおよそ8万頭のマスタングが生息しているが，毎年，何千頭もが[5]駆り集められて[6]畜舎や[7]牧場に閉じ込められ，またそうでないものは[8]繁殖抑制の[9]注射[10]を施されている。これはそれらに天敵がいないために生息数が[11]急増し，干ばつのためにすでに[13]悪化しつつある生態系[12]を傷めてしまったからである。この状況はまた，[15]草を食べるマスタングが自分たちの動物からえさ[16]を奪っていると感じる畜産農家[14]を憤慨させてきた。

活動家たちは，もし繁殖抑制プログラムがずっと以前に[17]開始されていたなら，現在の生息数危機は起きなかっただろうと主張し，このプログラムを大幅に拡大するよう要求している。これらの批判的な人々は駆り集めそのものも，[18]仲間から引き離され捕らわれて生きることも，これらの動物にとって非常に[19]精神的なストレスになると主張する。しかし政府機関は，[20]実現可能性の問題があり，繁殖抑制の強化を阻んでいると反論する。現在，研究が行われており，さまざまな利益団体が，解決法が近々見つかることを期待して意見を求められている。

カウボーイの仕事

19世紀，北米西部で飼われていた牛は，家畜とはいえ semi-feral（半野生の）状態で，広大な地域に散り散りになっていた。cowboy（カウボーイ）の重要な役目の1つは，そうした牛の roundup（駆り集め）だった。1カ所に集められた牛は，大都市に送られるため，市場や鉄道駅へと何日もかけて移送された。この長旅は cattle drive（キャトルドライブ）と呼ばれた。現代のカウボーイの活躍の場である rodeo（ロデオ）はスペイン語で「回り道」といった意味だが，南米では「駆り集め」の意味で用いられていた。

American Mustangs

1 ☐☐ **iconic** [aɪkɑ́(:)nɪk]	▶ emblematic, symbolic 形 象徴的な，偶像的な 名 icon
2 ☐☐ **roam** [roʊm] ①	▶ ramble, saunter, stroll, wander 動 (を) 歩き回る，(を) 徘徊する
3 ☐☐ **majestic** [mədʒéstɪk]	▶ splendid, magnificent, august, grandiose 形 堂々とした，威厳のある 名 majesty
4 ☐☐ **preserve** [prɪzə́:rv] ①	▶ reserve, sanctuary 名 自然保護区
5 ☐☐ **round up ～**	～を駆り集める，～を寄せ集める ● roundup「(家畜などの) 駆り集め」という名詞もある
6 ☐☐ **holding pen**	家畜を一時的に入れておく囲い柵
7 ☐☐ **pasture** [pǽstʃər]	▶ grass, meadow 名 牧場，牧草地
8 ☐☐ **fertility** [fə(:)rtíləti]	▶ the ability to produce babies 名 繁殖力，生殖力 形 fertile　⟷ infertility (不妊)
9 ☐☐ **injection** [ɪndʒékʃən]	▶ shot 名 注射 動 inject
10 ☐☐ **administer** [ədmínɪstər]	▶ dispense 動 (薬・治療など) を施す，を投与する〈to ～に〉 名 administration
11 ☐☐ **booming** [búːmɪŋ]	▶ roaring, thriving 形 急増する，急成長する 名 動 boom

12 ☐☐ **degrade** [dɪgréɪd]	▶ debase, deteriorate 動 の質を低下させる，を悪化させる 名 degradation ● de-（下げる）＋grade（地位）
13 ☐☐ **deteriorate** [dɪtíəriərèɪt]	▶ worsen, decline, degenerate 動 悪化する，衰える 名 deterioration ⇔ ameliorate
14 ☐☐ **outrage** [áʊtrèɪdʒ] ❶	▶ enrage, exasperate, infuriate 動 を憤慨させる，を激怒させる 名 憤慨，激怒
15 ☐☐ **graze** [greɪz]	動 （家畜などが）草を食べる
16 ☐☐ **deprive** *A* **of** *B*	A から B を奪う，A に B を与えない ● deprive *oneself* of ～（～を自ら手放す）
17 ☐☐ **commence** [kəméns]	▶ begin, start 動 開始する，始まる 名 commencement
18 ☐☐ **kin** [kɪn]	▶ relatives, kinfolk 名 親族，一族 ● 集合名詞で複数扱い
19 ☐☐ **traumatic** [trəmǽtɪk]	形 精神的に深く傷つける，トラウマになる 名 trauma 動 traumatize
20 ☐☐ **feasibility** [fìːzəbíləti]	▶ practicability, viability 名 実現可能性 形 feasible ⇔ unfeasibility
☐☐ **domesticate** [dəméstɪkèɪt]	▶ tame 動 を家畜化する，を飼い慣らす 名 domestication

自然・環境

1

California Strawberries

Some of the growing methods used to produce California's famous strawberry crop are controversial.

1　California ¹**dominates** the billion-dollar strawberry industry in the US thanks in large part to its ²**astoundingly** productive fields, which produce ³**yields** 20 times higher per acre than those of some rival growing areas. ⁴**Mouthwatering** and nutritious as California strawberries are, however,
5　environmentalists object strongly to the potentially ⁵**unsustainable** farming methods used to produce them.

　　California's ⁶**stunning** productivity is dependent on ⁷**prodigious** quantities of ⁸**pesticides** known as fumigants. Strawberries are highly susceptible to various diseases, so fumigants have become essential for
10　⁹**eradicating** soil-¹⁰**borne** pathogens that cause strawberries to ¹¹**wilt** and die. However, these have come ¹²**under fire** because they leave strawberries ¹³**laden** with chemical ¹⁴**residues** suspected to have detrimental health effects. In fact, the primary fumigant used for decades has been gradually ¹⁵**phased out**, leaving farmers ¹⁶**scrambling** to find
15　alternatives. Growers have shifted to alternative products, but at least one is a suspected ¹⁷**carcinogen**.

　　Fortunately, various new technologies are being ¹⁸**brought to bear** on the strawberry industry, such as non-chemical soil treatments and ¹⁹**tractor**-sized vacuums that will suck up pests. While these technologies
20　are in their ²⁰**infancy** and the costs are often ²¹**prohibitive**, there is hope that ways will be found to grow strawberries more sustainably in the near future.

🏴 (200 words)

ℓ.4　Mouthwatering and nutritious as California strawberries are, ... = Though California strawberries are mouthwatering and nutritious, ... :「～ではあるが」という〈譲歩〉を表す as の用法。

カリフォルニアのイチゴ

カリフォルニアの有名なイチゴを生産するのに使われている栽培方法の中には，物議を醸しているものがある。

カリフォルニアは，主に，ライバルの生産地域に比べて 1 エーカーあたり 20 倍の [3]生産高を誇る [2]驚くほど生産性の高い畑のおかげで，合衆国の 10 億ドル規模のイチゴ産業 [1]を支配している。しかし，カリフォルニアのイチゴは [4]食欲をそそり，栄養たっぷりではあるが，環境保護論者たちはそれらを生産するための潜在的に [5]持続可能でない農法に強く抗議している。

カリフォルニアの [6]驚くばかりの生産性は，[7]驚異的な量の燻煙剤と呼ばれる [8]殺虫剤のおかげである。イチゴはさまざまな病気に非常にかかりやすいため，イチゴを [11]しおれさせ，枯れさせてしまう土壌 [10]伝染性病原菌 [9]を根絶するためには，燻煙剤はなくてはならないものになっている。しかしながら，これらを用いるとイチゴが健康に有害な影響を与える疑いのある化学 [14]残留物 [13]漬けになるため，[12]非難の的になってきた。実際，何十年も用いられてきた主要な燻煙剤は徐々に [15]減らされ，農家は [16]慌てて代替品を探すことになった。生産者たちは代替製品に乗り換えたが，少なくともその 1 つは [17]発がん性物質の疑いがある。

幸い，非化学的な土壌処理法や害虫を吸い上げる [19]トラクター大の掃除機などさまざまな新しい技術がイチゴ産業に [18]もたらされつつある。これらの技術は [20]初期段階で費用はしばしば [21]法外ではあるが，近い将来イチゴをより持続可能な方法で栽培する方法が見つかる希望はある。

発がん性物質

carcinogenic（発がん性のある）ものには, ultraviolet radiation（紫外線）や asbestos（石綿，アスベスト）のように天然に存在するものもあるが, 食品を通じて取り込まれる chemical substance（化学物質）も人体への大きな危険である。代表的なのは food additive（食品添加物）と pesticide residue（残留農薬）で, 発がんのリスクによってさまざまな規制がかけられている。タバコの secondhand smoke（副流煙）にも多くの発がん性物質が含まれており, passive smoking（受動喫煙）を防ぐ取り組みが強化されている。

California Strawberries

1 ☐☐ **dominate** [dá(:)mɪnèɪt]	▶ command, control, predominate **動** を支配する，で支配的な地位を占める **名** dominance　**形** dominant
2 ☐☐ **astoundingly** [əstáʊndɪŋli]	▶ amazingly, astonishingly **副** 驚くほど，仰天するほど **動** astound　**形** astounding
3 ☐☐ **yield** [ji:ld]	▶ crop, harvest **名** 産出高，収穫高 **動** を産出する
4 ☐☐ **mouthwatering** [máʊθwɔ̀:ṭərɪŋ]	▶ appetizing **形** とてもおいしそうな ● water は「よだれが出る」という意味
5 ☐☐ **unsustainable** [ʌ̀nsəstéɪnəbl]	**形** 持続できない ⇄ sustainable
6 ☐☐ **stunning** [stʌ́nɪŋ]	▶ amazing, astonishing, staggering **形** 驚くべき，すばらしい **動** stun　**副** stunningly
7 ☐☐ **prodigious** [prədídʒəs]	▶ enormous, huge, tremendous **形** 驚異的な，莫大な
8 ☐☐ **pesticide** [péstɪsàɪd]	**名** 殺虫剤 ● pest（害虫）＋-cide（殺すもの）
9 ☐☐ **eradicate** [ɪrǽdɪkèɪt]	▶ eliminate, exterminate, wipe out **動** を根絶する，を一掃する **名** eradication
10 ☐☐ **borne** [bɔ:rn]	**形** （～で）運ばれる **動** bear ● airborne virus（空気感染するウイルス）
11 ☐☐ **wilt** [wɪlt]	▶ droop **動** （植物が）しおれる

12 ☐☐ **under fire**	非難の的になって，批判されて ● come under fire（非難を浴びる）
13 ☐☐ **laden** [léɪdən]	▶ full, loaded 形 いっぱいの〈with ～で〉，たくさん持った〈with ～を〉　● load（積む）の古語 lade の過去分詞から
14 ☐☐ **residue** [rézɪdjùː]	▶ remainder, remnant 名 残留物
15 ☐☐ **phase out ～**	～を段階的に廃止する ⇄ phase in
16 ☐☐ **scramble** [skrǽmbl]	▶ rush, hasten 動 慌ててする，我先にする〈to do ～しようと〉
17 ☐☐ **carcinogen** [kɑːrsínədʒən]	▶ a substance that can cause cancer 名 発がん性物質 形 carcinogenic
18 ☐☐ **bring ～ to bear**	～を向ける，～を利用する〈on ～に〉
19 ☐☐ **tractor** [trǽktər]	名 トラクター
20 ☐☐ **infancy** [ínfənsi]	▶ beginning, early stage 名 初期，萌芽期
21 ☐☐ **prohibitive** [prouhíbətɪv]	▶ exorbitant, outrageous, sky-high 形 （価格などが）法外な，途方もない
☐☐ **poisonous** [pɔ́ɪzənəs]	▶ toxic 形 有毒な，毒性のある 名 poison　⇄ nonpoisonous, nontoxic

The Centipede Controversy

A scientist discovers how much trouble you can get into if you fail to ensure that the creatures you are studying have been obtained legally.

1   Researcher Carles Doménech never imagined the controversy he would ¹**incite** when he published his research on a newly discovered ²**centipede** in a ³**prestigious** scientific ⁴**journal**. The new species, named *Scolopendra paradoxa*, was ⁵**procured** from collectors in the Philippines.

5   However, it was later discovered that Doménech had ⁶**unwittingly** ⁷**abetted** an illegal act by receiving the centipedes from collectors who had failed to obtain ⁸**permits** to export them to a foreign researcher. Though Doménech claims to be a ⁹**novice** researcher who was unaware of the proper research ¹⁰**protocols**, critics argue that he should have been
10   more ¹¹**diligent** in making sure his samples were obtained ¹²**legitimately** and that the ¹³**distinguished** journal that published his research should have done the same.

      This incident raises ¹⁴**thorny** questions about the ethics of scientific research and publication. While the concept of protecting every single
15   member of an endangered species is a ¹⁵**noble** one, in practice, ¹⁶**onerous** requirements for proof that specimens had not been ¹⁷**smuggled** or removed illegally could ¹⁸**hinder** research that benefits vulnerable species. Furthermore, the feasibility of a journal ¹⁹**endeavoring** to ascertain whether specimens had been acquired in compliance with the laws of so
20   many different countries is doubtful.   ▤ (194 words)

ムカデに関する論争

ある科学者は，研究対象の生物が合法的に入手されたことを保証できない場合，どれほど面倒なことになるのかを発見した。

　研究者のカルレス・ドメネクは [3]権威ある科学 [4]雑誌に新しく発見された [2]ムカデについての彼の研究を発表したとき，自分が [1]巻き起こす論争についてまったく想像もしなかった。Scolopendra paradoxa と名付けられたその新種は，フィリピンの収集家から [5]入手したものだった。

　しかし，後になって，ドメネクが，外国の研究者にムカデを輸出する [8]許可を得られなかった収集家からムカデを受け取ることで，[6]気づかないうちに違法行為 [7]を幇助していたことがわかった。ドメネクは，自分は [9]新米の研究者で正式な研究 [10]手続きについて知らなかったと主張しているが，批評家たちは，彼は標本が [12]合法的に入手されたことを確認することにもっと [11]念を入れるべきだったし，彼の研究を出版した [13]高名な雑誌も同様にすべきだったと論じている。

　この出来事は，科学研究と出版物の倫理について，[14]厄介な問題を提起している。絶滅危惧種の個体を１つ残らず保護するという概念は [15]崇高なものではあるが，実際には，その標本が [17]密輸入されたり違法に持ち去られたりしたものでないことの証明を求めるという [16]煩わしい条件が，絶滅の危機がある種の利益となるような研究 [18]を妨げる可能性がある。さらに，雑誌が，標本が実にさまざまな国々の法律にのっとって入手されたかどうかを究明する [19]努力をすることの実行可能性は疑わしい。

The Centipede Controversy

1 □□ **incite** [ɪnsáɪt] ❶	▶ cause, provoke, stir up 動 を誘発する，を引き起こす 名 incitement
2 □□ **centipede** [séntəpìːd]	名 ムカデ ● centi-（100 の）＋-pede（足）
3 □□ **prestigious** [prestíːdʒəs] ❶	▶ eminent, reputable, prominent 形 威信のある，名声の高い 名 prestige
4 □□ **journal** [dʒə́ːrnəl]	名（専門）雑誌 ● academic journal（学術誌）
5 □□ **procure** [prəkjúər]	▶ obtain, secure 動 を（苦労して）手に入れる，を入手する 名 procurement
6 □□ **unwittingly** [ʌnwítɪŋli]	▶ unconsciously, unknowingly 副 気づかずに，知らずに 形 unwitting ⇄ wittingly
7 □□ **abet** [əbét]	動（犯罪など）を幇助する，を教唆する ● aid and abet（を教唆幇助する）
8 □□ **permit** [pə́ːrmɪt]	▶ license, certificate 名 許可証，免許証 ● work permit（（外国人の）労働許可証）
9 □□ **novice** [ná(ː)vəs]	▶ beginner, neophyte, tenderfoot 名 初心者，新米 ⇄ expert, veteran
10 □□ **protocol** [próʊṭəkà(ː)l]	名（実験・治療などの）実施要領，プロトコル ● experimental protocol（実験プロトコル）
11 □□ **diligent** [dílɪdʒənt]	▶ hardworking, industrious, assiduous 形 勤勉な，熱心な〈in 〜に〉 名 diligence ⇄ lazy（怠惰な）

12 ☐☐ **legitimately** [lɪdʒítəmətli]	▶ legally, lawfully 副 合法的に 形 legitimate 名 legitimacy 反 illegitimately
13 ☐☐ **distinguished** [dɪstíŋgwɪʃt]	▶ eminent, noted, renowned 形 名高い，著名な
14 ☐☐ **thorny** [θɔ́ːrni]	▶ difficult, troublesome, prickly 形 （問題などが）厄介な，面倒な ● 「とげの多い」が本義
15 ☐☐ **noble** [nóʊbl]	▶ honorable, upright, virtuous 形 高潔な，気高い 名 nobility 副 nobly
16 ☐☐ **onerous** [óʊnərəs]	▶ burdensome, demanding, taxing 形 （仕事などが）煩わしい，面倒な
17 ☐☐ **smuggle** [smʌ́gl]	動 を密輸する 名 smuggling（密輸），smuggler（密輸業者）
18 ☐☐ **hinder** [híndər]	▶ hamper, impede, obstruct 動 を妨げる，を妨害する 名 hindrance
19 ☐☐ **endeavor** [ɪndévər] ❶	▶ strive, labor, exert *oneself* 動 （懸命に）努力する〈to do ～しようと〉 名 努力
☐☐ **poach** [poʊtʃ]	動 （を）密猟する 名 poaching（密猟），poacher（密猟者）
☐☐ **traffic** [trǽfɪk]	動 密売買をする〈in ～の〉 名 密売買 名 trafficking（密売買），trafficker（密売人）
☐☐ **embargo** [ɪmbáːrgoʊ]	名 禁輸，通商禁止〈on ～の〉 動 の通商を禁止する ● arms embargo（武器の禁輸）

自然・環境

3

Shark Teeth Used to Identify Biodiversity Loss

The teeth of sharks originally used to make weapons by Pacific Islanders were later found to be useful in estimating the diversity of sharks.

1   There is a ¹**scarcity** of data on shark populations before humans began to significantly change ocean biodiversity. Joshua Drew, a conservation biologist at Columbia University in New York, had an ²**ingenious** idea for ³**substantiating** the changes in shark diversity in the seas around the
5   Gilbert Islands. He had to go no further than the Field Museum of Natural History in Chicago, which holds a ⁴**copious** collection of weapons ⁵**crafted** by natives of the Gilbert Islands. The Gilbert Islanders were ⁶**adept** at making weapons from shark teeth. The teeth in the swords, lances, and other ⁷**fierce** weapons had been ⁸**perforated** and then ⁹**lashed**
10   with cords to small ¹⁰**recesses** drilled into wooden handles and spears.

Since sharks can be identified by their teeth, the weapons offered a valuable ¹¹**resource** for ¹²**monitoring** shark diversity over the span of 120 years, the date of the oldest weapons. Drew identified 19 different species, including three no longer found near the Gilbert Islands. The teeth were
15   gathered as the islanders fished off their own coasts, not through trading. This ¹³**implies** that the three shark species had once lived in the waters near the islands. Shark ¹⁴**finning**, a method of catching sharks in large numbers for their fins, had commenced near the islands over a hundred years ago. This ¹⁵**decimation** may account for the loss of shark species.

(221 words)

サメの歯でわかる生物多様性の損失

元来，太平洋諸島民によって武器を作るために使われていたサメの歯は，サメの多様性を推定するのに役立つことが後にわかった。

　人間が海洋生物の多様性に著しい変化を及ぼし始める以前の，サメの個体群についての資料は ^{1}不足している。ニューヨークのコロンビア大学の保全生物学者のジョシュア・ドゥルーは，ギルバート諸島周辺海域におけるサメの多様性の変化 ^{3}を実証する ^{2}独創的な考えを持っていた。彼はシカゴのフィールド自然史博物館以外を訪れる必要はなかった。そこにはギルバート諸島の原住民の ^{5}手で作られた ^{4}おびただしい数の武器が収蔵されている。ギルバート諸島の住民はサメの歯から武器を作ることに ^{6}熟達していた。剣や槍，その他の ^{7}強力な武器に取り付けられる歯は ^{8}穴をあけられ，それから木製の柄や槍にあけられた ^{10}穴に紐で ^{9}くくり付けられたのだった。

　サメの種は歯によって同定できるので，それらの武器は収蔵されている最も古い年代である 120 年前から今日までのサメの多様性 ^{12}を観察する貴重な情報 ^{11}源となった。ドゥルーはギルバート諸島近海ではもはや見られない 3 種を含む 19 種を特定した。それらの歯は交易を通じてではなく，島民が島の沿岸でサメを獲ったときに集められたものである。これはその 3 種のサメがかつてギルバート諸島近海に生息していたこと ^{13}を意味する。サメのヒレを獲るために多数のサメを捕獲する漁法であるフカ ^{14}ヒレ漁は，この海域で 100 年以上前から始まっていた。この ^{15}大量殺戮がサメの種の減少の原因かもしれない。

239

Shark Teeth Used to Identify Biodiversity Loss

1 ☐☐ **scarcity** [skéərsəti]	▶ shortage, lack, sparseness 名 不足, 乏しさ 形 scarce 🔄 abundance（豊富）
2 ☐☐ **ingenious** [ɪndʒíːniəs] ❶	▶ creative, inventive, resourceful, clever 形 独創的な,（案などが）巧みな 名 ingenuity（巧妙さ）
3 ☐☐ **substantiate** [səbstǽnʃièɪt]	▶ prove, vindicate, validate, corroborate 動 を実証する, を立証する 名 substantiation 形 substantial（実体のある）
4 ☐☐ **copious** [kóʊpiəs]	▶ abundant, plentiful, numerous, ample, profuse 形 おびただしい, 豊富な
5 ☐☐ **craft** [kræft]	▶ elaborate, work up, fashion, form 動 を（特別な技能を使って手で）作る
6 ☐☐ **adept** [ədépt] ❶	▶ talented, versed, skilled, proficient 形 熟練した〈at, in ～に〉 名 名人〈at, in ～の〉
7 ☐☐ **fierce** [fɪərs]	▶ powerful, formidable 形 強力な, どう猛な
8 ☐☐ **perforate** [póːrfərèɪt]	▶ pierce, penetrate, puncture 動 に穴をあける
9 ☐☐ **lash** [læʃ]	▶ fasten, tie, bind 動 をくくり付ける, を縛る
10 ☐☐ **recess** [ríːses]	▶ hollow, dent, concavity 名 穴, へこみ
11 ☐☐ **resource** [ríːsɔːrs]	▶ expedient, resort 名 手段, 資源

12 ☐☐ **monitor** [mά(:)nəṭər]	▶ observe, track **動** を観察する，を観測する
13 ☐☐ **imply** [ɪmpláɪ] ❶	▶ entail, indicate **動** を（必然的に）意味する，を暗示する **名** implication（含意）
14 ☐☐ **fin** [fɪn]	▶ cut off the fins from **動** （魚）のヒレを切り落とす **名** ヒレ
15 ☐☐ **decimation** [dèsəméɪʃən]	▶ massacre, slaughter **名** 大量殺戮 **動** decimate（を大量に殺す）
☐☐ **the Red List**	絶滅危惧種のリスト ● 国際自然保護連合（IUCN）が作成し，各国機関でも作成している
☐☐ **overfishing** [òʊvərfíʃɪŋ]	▶ overexploitation, excessive fishing **名** 魚の乱獲
☐☐ **aquaculture** [ά:kwəkʌ̀ltʃər]	▶ mariculture, sea farming, fish farming **名** （水産物の）養殖 ● aqua-（水）＋culture（栽培，養殖）

自然・環境

4

自然・環境 **5**

A Unique Life Form on Earth?

A NASA scientist claims to have found a form of life that is not related to any other organisms on Earth, but other scientists doubt her claim.

1   Biologist Paul Davies at Arizona State University was on a ¹**quest**. He asked researchers to search for life forms on Earth whose ²**makeup** is so ³**bizarre** as to indicate they do not spring up from our own ⁴**phylogenetic tree**, but from another entirely. This could be ⁵**de facto** evidence that there
5   was "a second ⁶**genesis**," and that multiple life origins on Earth may have occurred. It would also imply that life on other planets was likely.

   NASA biologist Felisa Wolfe-Simon believed she found such an organism in 2010. She and her research team discovered ⁷**bacteria** that thrived in ⁸**arsenic**-rich sediments. She ⁹**deduced** that, in order to live in
10   such a toxic environment, the bacteria must have ¹⁰**assimilated** arsenic into its DNA instead of the ¹¹**phosphorus** that is a key component of all other DNA.

   More recent studies do not ¹²**corroborate** Wolfe-Simon's deduction. They show that arsenic is not present in the bacteria's DNA, and that the
15   bacteria require phosphorus after all, linking them to other known species. While Wolfe-Simon is willing to make some ¹³**concessions**, she is not willing to ¹⁴**back down on** her argument that the bacteria are ¹⁵**singular**. After all, there is no other organism that flourishes in arsenic. Moreover, there is no proof showing that the arsenic-loving bacteria do not
20   ¹⁶**incorporate** the toxin in their ¹⁷**composition** in some way.

🇺🇸 (222 words)

地球上の無比の生き物？

ある NASA の科学者が，地球上の他のどの有機体とも関係のない生き物を発見したと主張しているが，他の科学者たちは彼女の主張を疑っている。

アリゾナ州立大学の生物学者ポール・デービーズはある ¹探求をしていた。彼は研究者たちに，地球上の生き物でありながら ²構造が非常に ³風変わりで，既存の ⁴系統樹から発生したものでなくまったく別の起源を持つような生き物を探すよう呼びかけた。このことは「第二の ⁶発生」があって，地球上に複数の生命の起源が生じていたという ⁵事実上の証拠になり得る。それは他の惑星に生命が存在し得ることをも暗に示す。

NASA の生物学者フェリッサ・ウルフ・サイモンは 2010 年にそのような有機体を発見したと考えた。彼女と彼女の研究チームは ⁸ヒ素を豊富に含む堆積物の中で力強く成長する ⁷バクテリアを発見した。彼女は，そのような有毒な環境の中で生きるために，そのバクテリアは他のすべての（生き物の）DNA の重要な構成要素である ¹¹リンの代わりにヒ素をその DNA ¹⁰に取り込んだに違いない ⁹と推論した。

もっと最近の研究はウルフ・サイモンの推論 ¹²を裏づけるものではない。ヒ素がバクテリアの DNA には存在しないこと，結局のところバクテリアにはリンが必要なことを明らかにして，そのバクテリアを既知の他の種と結びつけている。ウルフ・サイモンはいくらか ¹³譲歩することには前向きだが，そのバクテリアが ¹⁵まれに見るものだという主張 ¹⁴を撤回する気はない。なにしろ，ヒ素の中で生育する有機体は他に存在しないし，その上，ヒ素を好むバクテリアが何らかの方法でその ¹⁷組織の中に毒素 ¹⁶を組み入れてはいないことを示す証拠もないからである。

自然・環境

5

天地創造

聖書の Genesis（『創世記』）によると，神は 6 日間で天と地と動植物などを作った。これが the Creation（天地創造）であり，キリスト教の教義では，すべての生命の起源はここにあるとされる。second genesis（第二の発生）は，聖書の天地創造を first genesis と考えることを前提とした表現である。もっとも，phylogenetic tree（系統樹）はダーウィンの進化論に基づく概念だから，この英文の科学者たちが天地創造を信じているわけではない。既知の生物とはまったく系統が異なる生物の起源を指す便利な表現として second genesis が用いられているにすぎない。

A Unique Life Form on Earth?

1 ☐☐ **quest** [kwést]	▶ search, pursuit, hunt 名 探求, 追究 ● be on a quest(探求している)
2 ☐☐ **makeup** [méɪkʌ̀p]	▶ composition, constitution, framework 名 構造, 構成 ● make up 〜(〜を構成する)
3 ☐☐ **bizarre** [bɪzάːr] ❶	▶ strange, peculiar 形 奇妙な, 奇怪な
4 ☐☐ **phylogenetic tree**	生物の進化系統樹
5 ☐☐ **de facto**	▶ actual, virtual, real 事実上の ● [deɪ fǽktoʊ] と発音する
6 ☐☐ **genesis** [dʒénəsɪs]	▶ beginning, origin, outset 名 発生, 起源
7 ☐☐ **bacteria** [bæktíəriə]	▶ germs, microbes, microorganisms 名 バクテリア, 細菌 ● bacterium の複数形だが, 単数としても扱われる
8 ☐☐ **arsenic** [άːrsənɪk]	名 ヒ素
9 ☐☐ **deduce** [dɪdjúːs]	▶ infer, conclude, educe 動 を(一般原理などから論理的に)推論する 名 deduction(推論)
10 ☐☐ **assimilate** [əsíməlèɪt]	▶ absorb, imbibe, take in 動 (栄養など)を吸収する 名 assimilation
11 ☐☐ **phosphorus** [fά(ː)sfərəs]	名 リン

12 ☐☐ **corroborate** [kərá(:)bərèɪt]	▶ confirm, substantiate, back up **動** を裏づける，を確証する **名** corroboration **形** corroborative
13 ☐☐ **concession** [kənséʃən]	▶ compromise, allowance **名** 譲歩 **動** concede（を（譲歩して）認める）
14 ☐☐ **back down on ～**	▶ back off, retract （発言など）を撤回する，～を取り消す
15 ☐☐ **singular** [síŋɡjʊlər]	▶ unique, rare, uncommon **形** まれな，無二の **名** singularity
16 ☐☐ **incorporate** [ɪnkɔ́ːrpərèɪt]	▶ include, contain, merge **動** を組み入れる，を取り込む〈into ～に〉 **名** incorporation
17 ☐☐ **composition** [kà(:)mpəzíʃən]	▶ structure, framework, conformation **名** 組織，組成 **動** compose（を構成する，を組織する）
☐☐ **fallacy** [fǽləsi]	▶ misapprehension, misconception **名** 誤った推論

自然・環境

5

LEDs May Color the Night Sky Blue

Light pollution is a serious problem that can cause great harm to animals, and experts are concerned that the increased use of LED lights is making the problem worse.

1　　Much has been written about ¹**light pollution**, also known as ²**skyglow**. Skyglow is ³**artificial** light that has been ⁴**cast** outward from cities. Thousands of ⁵**nocturnal** species have been affected — and generally not in beneficial ways. Animal migration, reproduction, and
5　feeding behaviors have all been ⁶**stunted** or impacted. Birds have ⁷**collided into** illuminated skyscrapers, while turtles have been ⁸**beached** when following lights on land.

　　Now the nighttime sky may even change color. LEDs, light-emitting diodes, have gained popularity since they offer ⁹**distinct** benefits, such as
10　lower electricity bills and a longer ¹⁰**lifespan**. As LED lights ¹¹**catch on**, the nighttime sky may be altered to a blue color as opposed to the reddish light cast out by ¹²**incandescent** bulbs. Researchers can only speculate how blue skyglow will affect nocturnal creatures. However, one study has been carried out so far. In the city of Berlin, where many yellow-orange
15　lights have been ¹³**supplanted** by LEDs, researchers determined that LEDs do provide a blue ¹⁴**tinge** to the sky on clear nights — and increase the skyglow effect.

　　Biophysicist Mark Rea is fully cognizant of the hazards related to LEDs, but argues that ¹⁵**ameliorating** the skyglow they cause may be
20　possible by, for example, directing light downwards rather than up. Furthermore, since the brightness of light is more important than where it falls on the color ¹⁶**spectrum**, he stresses that precise studies are ¹⁷**imperative** so wasteful usage of lighting can be reduced.

🏴󠁧󠁢󠁥󠁮󠁧󠁿🇬🇧 (235 words)

LED は夜空を青色に染めるかもしれない

光害は動物に大きな害を引き起こし得る深刻な問題であり,専門家は LED 照明の使用の増加が問題を悪化させていると心配している。

²夜空が明るくなることとしても知られている ¹光害についてはこれまで多くのことが書かれている。それは都市から外に向かって ⁴放たれてきた ³人工の光である。何千もの ⁵夜行性の種が影響を受けている――概して有益でない形で。動物の移動,繁殖,摂餌行動のすべてが ⁶妨げられたり,影響を受けたりしてきている。鳥はライトアップされた超高層ビル ⁷に衝突し,カメは陸上の光に導かれて ⁸浜に上がってきている。

今や夜空の色さえもが変わるかもしれない。より安い電気代やより長い ¹⁰寿命といった ⁹明確な利点を提供するという理由で,発光ダイオード（LED）が普及してきた。LED 照明が ¹¹人気を博すと,夜空は ¹²白熱電球が放つ赤みがかった光とは対照的に青色に変えられるかもしれない。研究者たちは青い夜空が夜行性の生き物にどのような影響を与えるかを推測するしかない。しかし,これまでに一度調査が行われた。ベルリンの街では多くの黄色がかったオレンジ色の街灯が LED に ¹³取って代わられたのだが,研究者たちは,そこでは晴れた夜には LED が空に青みがかった ¹⁴色合いを与えていて,夜空が明るくなる効果が増していることを突き止めた。

生物物理学者マーク・レイは LED に関連する危険を十分に認識しているが,例えば,光を上ではなく下に向けることで,LED が要因となる夜空の明るさ ¹⁵を改善することができるかもしれないと主張する。さらに,光が色の ¹⁶スペクトルのどこに位置するかということよりも光の明るさの方が重要なので,照明の無駄遣いが減らせるように,正確な調査が ¹⁷不可欠であると彼は強調する。

LEDs May Color the Night Sky Blue

1 ☐☐ **light pollution**	光害
2 ☐☐ **skyglow** [skáɪɡlòʊ]	名 人工の光によって夜空が明るくなること
3 ☐☐ **artificial** [à:rṭɪfíʃəl] ❶	▶ synthetic, manufactured, man-made 形 人工的な ⟷ natural（自然の）
4 ☐☐ **cast** [kæst]	▶ emit, radiate, give off, send out 動（光）を放つ，を照射する
5 ☐☐ **nocturnal** [nɑ(:)ktə́:rnəl]	形 夜行性の ⟷ diurnal（昼行性の）
6 ☐☐ **stunt** [stʌnt]	▶ inhibit 動 を妨げる
7 ☐☐ **collide into ～**	▶ crash into, bump into ～に衝突する，～にぶつかる
8 ☐☐ **beach** [bi:tʃ]	▶ strand, run aground, run ashore 動 を浜に乗り上げさせる
9 ☐☐ **distinct** [dɪstíŋkt]	▶ well-defined, obvious, prominent, pronounced 形 明確な，はっきりした
10 ☐☐ **lifespan** [láɪfspæn]	▶ lifetime, life 名（物・人の）寿命
11 ☐☐ **catch on**	▶ boom, take off, thrive, flourish 人気が出る，はやる

12 ☐☐ **incandescent** [ìnkəndésənt]	▶ white-hot 形 白熱光を発する
13 ☐☐ **supplant** [səplǽnt]	▶ supersede, displace, replace 動 に取って代わる
14 ☐☐ **tinge** [tɪndʒ]	▶ shade, tone, hue, tint 名 色合い
15 ☐☐ **ameliorate** [əmíːliərèɪt]	▶ improve, better, mitigate 動 を改善する ⇔ deteriorate（を悪化させる）
16 ☐☐ **spectrum** [spéktrəm]	名 スペクトル 形 spectral ● 赤から紫までの光の帯のこと
17 ☐☐ **imperative** [ɪmpérətɪv]	▶ important, necessary, crucial, mandatory, urgent 形 必須の，緊急の
☐☐ **fluorescent light**	蛍光灯 ● fluor-（蛍光）＋escent（の光を放つ）
☐☐ **noise pollution**	騒音公害

Pythons Pose a Danger to Florida's Habitat

Large snakes known as pythons that were kept as pets in Florida have escaped into the wild and become an invasive species.

1　　Recent discoveries of gigantic Burmese pythons in the Everglades, a region in Florida ¹**renowned** for its ²**biodiversity**, are of great concern to environmentalists. These ³**robust** creatures can be nearly 20 feet long and carry dozens of eggs. Pythons are an ⁴**invasive species** that ⁵**jeopardize**
5　the survival of a wide variety of ⁶**native species**, which they ⁷**prey on**. Both the creatures' size and the number of eggs indicate that pythons are thriving in their newfound home. Population estimates range from thousands to hundreds of thousands.

　　The pythons are the ⁸**offspring** of pets that were either purposely
10　abandoned in the Everglades or were ⁹**inadvertently** allowed to escape by their owners. Local conservationists are trying to understand more about the snakes and the dangers they ¹⁰**pose** in their efforts to ¹¹**curtail** their spread. They have already conceded that it will be extremely difficult, if not impossible, to eradicate them.

15　　Florida ¹²**holds the title of** being the ¹³**ecosystem** that has been hardest hit by invasive reptiles and amphibians. There has been an ¹⁴**influx** of more than 60 non-native species to Florida since the mid-1800s, and many are now known to have become established there. Invasive species have become a ¹⁵**pervasive** problem for conservationists, who are
20　attempting to ¹⁶**gauge** the extent of the problem as well as ¹⁷**crack down on** ¹⁸**derelict** pet owners. 　　　　　　　　　　　■■■ (218 words)

タイトル　python：ニシキヘビ。
ℓ.7　　　Population estimates range ... ：主語を間違えないように注意。Population estimates が
　　　　　主語。

ニシキヘビ，フロリダの生息地に危険をもたらす

フロリダ州でペットとして飼われていたニシキヘビとして知られる大きなヘビが野生に逃げ，外来種となった。

[2]多様な生態系が存在することで[1]有名なフロリダ州のエバーグレーズ国立公園で，最近巨大なビルマニシキヘビが見つかったことは環境問題の専門家たちにとって大きな懸念となっている。これらの[3]頑強な生物たちは体長が約20フィートに及ぶことがあり，多くの卵を抱えている。ニシキヘビは多様な[6]在来種の生存[5]を脅かす[4]外来種で，それら在来種[7]を捕食する。その大きさと卵の数の両方から，ニシキヘビが新しく見つけた生息地で繁栄していることがうかがえる。推定個体数は数千から数十万に及ぶ。

そのニシキヘビたちはエバーグレーズに故意に捨てられたか，飼い主の[9]不注意で逃げ出したペットの[8]子孫である。現地の自然保護活動家たちは，それが広がるの[11]を抑えるために，このヘビそのものと，ヘビ[10]がもたらす危険についてもっと知ろうとしている。彼らはすでにニシキヘビを根絶することは極めて困難，おそらく不可能だろうと認めている。

フロリダ州は外来種の爬虫類や両生類によって最も大きな被害を受けた[13]生態系である[12]という称号を持っている。1800年代半ば以降60以上の外来種がフロリダに[14]流入し，その多くがそこに定着したことが現在わかっている。外来種は自然保護活動家たちにとって[15]広範囲にわたる問題となっており，彼らは[18]怠慢なペットの飼い主たち[17]を厳しく取り締まるとともに問題の程度[16]を測ろうとしている。

Pythons Pose a Danger to Florida's Habitat

1 ☐☐ **renowned** [rɪnáʊnd]	▶ celebrated, illustrious, notable 形 有名な，誉れ高い〈for 〜で〉 名 renown（名声）
2 ☐☐ **biodiversity** [bàɪoʊdəvə́ːrsəṭi]	▶ biological diversity 名 生物の多様性 ● bio- は「生命，生物」
3 ☐☐ **robust** [roʊbʌ́st]	▶ vigorous, sturdy, rugged, lusty 形 強健な，たくましい，強い
4 ☐☐ **invasive species**	▶ alien species, introduced species 外来種
5 ☐☐ **jeopardize** [dʒépərdàɪz] ❶	▶ endanger, threaten, imperil 動 を脅かす，を危険にさらす 名 jeopardy（危険）
6 ☐☐ **native species**	▶ domestic species, local species 在来種
7 ☐☐ **prey on 〜**	▶ hunt, eat, feed on, live on 〜を捕食する，〜をえさとして食べる ● 名詞の prey は「えさ（となる動物）」
8 ☐☐ **offspring** [ɔ́(ː)fsprìŋ] ❶	▶ descendant, progeny 名（人・動植物の）子，子孫 ⇔ ancestor, forefather（先祖）
9 ☐☐ **inadvertently** [ìnədvə́ːrtəntli]	▶ inattentively, unintentionally, accidentally 副 不注意で，うっかり ⇔ deliberately
10 ☐☐ **pose** [poʊz]	▶ present, cause, produce 動（問題など）をもたらす，を引き起こす
11 ☐☐ **curtail** [kəːrtéɪl]	▶ restrict, curb, rein in, reduce, cut down 動 を制限する，を削減する 名 curtailment

12 ☐☐ **hold the title of ~**	〜の称号を持っている，〜で一番である
13 ☐☐ **ecosystem** [íːkousìstəm]	▶ ecosys **名** 生態系
14 ☐☐ **influx** [ínflʌks]	▶ inundation，inflow **名** 到来，流入 ⇄ efflux（流出，発散）
15 ☐☐ **pervasive** [pərvéisiv]	▶ prevalent，widespread，ubiquitous **形** 広範な，蔓延した **動** pervade　**名** pervasion
16 ☐☐ **gauge** [ɡeidʒ] ❶	▶ appraise，assess，evaluate，estimate，size up **動** を測定する，を見積もる
17 ☐☐ **crack down on ~**	▶ clamp down on，get tough on 〜を厳しく取り締まる，〜に断固とした態度をとる
18 ☐☐ **derelict** [dérəlìkt]	▶ negligent，slack，neglectful **形** 怠慢な
☐☐ **predator** [prédəṭər]	▶ an animal that kills and eats other animals **名** 捕食者 **形** predatory（捕食性の）
☐☐ **natural selection**	（生物の）自然淘汰 ⇄ artificial selection（人為淘汰）

Global Warming May Increase Biodiversity

While some people fear global warming will cause many species to go extinct, one analysis of geological records indicates warm temperatures may increase biodiversity.

1　　Most environmentalists associate global warming with loss of biodiversity. While increased temperatures will prove [1]**lethal** to many species and lead to mass extinctions, this basic [2]**premise** may be flawed over the long run. Peter Mayhew, an evolutionary ecologist at the
5　University of York, found that initial [3]**assessments** were based on all geological periods equally. He argues that this approach is [4]**unsound**, for some geological eras are more thoroughly researched than others. Therefore, in his own analysis, Mayhew included only well-sampled periods and [5]**tallied up** the species known to exist during those periods.

10　　Ironically, based on fossil records, there is an [6]**inverse correlation** between biodiversity and temperatures. This may [7]**defy** logic, but it explains an [8]**anomaly** that has plagued scientists for decades. While many have assumed that warmer periods of Earth have been inhospitable to biodiversity, it is widely known that tropical areas support the most
15　[9]**diverse** range of life forms. Tropical areas will increase with global warming.

　　Mayhew acknowledges that rapid climate change will put a [10]**strain** on [11]**habitats** around the world and he is hardly optimistic about the short term. After all, it takes millions of years for new species to evolve.
20　However, while global warming will cause major environmental [12]**fracture** and upset the [13]**equilibrium** in many of the Earth's ecosystems, he believes the [14]**implicit** assumption that biodiversity will remain [15]**irretrievably** damaged may be [16]**ill-founded**.　　　(226 words)

地球温暖化は生物多様性を増大させるかもしれない

地球温暖化によって多くの種が絶滅することを懸念する人々がいる一方で，地質学的記録の1つの分析では，温暖な気温は生物多様性を高める可能性があることが示されている。

ほとんどの環境保護主義者は地球温暖化を生物多様性の喪失と結びつけて考える。気温の上昇は多くの種にとって ¹致命的で大量絶滅をもたらすが，長期的に考えるとこの根本的な ²前提には欠陥があるかもしれない。ヨーク大学の進化生態学者ピーター・メイヒューは，初期の ³評価はすべての地質学上の時代を均等に扱っていたことを発見した。彼はこの手法は ⁴信用できないと主張する。というのも，地質時代の中には徹底して研究がなされている時代とそうでない時代があるからだ。したがって，メイヒューは自分の分析には十分に標本が取れている時代のみを含み，それらの時代に存在していたことが知られている種 ⁵を集計した。

皮肉なことに，化石標本に基づくと，生物多様性と気温の間には ⁶逆相関がある。これは論理 ⁷に反するかもしれないが，数十年間にわたり科学者たちを悩ませてきた ⁸矛盾を説明する。多くの科学者たちは地球の気温が暖かい時期の方が多様な生物の生存に適さなかったと仮定してきたが，その一方で熱帯地方が最も ⁹多様な生命体が生息する地域であることは広く知られている。熱帯地方は地球温暖化とともに拡大する。

メイヒューは急激な気候変動が世界中の ¹¹生息地に ¹⁰負担をかけることを認めており，短期については少しも楽観していない。そもそも新しい種が進化するには何百万年もの時間がかかる。しかしながら，地球温暖化が大規模な環境 ¹²破壊を引き起こし，地球上の多くの生態系の ¹³均衡を乱す一方で，生物多様性は ¹⁵回復できないほどに破壊されたままであり続けるという ¹⁴暗黙の仮定には ¹⁶根拠がないかもしれないと彼は考えている。

さまざまな土壌浸食

生態系に影響を与えるものとして soil erosion（土壌浸食）がある。その地域で植物が育たなくなってしまい，その結果，その植物をえさとする動物がいなくなるのである。他に，coastal erosion（海岸浸食），wind erosion（風食（風，特に砂嵐による浸食）），gravity erosion（重力浸食）がある。

Global Warming May Increase Biodiversity

1 ☐☐ **lethal** [líːθəl]	▶ fatal, deadly, mortal 形 致命的な，致死性の 〈to ～にとって〉
2 ☐☐ **premise** [prémɪs] ⓘ	▶ proposition, assumption, postulation, surmise, hypothesis 名 前提，仮定
3 ☐☐ **assessment** [əsésmənt]	▶ valuation, estimation 名 評価，査定 動 assess
4 ☐☐ **unsound** [ʌnsáʊnd]	▶ ill-founded, unreliable, dubious, fallacious 形 （議論などが）信頼できない，根拠が確かでない ⇔ sound（しっかりした，確かな根拠のある），strong
5 ☐☐ **tally up ～**	▶ count up, enumerate ～を数え上げる
6 ☐☐ **inverse correlation**	▶ opposite [negative] correlation 逆相関 ⇔ positive correlation（正相関）
7 ☐☐ **defy** [dɪfáɪ]	▶ contravene, contradict 動 （論理・確率など）に反する 名 defiance 形 defiant
8 ☐☐ **anomaly** [ənɑ́(ː)məli]	▶ irregularity, inconsistency, incongruity, aberration 名 矛盾，変則
9 ☐☐ **diverse** [dəvə́ːrs]	▶ sundry, manifold, miscellaneous 形 多様な，種々の 動 diversify 名 diversity
10 ☐☐ **strain** [streɪn]	▶ burden, load 名 負担，重圧 ● put a strain on ～（～に負担をかける）
11 ☐☐ **habitat** [hǽbɪtæt]	▶ habitation 名 生息地

12 □□ **fracture** [fræktʃər]	**名** 破壊 ● 通常は「骨折」の意味で使われるが，ここでは environmental fracture で「環境破壊」
13 □□ **equilibrium** [ìːkwɪlíbriəm]	▶ balance, equipoise, parity **名** 均衡，平衡
14 □□ **implicit** [ɪmplísɪt]	▶ unexpressed, tacit, deducible **形** 暗黙的な ⇔ explicit（明示的な，はっきりした）
15 □□ **irretrievably** [ìrɪtríːvəbli]	▶ irreversibly, irrecoverably, irremediably **副** 回復できないほど，元通りにならないくらいに
16 □□ **ill-founded** [ìlfáʊndɪd]	▶ groundless, baseless, unjustified, unsound **形** 根拠に基づかない
□□ **stratum** [stréɪṭəm]	▶ layer, bed **名** 地層 ● 複数形は strata
□□ **deforestation** [diːfɔ(ː)rɪstéɪʃən]	▶ destruction of forests **名** 森林破壊 **動** deforest ⇔ afforestation（植林）
□□ **desertification** [dɪzə̀ːrṭəfɪkéɪʃən]	▶ the process of becoming or making an area a desert **名** 砂漠化

自然・環境

8

The Impending Menace of Antarctic Methane

A scientist has warned that there could be large amounts of methane that will escape into the atmosphere and increase global warming if ice in Antarctica melts.

1　　For most of the last hundred million years, Antarctica was [1]**substantially** warmer due to higher levels of carbon dioxide in the atmosphere. Much of it was covered in dense forests, with deep bays stretching into its interior. Jemma Wadham and a team of researchers from
5　the University of Bristol, Great Britain, theorize that deep layers of plant [2]**sediments** would have collected in those bays, hosting [3]**multitudes of** [4]**methane**-producing microbes. The sediments are now covered by kilometers of ice but the microbes are still producing methane gas, which could potentially be an even bigger [5]**menace** than the less powerful
10　greenhouse gas, carbon dioxide.

　　Wadham [6]**has yet to** detect methane or methane-producing microbes under the Antarctic [7]**ice sheet**, but this does not lessen the [8]**credence** of her theory among researchers. Though her ideas are only [9]**hypothetical**, microbes have been found in almost every environment, including those
15　considered [10]**inhospitable** to most forms of life, such as boiling waters near underground volcanoes and at highly-pressurized, pitch black settings on [11]**ocean floors**.

　　Wadham estimates that there may be over 100 billion tons of gas [12]**built up** under the ice sheet. Unless greenhouse gas emissions [13]**abate**,
20　ice sheets will [14]**inevitably** melt in the coming decades. Much of this methane will [15]**ultimately** escape into the atmosphere, causing further global warming. This and other scenarios could [16]**add up to** a global warming [17]**tipping point**. Some researchers fear that [18]**impending** global climate change could happen much more rapidly than previously believed,
25　[19]**spelling** an [20]**unprecedented** environmental catastrophe.　　■ (247 words)

差し迫る南極メタンの脅威

南極大陸の氷が溶けると，大量のメタンが大気中に流出し，地球温暖化を促進する可能性があると，ある科学者が警告している。

　この1億年のほとんどの間，大気中の二酸化炭素の増加によって南極の気温は[1]著しく高かった。南極の大半はうっそうとした森林で覆われ，深い湾が内陸に切れ込んでいた。英国ブリストル大学のジェマ・ワダムらの研究チームは，植物の深い[2]堆積層がそれらの湾の下に積み重なって[4]メタンを発生する[3]多数の微生物が生息しているという仮説を立てている。今，堆積物は厚さ数キロメートルの氷によって覆われているが，微生物はメタンガスを発生し続けており，それはより弱い温室効果のある二酸化炭素よりもさらに大きな[5]脅威となる可能性がある。

　ワダムは[6]まだ南極の[7]氷床下にメタンやメタンを発生する微生物を見つけていないが，このことで彼女の理論の[8]信頼性が研究者間で下がることはない。彼女の見解は[9]仮説にすぎないが，微生物は，海底火山周辺で噴出する熱水や[11]海底の高圧で真っ暗な環境など，ほとんどの生物の[10]生存に適さないと考えられる環境を含むほぼすべての環境で見つかっている。

　ワダムは氷床の下には1,000億トンを超えるガスが[12]蓄積されている可能性があると推定している。温室効果ガスの排出量が[13]減少しない限り，今後数十年の間に氷床は[14]必ず溶けるだろう。氷床下のメタンのほとんどが[15]最終的に大気中に流出し，さらなる地球温暖化を引き起こすことになる。このことや他の状況が[16]結局地球温暖化の[17]分岐点になるかもしれない。[18]差し迫る地球規模の気候変動がこれまで考えられていたよりもよりいっそう急激に起こり，[20]前例のない環境の大惨事[19]をもたらすことを恐れている研究者もいる。

The Impending Menace of Antarctic Methane

1 ☐☐ **substantially** [səbstǽnʃəli]	▶ markedly, appreciably, significantly 副 著しく、相当 形 substantial（かなりの）
2 ☐☐ **sediment** [sédɪmənt]	▶ accumulation, deposit, silt, alluvium 名 堆積物 名 sedimentation（堆積（作用）） 形 sedimentary
3 ☐☐ **multitudes of ~**	多数の～ ● a multitude of ~ も同じ意味
4 ☐☐ **methane** [méθeɪn]	▶ marsh gas, swamp gas 名 メタン
5 ☐☐ **menace** [ménəs] ❶	▶ threat 名 脅威　動 の脅威となる 形 menacing（脅威となるような、威嚇的な）
6 ☐☐ **have yet to do**	まだ～していない
7 ☐☐ **ice sheet**	（南極・グリーンランドの）氷床、地表を覆う広大な氷塊
8 ☐☐ **credence** [krí:dəns]	▶ credibility, trustworthiness, reliability 名 信用、信頼
9 ☐☐ **hypothetical** [hàɪpəθétɪkəl]	▶ suppositional, theoretical, assumed 形 仮説的な、憶測に基づく 名 hypothesis（仮説）
10 ☐☐ **inhospitable** [ìnhɑ(:)spítəbl]	▶ uninhabitable, unwelcoming, harsh, bleak 形 生存に適さない ⇔ hospitable（快適な）
11 ☐☐ **ocean floor**	▶ seabed, seafloor 海底

12 ☐☐ **build up 〜**	▶ accumulate, increase, add up, bulk up 〜を蓄積する
13 ☐☐ **abate** [əbéɪt]	▶ dwindle, wane, diminish, subside, ease off **動** 減少する，弱まる，和らぐ
14 ☐☐ **inevitably** [ɪnévətəbli]	▶ inescapably, perforce **副** 必ず，不可避的に **形** inevitable（避けられない）
15 ☐☐ **ultimately** [ʌ́ltɪmətli]	▶ eventually, in the end, finally **副** 最終的に
16 ☐☐ **add up to 〜**	▶ amount to, lead to, result in 〜という結果になる
17 ☐☐ **tipping point**	（蓄積が一気に大きな影響力を持つようになる） 分岐点，結果が定まる瞬間
18 ☐☐ **impending** [ɪmpéndɪŋ]	▶ imminent, approaching, urgent, pressing **形** 差し迫った，まさに起ころうとしている
19 ☐☐ **spell** [spel]	▶ cause, mean, lead to **動** （災いなど）をもたらす，を招く
20 ☐☐ **unprecedented** [ʌnprésədenֺtɪd]	▶ unexampled, unheard-of, unparalleled **形** 前例のない **⇔** precedented（前例のある）

自然・環境

9

How Fresh Water Fortifies Hurricanes

Research has revealed that when tropical storms pass over fresh water, they can become stronger as fresh water tends to be warmer.

1 Hurricanes, typhoons, and other tropical storms are known to gather strength over warm water, converting the heat into wind motion. Fortunately, the winds of strong storms stir the warm surface of the oceans with colder waters from the depths, **¹bringing about** a drop in
5 temperatures and causing storms to deteriorate.

This natural **²propensity**, though, is impeded when fresh water is introduced to ocean surfaces by river mouths or intense rainfall. Since fresh water is less dense than salt water, it sits on the surface. An **³analogy** would be oil sitting on the surface of water. This **⁴inherent** effect of fresh
10 water on ocean water creates a "barrier level" that **⁵inhibits** the mixing action of waves, thereby keeping ocean surfaces warmer and generating stronger storms.

Karthik Balaguru of Pacific Northwest National Laboratory undertook an analysis of 587 tropical storms in three different oceans, and
15 discovered that storms located over barrier levels cooled down 36 percent less than storms in other areas. Though only 10 to 23 percent of tropical storms cross barrier levels, the **⁶implications** are staggering. Balaguru said that studies show that hurricanes can quickly **⁷augment** as they go over oceans covered by fresh water. He **⁸surmises** that storms intensify by
20 up to 50 percent over river **⁹outlets** and in areas of heavy rainfall, making them more devastating. Balaguru hopes that regions **¹⁰prone to** having barrier levels can be monitored for **¹¹salinity** in order to **¹²keep track of** how hurricanes might behave.　　　🇬🇧 (242 words)

淡水がいかにしてハリケーンを強化するか

研究により，熱帯暴風雨が淡水の上を通るとき，淡水の方がより温かい傾向があるため，（暴風が）強化されることが明らかになった。

　ハリケーンや台風，その他の熱帯暴風雨は温かい水の上で勢力を増し，熱を風の運動に換えることがわかっている。幸い，勢力の強い嵐の風が温かい海面を深海の冷たい水とかき混ぜて温度の低下[1]を引き起こし，嵐の勢力は弱まる。

　しかし，河口から，または集中豪雨によって淡水が海面にもたらされると，この自然界に備わっている[2]性質は妨げられる。淡水は海水よりも密度が低いので，海面の上にとどまる。油が水面に浮くのと[3]似た現象である。この淡水が海水の上にとどまるという[4]固有の現象は波によるかき混ぜ作用[5]を抑制する「境界面」を生み，その結果，海面は温かいままに保たれ，より勢力の強い嵐を引き起こす。

　パシフィック・ノースウェスト国立研究所のカーティク・バラグルは3つの異なる海洋で起きた587の熱帯暴風雨について分析を行い，温度の低下は境界面上の嵐の方がそれ以外の場所の嵐よりも36%少ないことを発見した。境界面上を通過する熱帯暴風雨は全体の10%から23%にすぎないが，そこから[6]予想されることは驚くべきものである。研究によって，淡水に覆われた海上を通過するハリケーンはその勢力が急激に[7]増す可能性があることがわかっているとバラグルは述べている。彼は[9]河口の上空や大雨の地域では，嵐はその勢力を最大で50%増し，より破壊的なものとなる[8]と推測している。ハリケーンの勢力がどのようになるか[12]を追跡するために，境界面[10]の影響を受けやすい海域の[11]塩分濃度を観測することをバラグルは望んでいる。

熱帯性低気圧

暴風を伴う熱帯性低気圧は発生地域によって呼び名が異なる。hurricane は大西洋北部や太平洋北東部などで発生するもの。cyclone はインド洋と太平洋南部で発生するもの。typhoon は太平洋北西部や南シナ海で発生するもの。

How Fresh Water Fortifies Hurricanes

1 ☐☐ **bring about ～**	▶ set off, touch off, cause ～を引き起こす, ～をもたらす
2 ☐☐ **propensity** [prəpénsəti]	▶ tendency, inclination, proclivity **名**(好ましくない)性質, 傾向
3 ☐☐ **analogy** [ənǽlədʒi]	▶ similitude, resemblance, parallel **名** 類似したもの[現象] **形** analogous(類似の)
4 ☐☐ **inherent** [ɪnhíərənt]	▶ intrinsic, innate, immanent **形** 本来の, もともと持っている **名** inherence(固有, 本来性)
5 ☐☐ **inhibit** [ɪnhíbət]	▶ hinder, hold back, hamper, impede, deter **動** を抑制する, を抑止する **名** inhibition
6 ☐☐ **implication** [ìmplɪkéɪʃən]	▶ consequence, ramifications, repercussions **名**(通例 -s)予想される結果[影響]
7 ☐☐ **augment** [ɔːgmént]	▶ strengthen, reinforce, intensify **動** 増大する, を増加させる
8 ☐☐ **surmise** [sərmáɪz]	▶ guess, assume, conjecture, presume **動** を推測する, だと考える **名** 憶測
9 ☐☐ **outlet** [áʊtlèt] ❶	▶ mouth, estuary **名** 河口
10 ☐☐ **be prone to ～**	▶ be susceptible to, be vulnerable to, be liable to ～の影響を受けやすい
11 ☐☐ **salinity** [səlínəti]	**名** 塩分(濃度) **形** saline(塩の, 塩を含む)

12 ☐☐ **keep track of ～**	▶ chronicle, record ～の経過を追跡する，～を記録する
☐☐ **low atmospheric pressure**	▶ depression, cyclone 低気圧 ⮂ high atmospheric pressure, anticyclone
☐☐ **front** [frʌnt] ❶	名（気象の）前線 ● a warm [cold] front（温暖［寒冷］前線）
☐☐ **tornado** [tɔːrnéɪdou] ❶	▶ whirlwind, windstorm, twister 名 竜巻
☐☐ **landslide** [lǽndslàɪd]	▶ landslip, mudslide 名 土砂崩れ
☐☐ **oceanography** [òuʃəná(ː)grəfi]	名 海洋学 名 oceanographer（海洋学者） 形 oceanographic(al)
☐☐ **brackish water**	汽水

自然・環境

10

265

How a Book Saved the Bald Eagle

Rachel Carson's famous book *Silent Spring* raised public awareness of the dangers of agricultural chemicals and helped save America's bald eagles.

1　Rachel Carson's *Silent Spring*, first published in 1962, turned out to be a major [1]**breakthrough** in the environmental movement. Carson [2]**spelled out** how the contamination caused by the [3]**synthetic** [4]**insecticide** DDT was wreaking havoc on bird populations throughout the US. If nothing 5 had been done to [5]**curb** the [6]**widespread** use of DDT and other pesticides, all bird species would have been [7]**imperiled**. In the book, she asked us to [8]**mull over** a world without birdsong. At the time of the book's publication, fewer than 500 [9]**nesting pairs** of bald eagles remained in the US. The bald eagle, symbol of America, was [10]**on the brink of** 10 [11]**extinction**.

Many Americans [12]**were taken aback** by Carson's claims. Thanks partly to her book, a series of environmental protection laws were [13]**hammered out** in the American Congress, including the banning of DDT in 1972. Many environmentalists were [14]**skeptical** that the laws 15 would do enough or that they would be sufficiently [15]**enforced**. They knew that the pesticide had already been widely [16]**dispersed** and that birds would continue to face exposure to it. However, the banning of DDT and the [17]**implementation** of other programs to save birds, such as a pioneering program to breed [18]**endangered** captive birds and later release 20 them into the wild, had positive outcomes. As of 2019, there were more than 70,000 breeding pairs of bald eagles in the lower 48 states of the US. Rachel Carson and other environmentalists have worked hard to ensure that springs remain anything but silent.

(248 words)

ℓ.3　DDT：dichlorodiphenyltrichloroethane（ジクロロジフェニルトリクロロエタン）の略。かつて殺虫剤として使われていた。

ℓ.23　springs remain ...：つまり「必ず鳥の声が聞けるようになる」ことを意味している。

1冊の本がハクトウワシをどのように救ったか

レイチェル・カーソンの有名な著書『沈黙の春』は，農薬の危険性に対する人々の意識を高め，アメリカのハクトウワシを救うのに役立った。

　1962年に最初に出版されたレイチェル・カーソンの『沈黙の春』は，環境保護運動を大きく[1]進展させるものとなった。カーソンは[3]合成[4]殺虫剤DDTによる汚染が合衆国全土の鳥の個体数にいかに甚大な被害を与えているか[2]をはっきり述べた。もし[6]広範に使用されているDDTやその他の殺虫剤の使用[5]を制限するために何もなされていなかったら，鳥の種はみな[7]危険にさらされていただろう。その著書の中で，彼女は私たちに鳥のさえずる声がしない世界[8]について考えるように求めた。出版当時，合衆国にはハクトウワシの[9]つがいは500も残っていなかった。合衆国の象徴であるハクトウワシは[11]絶滅[10]の危機に瀕していたのだ。

　多くのアメリカ人はカーソンの主張に[12]驚いた。彼女の著書のおかげもあって，1972年のDDTの使用禁止を含む一連の環境保護法がアメリカ連邦議会で[13]徹底的に検討された末に成立した。多くの環境保護論者はそういった法律が十分に機能するか，あるいは十分に[15]施行されるかについて[14]懐疑的だった。彼らは，殺虫剤はすでに広く[16]散布されており，鳥たちはそれにさらされ続けることをわかっていた。しかしDDTの使用を禁止し，鳥を救うためのその他のプログラム（例えば[18]絶滅が危惧される鳥を飼育下で繁殖させ，後に自然に放すという先駆的なプログラムなど）を[17]実施したことは良い結果をもたらした。2019年現在，アラスカとハワイを除く米国本土48州には70,000組以上のハクトウワシのつがいがいた。レイチェル・カーソンをはじめとする環境保護論者たちは，春が決して沈黙したままにならないよう努力を続けてきた。

How a Book Saved the Bald Eagle

1 ☐☐
breakthrough
[bréɪkθrùː]

▶ advance, development, improvement, progress
名 進展，（問題の）打開

---

2 ☐☐
spell out 〜

▶ elucidate, clarify, make clear, explain
〜をはっきり述べる

---

3 ☐☐
synthetic
[sɪnθétɪk] ⚠

▶ artificial, man-made, manufactured
形 合成の，人工の

---

4 ☐☐
insecticide
[ɪnséktɪsàɪd]

▶ larvicide, pesticide
名 殺虫剤
● insect（虫）+-(i)cide（殺すもの）

---

5 ☐☐
curb
[kəːrb]

▶ restrain, hold back, repress, check, subdue
動 を抑制する

---

6 ☐☐
widespread
[wáɪdsprèd]

▶ extensive, common, rampant, prevalent, pervasive
形 広範な，普及した

---

7 ☐☐
imperil
[ɪmpérəl]

▶ endanger, jeopardize, threaten
動 を危険にさらす，を危うくする

---

8 ☐☐
mull over 〜

▶ ponder, meditate on, contemplate, ruminate on
〜をじっくり考える

---

9 ☐☐
nesting pair

▶ mates, brace
（鳥などの）つがい

---

10 ☐☐
on the brink of 〜

▶ on the verge of, on the threshold of
〜に瀕して，〜の瀬戸際で

---

11 ☐☐
extinction
[ɪkstíŋkʃən]

▶ extermination, eradication, elimination
名 絶滅，死滅
形 extinct（絶滅した）

12 ☐☐ **be taken aback**	▶ be staggered, be stunned, be astounded びっくりする，驚きのあまり呆然とする ● be taken back とも言う
13 ☐☐ **hammer out ～**	▶ agree on, thrash out, decide on, work out ～の合意に達する，～を苦労の末に生み出す
14 ☐☐ **skeptical** [sképtɪkəl]	▶ doubtful, distrustful, incredulous 形 懐疑的な 名 skepticism（懐疑（論）），skeptic（疑い深い人）
15 ☐☐ **enforce** [ɪnfɔ́ːrs]	▶ implement, execute, impose, administer 動 （法律など）を施行する，を執行する
16 ☐☐ **disperse** [dɪspə́ːrs]	▶ scatter, disseminate 動 を分散させる，を広める 名 dispersion（散乱，散布）
17 ☐☐ **implementation** [ìmplɪmentéɪʃən]	▶ enforcement, execution, operation 名 （戦略・計画などの）実行，（契約などの）履行 動 implement
18 ☐☐ **endangered** [ɪndéɪndʒərd]	▶ threatened, imperiled, jeopardized 形 絶滅の危機に瀕した 動 endanger（を危険にさらす）
☐☐ **environmentalism** [ɪnvàɪərənméntəlìzm]	▶ conservationism, preservationism 名 環境保護（主義［政策，活動］）
☐☐ **fungicide** [fʌ́ŋɡɪsàɪd]	名 かび取り剤，殺菌剤
☐☐ **blight** [blaɪt]	名 （植物の）胴枯れ病

Nutrition Information Overload

When supporting people's efforts to lose weight, helping them deal with their emotional needs and weaknesses may be more effective than providing calorie information.

Nutritionists have long assumed that education is ¹**crucial** to getting people to improve their diets. That is why many cities around the world now make it ²**mandatory** for restaurants to provide information on their menus about the ³**nutritional value** of their food offerings, including calorie counts. However, researchers were ⁴**baffled** to discover that large-scale public ⁵**interventions** seemed to have little effect when it came to people's dietary choices. Surveys showed that only about one in seven people even bothered to notice the nutritional information on menus, and even those that did notice ⁶**were apt to** choose high-calorie selections. While nutritionists have not ⁷**ruled out** education as a key tool, they realize that making healthful food choices can be ⁸**daunting** for many people, who are so overwhelmed with the ⁹**overload** of information that they ¹⁰**tune** it **out**.

A number of obstacles block people from making healthy choices. The first is people's ¹¹**perspective** on ¹²**payoffs**. While most would ¹³**profess** interest in improving their nutritional ¹⁴**intake**, their choices often ¹⁵**contradict** their good intentions, because food offers an immediate payoff when they feel stressed, depressed, or bored. In addition, many people have negative self-images and ¹⁶**are resigned to** being fat or unhealthy. Knowledge is helpful ¹⁷**to an extent**, but it is easy to underestimate the amount of effort required to make major lifestyle changes. We often ¹⁸**undermine** our own efforts. That is why, before attempting challenging lifestyle changes, we should first ¹⁹**address** our emotional needs and weaknesses.

(243 words)

栄養成分表が過重負担に

体重を減らす努力をサポートする際，感情面のニーズや弱さに対処するのを助ける方がカロリー情報を与えるよりも効果的かもしれない。

　栄養学者は長い間，食生活を改善させるには人々に知識を与えることが [1]極めて重要であると考えてきた。そのため，今日世界の多くの都市で飲食店が提供する料理のカロリー摂取量を含む，[3]栄養価の情報をメニューに表示することが [2]義務となっている。しかし研究者たちは，食べ物の選択に関して言えば，その大規模な公的 [5]介入にほとんど効果はないらしいことを発見し，[4]困惑した。複数の調査によれば，メニューに載っている栄養成分にわざわざ注目しようという人はおよそ 7 人に 1 人にすぎず，注目した人たちですら高カロリーのものを選ぶ [6]傾向があった。栄養学者は知識を与えることが重要な手段であるということ [7]を排除してはいないが，健康に良い食べ物を選ぶことは多くの人にとって [8]難しいということを理解している。人々はあまりの情報 [9]過多に圧倒されてしまい，それ [10]から目を背けてしまうのだ。

　人々が健康に良い選択をするのを妨げる多くの障害がある。まずは人々の [12]見返りに対する [11]見方である。たいていの人が栄養 [14]摂取の改善に関心がある [13]と公言するものの，彼らの選択はしばしばその立派な心構え [15]に矛盾する。なぜならストレスを抱えていたり，気が滅入っていたり，うんざりしていたりするときに，食べ物はすぐさま見返りを提供してくれるからである。その上，多くの人が否定的な自己イメージを持っており，肥満や不健康でいること [16]を甘受している。知識は [17]ある程度は有益だが，生活スタイルを大きく変えるために必要な努力の量は軽視されやすい。私たちは自分の努力 [18]を台なしにすることが多い。だから，骨の折れるような生活スタイルの変更を試みる前に，まず感情的な欲求と弱点 [19]に注意を向けるべきなのである。

カロリー計算

「（カロリー計算によって得られる）カロリー摂取量」は英語では普通 calorie counts と言う。「（ダイエットのために）カロリーを計算する」は count calories，「カロリーを燃焼する」は burn off calories と言う。

Nutrition Information Overload

1 ☐☐ **crucial** [krúːʃəl]	▶ vital, essential 形 極めて重要な ● be crucial to [for] 〜（〜に極めて重要である）
2 ☐☐ **mandatory** [mǽndətɔ̀ːri]	▶ obligatory, compulsory, imperative 形 義務的な，必須の 名 mandate（権限，委任）
3 ☐☐ **nutritional value**	▶ food value 栄養価，栄養的価値
4 ☐☐ **baffle** [bǽfl]	▶ confuse, perplex, bewilder, confound 動 を困惑させる，を途方に暮れさせる 名 bafflement 形 baffling
5 ☐☐ **intervention** [ìntərvénʃən]	▶ interference 名 介入，干渉 動 intervene（干渉する，介入する）
6 ☐☐ **be apt to *do***	▶ be inclined to *do*, be prone to *do*, be likely to *do*, be liable to *do* 〜する傾向がある，〜しがちである
7 ☐☐ **rule out 〜**	▶ dismiss, exclude, eliminate, preclude （可能性など）を排除する，〜を除外する
8 ☐☐ **daunting** [dɔ́ːntɪŋ]	▶ deterring, discouraging, intimidating 形 （課題などが）困難な，ひるませる 動 daunt
9 ☐☐ **overload** [óuvərlòud]	▶ superfluity, excess, overabundance, glut 名 詰め込みすぎ，過重
10 ☐☐ **tune out 〜**	〜から目を背ける，〜を無視する ●「視聴していたチャンネルから他に移る」というのがもともとの意味
11 ☐☐ **perspective** [pərspéktɪv]	▶ view(point), standpoint, position 名 見方，観点，見地

12 ☐☐ **payoff** [péɪɔ̀(ː)f]	▶ reward, recompense, compensation 名 報い，報酬 ● pay off は「成果が上がる，利益を生む」
13 ☐☐ **profess** [prəfés] ❶	▶ declare, proclaim, assert 動 を公言する，を明言する ● pro-（公に）＋fess（言う）
14 ☐☐ **intake** [íntèɪk]	▶ consumption, ingestion, uptake, inhalation 名（飲食物・栄養などの）摂取（量），（空気などの）吸入（量）
15 ☐☐ **contradict** [kà(ː)ntrədíkt]	▶ conflict with, disagree with 動 に矛盾する，に反論する 名 contradiction 形 contradictory
16 ☐☐ **be resigned to** *doing*	▶ be reconciled to *doing*, reconcile *oneself* to *doing* 甘んじて～する，あきらめて～する
17 ☐☐ **to an extent**	▶ somewhat, partly ある程度 ● to some [a certain] extent とも言う
18 ☐☐ **undermine** [ʌ̀ndərmáɪn]	▶ spoil, weaken, mar 動 をだめにする，を阻害する ● undermine his credibility（彼の信用を傷つける）
19 ☐☐ **address** [ədrés]	▶ attend to, tackle, deal with 動 に注意を向ける，（問題など）に取り組む
☐☐ **obesity** [oʊbíːsəti]	▶ corpulence, overweight, fatness 名 肥満 形 obese（肥満体の）
☐☐ **malnutrition** [mæ̀lnjutríʃən]	▶ undernourishment, malnourishment 名 栄養失調 ⇔ overnutrition（栄養過多）

Maine's Lobster Surplus

During the mid-2010s, there was a lobster surplus in Maine, affecting fishermen's livelihoods with lower prices for their catch and increased license fees.

1   Maine has always been renowned for its lobsters, but it has never experienced anything like the ¹**surge** in the number ²**hauled in** during the mid-2010s. The excess of ³**crustaceans** sent prices ⁴**tumbling**. Seafood restaurants and other businesses ⁵**were swamped with** lobsters and
5   promoted them like never before to get rid of excess stock. Some businesses even resorted to ⁶**gimmicks** to move lobsters: a massage parlor and a tire shop, for example, offered a free lobster with every purchase.

Businesses were not alone. The governor of Maine kicked off a promotional campaign by proclaiming August as "Maine Lobster Month."
10   A television advertisement ⁷**beseeched** the state's citizens to support local fishermen by eating more lobster. A team of fishermen that ⁸**sat on** the Maine Lobster Advisory Council ⁹**unanimously** gave their ¹⁰**endorsement** for a $3 million national marketing effort designed to encourage consumption.

15   The ¹¹**proliferation** of the crustaceans may have benefitted lobster lovers, but it had its ¹²**drawbacks** for the fishermen. They saw their earnings ¹³**taper off**. Some no longer found it ¹⁴**viable** to continue working. With the ¹⁵**glut** ¹⁶**nibbling away at** their incomes, fishermen ¹⁷**balked at** the state legislature's proposal to increase fishing license fees
20   to pay for additional lobster promotion costs, but eventually ended up losing the fight. In recent years, Maine's efforts to promote lobster seem to have ¹⁸**paid off**, as demand and prices have both risen.   (227 words)

ℓ.2   the number hauled in ... : the number of lobsters hauled in ということ。

274

メイン州のロブスター，供給過剰に

2010年代半ば，メイン州ではロブスターの供給過剰が起き，漁獲に対する価格の低下や漁業権料の引き上げによって漁師の生活に影響をもたらした。

　メイン州はいつもロブスターで有名であったが，2010年代半ばのような[2]**水揚げ量**の[1]**急激な増加**はこれまでに経験したことがない。この[3]**甲殻類**の過剰な豊漁は価格の[4]**暴落**を招いた。シーフードの飲食店やその他の店にはロブスター[5]**が押し寄せ**，過剰在庫を処分するためにかつてない売り込みを行った。ロブスターをさばくための[6]**策略**に打って出る業種もあった。例えば，マッサージ店やタイヤ販売店では，利用者にもれなくロブスターを無料でプレゼントしていた。

　こういった取り組みは商業だけにとどまらなかった。メイン州の知事はロブスター販売促進キャンペーンを始めるにあたって，8月を「メイン州ロブスター月間」と宣言した。テレビ広告ではもっとロブスターを食べて地元の漁師を支援することを州民[7]**に嘆願した**。メイン州ロブスター諮問委員会[8]**の委員である**漁師たちは，消費を促すことを意図した300万ドルの全国的なマーケティング活動を[9]**満場一致で**[10]**支持**した。

　この甲殻類の[11]**豊漁**はロブスター好きに利益を与えたかもしれないが，漁師たちには[12]**不利益**をもたらした。彼らは収入が[13]**先細りになる**のを目の当たりにしたのだ。中には仕事を続けることはもはや不[14]**可能**だと考えた人もいた。[15]**供給過剰**が漁師の収入[16]**を少しずつ減らしている**中，彼らは追加のロブスター販売促進費用を賄うために漁業権料を引き上げるという州議会の提案への同意[17]**をしぶった**が，結局は戦いに敗れた。近年では，ロブスターの販売を促進するメイン州の取り組みは[18]**実を結んだ**ようで，需要と価格の両方が上昇した。

Maine's Lobster Surplus

1 ☐☐ **surge** [sə:rdʒ]	▶ upswing, leap, rise, increase **名** 高まり，急増 〈in ～の〉 **動** 高まる，急増する
2 ☐☐ **haul in ～**	▶ pull in ～を引き入れる，～をたぐり込む
3 ☐☐ **crustacean** [krʌstéɪʃən]	▶ shellfish **名** 甲殻類（の動物）　**形** 甲殻類の ● crust（甲殻）
4 ☐☐ **tumble** [tʌ́mbl] ❶	▶ plummet, plunge, nosedive **動**（価格などが）急落する，暴落する ● send prices tumbling（価格を急落させる）
5 ☐☐ **be swamped with ～**	▶ be inundated with, be overwhelmed with ～を手に負えないくらい与えられる，～で忙殺 されている
6 ☐☐ **gimmick** [gímɪk]	▶ trick, ploy, artifice **名** 策略，（注意を引きつける）巧妙な仕掛け
7 ☐☐ **beseech** [bɪsíːtʃ]	▶ implore, supplicate, entreat, beg **動** に嘆願する，に懇願する 〈to do ～するように〉
8 ☐☐ **sit on ～**	▶ serve on, be a member of （委員会など）の一員である
9 ☐☐ **unanimously** [junǽnɪməsli]	▶ solidly **副** 満場一致で
10 ☐☐ **endorsement** [ɪndɔ́ːrsmənt]	▶ backing, patronage, support, sanction, approval **名** 支持，是認 **動** endorse
11 ☐☐ **proliferation** [prəlìfəréɪʃən]	▶ leap, mushrooming, run-up **名** 急増，激増 **動** proliferate（急増する）

12 ☐☐ **drawback** [dróːbæk]	▶ disadvantage, flaw, downside, imperfection, defect **名** 不利な点，短所
13 ☐☐ **taper off**	▶ dwindle, shrink, wane, peter out, slacken off 先細りになる，漸減する
14 ☐☐ **viable** [váɪəbl]	▶ doable, workable, practicable, feasible **形** 実行可能な，実現性のある **名** viability
15 ☐☐ **glut** [ɡlʌt]	▶ surplus, excess, surfeit, overabundance **名** （商品の）供給過剰，過多 **⇔** shortage, dearth（不足）
16 ☐☐ **nibble away at ～**	▶ dwindle, diminish, taper off ～を少しずつ減らす ● nibble は「（ネズミなどが）かじる」の意味
17 ☐☐ **balk at ～**	▶ recoil from, hesitate about, flinch from ～をしぶる，～に尻込みする ● 特に英では baulk とも綴る
18 ☐☐ **pay off**	▶ be successful, provide a return, be profitable 成果が上がる，利益を生む
☐☐ **crawfish** [króːfiʃ]	▶ crayfish, spiny lobster **名** イセエビ，ザリガニ
☐☐ **fishery** [fíʃəri]	▶ fishing (industry) **名** 漁業，水産業

自然・環境 **14**

A Sheep Survival Strategy

A recent experiment has supported the "selfish herd" theory, which says that sheep will selfishly try to move to the center of their flock when danger approaches.

1   Sheep have a reputation for blindly following each other, regardless of the situation. Now, researchers are finding out that their [1]**flocking** tendencies are far from [2]**outrageous** and [3]**haphazard**. Instead, their movements are as [4]**coherent** as they are deliberate. When approached by
5   predators, sheep will [5]**scurry** towards the center of their flock, [6]**maneuvering** for [7]**optimum** safety at the expense of those left at the periphery, who are exposed to the predators.

This "selfish [8]**herd**" theory was first [9]**postulated** in 1973 by W. D. Hamilton, a British evolutionary biologist. The theory was recently
10   verified thanks to an ingenious experiment undertaken by researchers at the University of London and the University of Cambridge, which entailed attaching GPS [10]**tracking devices** to 46 sheep and a sheepdog. Researchers reasoned the sheepdog would elicit a flocking response similar to that of a predator. When the sheepdog approached, the sheep
15   went into a [11]**swirling** [12]**frenzy**. Detailed analyses of their movements showed that, instead of a [13]**disorderly** [14]**flight**, the sheep were [15]**adhering to** a proven survival strategy.

Andrew King of the University of London Royal [16]**Veterinary** College [17]**asserted** that the findings have broad implications. He thinks
20   that understanding how these rules work can [18]**hint at** similar systems and common principles across species.   (204 words)

羊の生き残り戦略

最近の実験が「利己的な群れ」理論を支持した。その理論は，羊は危険が迫ったとき利己的に群れの中心へ移動しようとすることを述べている。

どんな状況であっても，羊はやみくもにお互いの後をついていくものと言われている。今，研究者たちは羊の ¹群れをなす傾向は決して ²理不尽でも ³場当たり的でもないことを解明しつつある。それどころか，羊たちの動きは，意図的であると同時に，⁴筋が通っている。捕食動物が近づくと，羊は群れの中心に向かって ⁵慌てて走り，周縁に取り残されて捕食動物にさらされる仲間を犠牲にして ⁷最適の安全を得ようと ⁶画策する。

この「利己的な ⁸群れ」理論は 1973 年にイギリス人進化生物学者，W・D・ハミルトンが初めて ⁹仮説を立てた。近年，ロンドン大学とケンブリッジ大学の研究者たちが行った巧妙な実験のおかげで，その仮説は実証された。その実験では 46 頭の羊と 1 匹の牧羊犬に GPS ¹⁰追跡装置を取り付けた。研究者たちは捕食動物が引き出すのと似たような群れの反応を牧羊犬が引き出すだろうと推論した。牧羊犬が近づくと，羊たちは ¹¹ぐるぐる回り ¹²狂乱状態になった。羊の動きを詳しく分析した結果，羊は ¹³無秩序に ¹⁴逃走しているのではなく，立証済みの生き残り戦略 ¹⁵に従っていることがわかった。

ロンドン大学王立 ¹⁶獣医学校のアンドリュー・キングは，この発見には幅広い影響力がある ¹⁷と断言した。このような法則がどう働くかを理解できれば，種の枠を越えて類似の体系と共通の原則 ¹⁸を示唆することができるとキングは考える。

A Sheep Survival Strategy

1 ☐☐ **flock** [flɑ(:)k]	▶ gather, congregate, huddle 動 群がる，集まる 名 （羊・鳥などの）群れ
2 ☐☐ **outrageous** [aʊtréɪdʒəs] ❶	▶ irrational, unreasonable 形 途方もない，無法な
3 ☐☐ **haphazard** [hæphǽzərd]	▶ arbitrary, random, disorganized 形 でたらめな 副 haphazardly
4 ☐☐ **coherent** [koʊhíərənt]	▶ consistent, reasonable, legitimate 形 筋の通った，首尾一貫した 名 coherence（一貫性）
5 ☐☐ **scurry** [skə́:ri]	▶ hurry, dash, scuttle 動 慌てて走る，急ぐ
6 ☐☐ **maneuver** [mənú:vər] ❶	▶ contrive, scheme, intrigue 動 作戦的に行動する 名 策略
7 ☐☐ **optimum** [á(:)ptɪməm]	▶ best, optimal, most favorable 形 （ある条件下で）最適な，最高の 名 最適条件
8 ☐☐ **herd** [hə:rd] ❶	▶ flock, pack, swarm 名 （動物の）群れ 動 群れをなす
9 ☐☐ **postulate** [pá(:)stʃəlèɪt]	▶ assume, presuppose, hypothesize 動 を仮定する 名 postulation
10 ☐☐ **tracking device**	▶ tracking system 追跡装置
11 ☐☐ **swirl** [swə:rl] ❶	▶ whirl, twirl 動 ぐるぐる回る，渦巻く 名 渦巻き

12 ☐☐ **frenzy** [frénzi]	▶ delirium, lunacy, turmoil **名** 狂乱，取り乱した状態
13 ☐☐ **disorderly** [dɪsɔ́ːrdərli]	▶ chaotic, confused, disorganized **形** 無秩序の，混乱した **名** disorder
14 ☐☐ **flight** [flaɪt]	▶ getaway **名** 逃走，逃亡 **動** flee
15 ☐☐ **adhere to ～**	▶ follow, observe, abide by, stand by （規則など）を（頑なに）守る，～に従う ● 動詞 adhere は「くっつく」という意味
16 ☐☐ **veterinary** [vétərənèri]	**形** 獣医の
17 ☐☐ **assert** [əsə́ːrt]	▶ affirm, contend, profess **動** を断言する **形** assertive（積極的な，独断的な）
18 ☐☐ **hint at ～**	▶ imply, infer, allude to ～をほのめかす
☐☐ **discreet** [dɪskríːt]	▶ prudent, cautious, circumspect, wary **形** 配慮のある，慎重な **名** discretion
☐☐ **scapegoat** [skéɪpgòut]	▶ victim, substitute **名** 身代わり，他人の罪を負う者，スケープゴート ● make a scapegoat of ～（～を身代わりにする）

自然・環境

14

Baring the Truth about Bear Intelligence

Though often regarded as lacking intelligence, bears seem to possess important intellectual abilities, such as being able to count.

1   People often imagine bears as the big, clumsy brutes of the animal kingdom, but they are actually much more intelligent than people ¹**give** them **credit for**. Though their brains are not as large as those of primates, they are the biggest among all ²**carnivores**. Some studies provide
5   evidence that they can ³**put** those brains **to work** to undertake surprisingly complex tasks. A psychological study suggests that bears may show abilities similar to those of humans, despite being previously ⁴**disregarded** by ⁵**cognitive scientists**.

During the experiment, three bears at a zoo were allowed to approach
10   a touch-screen computer. They were encouraged to touch images, and were given a ⁶**morsel** of food if they accomplished the task correctly. The bears were able to discern the number of dots on images, even when the dots were moving about in a ⁷**follow-up** experiment. This provided evidence that bears can count. The bears excelled, even though the tests
15   ⁸**entailed** performing tasks that relied on visual ⁹**acuity**, not seen as a bear's ¹⁰**forte**. They have other skills at their disposal, such as strength, speed, and smell. Their sense of smell, for example, is a thousand times greater than a human's.

As to how bears came to be so smart, researchers deduced that they
20   are ¹¹**inveterate** ¹²**scroungers** that must use ¹³**ingenuity** to ¹⁴**get through** winters or times of environmental stress when food is ¹⁵**scarce**.

▧ (227 words)

タイトル　Baring：bear とかけて同音の bare（を明らかにする）を用いている。

熊の知性の真実をくまなく明かす

熊はしばしば知能が低いと見なされるが, 数を数えられるなど重要な知的能力を持っているようだ。

　人々はよく熊を動物界の大きく不器用な獣だと考えるが, 実際は人々が [1]思っているよりずっと知能が高い。熊の脳は霊長類の脳ほど大きくはないが, すべての [2]肉食動物の中では最も大きい。いくつかの研究は, 熊は脳 [3]を働かせ, 驚くほど複雑な課題をやってのけることができるという証拠を示している。ある心理学研究は, 以前は [5]認知科学者たちに [4]無視されていたが, 熊が人間と似たような能力を示す可能性を示唆する。

　その実験中, ある動物園の 3 頭の熊はタッチスクリーンのコンピュータに近づくことを許された。その熊たちは, 画像にさわるよう促され, その課題を正しく成し遂げることができれば食べ物を [6]ひと口与えられた。熊たちは画像上の点の数を識別することができ, [7]続いて行われた実験で点が動き回っているときにも識別することができた。これは熊が数を数えることができるという証拠になった。このテストは熊の [10]得意分野とは考えられていない視覚的 [9]鋭敏さに頼る課題を成し遂げること [8]を含んでいたにもかかわらず, 熊たちは卓越していた。彼らは, 体力, 素早さ, 嗅覚など他の技能も自由に使うことができる。例えば, 熊の嗅覚は人間の嗅覚より千倍も優れている。

　熊がいかにしてこれほど賢くなったのかについて, 研究者たちは, 熊は [11]常習的に [12]食べ物を探し回る動物であり, 食べ物が [15]不足する冬や環境ストレスの時期 [14]を乗り切るために [13]知恵を働かさなければならないからだと推測した。

Baring the Truth about Bear Intelligence

1 ☐☐ **give _A_ credit for _B_**	A を B であると思う
2 ☐☐ **carnivore** [kɑ́:rnəvɔ̀:r]	▶ predator 名 肉食動物　形 carnivorous ● herbivore（草食動物）, omnivore（雑食動物）
3 ☐☐ **put ～ to work**	▶ exercise, exert ～を働かせる
4 ☐☐ **disregard** [dìsrɪgɑ́:rd]	▶ ignore, neglect, depreciate 動 を無視する, を軽視する
5 ☐☐ **cognitive scientist**	認知科学者
6 ☐☐ **morsel** [mɔ́:rsəl]	▶ mouthful, bite, nibble 名 ひと口（分）〈of 食べ物の〉
7 ☐☐ **follow-up** [fɑ́(:)loʊʌp]	▶ continuing 形（調査が）追跡の, 引き続いての 名 追跡調査
8 ☐☐ **entail** [ɪntéɪl]	▶ involve, necessitate 動 を含む, を伴う
9 ☐☐ **acuity** [əkjúːəti]	▶ acuteness 名（感覚の）鋭さ, 鋭敏さ 形 acute
10 ☐☐ **forte** [fɔːrt]	▶ advantage, strong point, long suit 名 得意なこと
11 ☐☐ **inveterate** [ɪnvétərət]	▶ chronic, habitual, confirmed 形 常習的な, 慢性の

12 ☐☐ **scrounger** [skráʊndʒər]	▶ seeker, gatherer **名** 探し回る人［動物］ **動** scrounge
13 ☐☐ **ingenuity** [ìndʒənjúːəti] ❶	▶ creativity, inventiveness **名** 工夫，創意 **形** ingenious（創意工夫に富む，利口な）
14 ☐☐ **get through ～**	▶ survive, endure, bear ～を乗り切る，～を切り抜ける
15 ☐☐ **scarce** [skeərs] ❶	▶ scanty, deficient, in short supply **形**（必要な物が）不足して，欠乏して **名** scarcity
☐☐ **hibernate** [háɪbərnèɪt]	▶ lie dormant, lie torpid **動** 冬眠する **名** hibernation
☐☐ **quadrupedal** [kwɑ̀(ː)drúːpedəl]	▶ using all four feet for walking or running **形** 四足歩行の ● quadru-（4）＋ped-（足）＋-al（形容詞語尾）

Disease Killing Animals Worldwide

The diseases caused by fungi have become an increasingly serious problem as a result of increases in global trade and human activities that help to spread them.

1 ¹**Fungi** are an integral part of ecosystems, for they transfer nitrogen and phosphorus from the soil to the roots of trees. However, certain varieties are lethal, ²**annihilating** animals and even wiping out entire species. In fact, in one study, researchers discovered fungi-caused

5 extinctions accounted for 65 percent of pathogen-related species extinctions in the last 50 years. The best-known of the lethal varieties is commonly known as chytrid, which has infected over 500 species of frogs and salamanders worldwide, pushing many to the brink of extinction.

The ³**circulation** of fungi has been a direct result of global trade in

10 plants and animals as well as human intervention in ⁴**wilderness areas**. Fungi ⁵**covertly** embed themselves in almost any life form, including those not susceptible to disease, easily hitching a ride on live ⁶**freight**. Fungi can lie ⁷**dormant** for years, waiting for the right conditions to spread and grow. One known instance of this is the fungus causing a ⁸**die-**

15 **off** of California native oak trees and the ⁹**clear-cutting** of vast areas. Before causing a ¹⁰**pandemic**, the fungus is believed to have attached itself to a rhododendron, an ¹¹**ornamental** plant imported from Asia. On arrival in California, the fungus transferred to trees and caused an ecological disaster.

20 Fungi are known to quickly evolve, increasing their chances of survival. Unfortunately, this ability has led to the creation of several ¹²**formidable** new pathogens, with fatal ¹³**repercussions**. ¹⁴**Ongoing** ¹⁵**infestations** of these new killers are certain to ¹⁶**condemn** further species **to** extinction. 　🇬🇧 (244 words)

ℓ.17　rhododendron：シャクナゲ

世界中で動物に死をもたらしている病気

菌類によって引き起こされる病気は，それらを広めるのを助ける世界的な貿易や人間活動の増加の結果，ますます深刻な問題になっている。

^{1}菌類は，窒素やリンを土壌から木の根に運ぶので，生態系には不可欠な要素である。しかし種類によっては，死をもたらし，動物^{2}を大量に殺したり種全体を全滅させたりするものさえある。事実，ある研究では，菌類が引き起こした絶滅は，過去 50 年間で病原体が関わった種の絶滅の 65％を占めることがわかった。死をもたらす種類で最も有名なのはツボカビという名で一般的に知られており，世界中で 500 を超えるカエルやサンショウウオの種に感染し，多くを絶滅の瀬戸際に追い込んでいる。

菌類の^{3}拡散は，地球規模の植物や動物の取引や，人間が^{4}自然保護区域に立ち入ることが直接の原因である。菌類はほぼどのような生命体にも^{5}密かに入り込み，中には病気にかからないものもいるが，いずれにせよ生きた^{6}貨物にたやすく便乗して移動していく。菌類は長年^{7}休眠状態でいて，蔓延し成長するためのちょうど良い条件になるのを待つことができる。有名な一例は，カリフォルニアに自生する樫の木を^{8}大量に死滅させ広大な地域の^{9}皆伐を引き起こした菌類である。^{10}世界的流行病を起こす前，その菌はアジアから^{11}観賞用植物として輸入された 1 本のシャクナゲについていたと考えられている。カリフォルニアに着くと，その菌は木々に移動し生態系に大惨事を引き起こした。

菌類は，素早く進化していくことで知られており，それにより生存の可能性を高める。残念ながらこの能力によって致命的な^{13}影響を持ついくつもの^{12}恐ろしい新病原菌が作り出された。こうした新しい殺し屋の^{15}蔓延^{14}が続くと，さらなる種の絶滅^{16}を運命づけることは間違いない。

Disease Killing Animals Worldwide

1 ☐☐
fungi
[fʌ́ŋgiː]
- ▶ fungoid
- 名 菌類
- ● fungus（菌）の複数形

2 ☐☐
annihilate
[ənáɪəlèɪt] ❶
- ▶ decimate, kill off, wipe out
- 動 を大量に殺す
- 名 annihilation

3 ☐☐
circulation
[sə̀ːrkjuléɪʃən]
- ▶ distribution, currency, spread
- 名 広がり，流通
- 動 circulate

4 ☐☐
wilderness area
- ▶ nature reserve, wildlife preserve
- 自然保護区域

5 ☐☐
covertly
[kóʊvərtli]
- ▶ secretly, stealthily, surreptitiously
- 副 密かに，こっそり
- 形 covert ⇔ overtly（明白に，公然と）

6 ☐☐
freight
[freɪt] ❶
- ▶ cargo, bulk, load
- 名 貨物，積み荷

7 ☐☐
dormant
[dɔ́ːrmənt]
- ▶ asleep, inactive
- 形 休眠［冬眠］している
- 名 dormancy

8 ☐☐
die-off
[dáɪɔ̀(ː)f]
- ▶ mass mortality, extinction, annihilation
- 名 （動植物の種の）大量死，絶滅

9 ☐☐
clear-cutting
[klìərkʌ́tɪŋ]
- ▶ clear-cut logging
- 名 皆伐，ある地域の木をすべて伐採すること

10 ☐☐
pandemic
[pændémɪk]
- ▶ epidemic, infectious [epizootic] disease
- 名 全国［世界］的流行病
- 形 （病気などが）広範囲で流行する

11 ☐☐
ornamental
[ɔ̀ːrnəmén̬əl]
- ▶ decorative
- 形 （植物が）観賞用の，装飾用の
- 名 ornament

12 ☐☐ **formidable** [fɔ́ːrmɪdəbl]	▶ daunting, burdensome 形 恐ろしい，手ごわい
13 ☐☐ **repercussion** [rìːpərkʌ́ʃən]	▶ backlash, aftermath 名 (好ましくない) 影響，反動
14 ☐☐ **ongoing** [á(ː)ngòuɪŋ]	▶ continuing, current, progressing 形 継続中の
15 ☐☐ **infestation** [ìnfestéɪʃən]	▶ invasion, proliferation, rampancy 名 蔓延，横行 動 infest ((病気などが) (場所) に蔓延する)
16 ☐☐ **condemn _A_ to _B_**	A に B を運命づける ● 通例受身形で用いる
☐☐ **prevalence** [prévələns] ❶	▶ pervasiveness, infestation, spread 名 蔓延 〈of ～の〉 形 prevalent (蔓延している)

確認テスト

1 次の日本語の意味の単語を下の❶〜⓰の中から選んで書きなさい。

（1）堂々とした，威厳のある （　：　　　　　　　　　　　）
（2）残留物 （　：　　　　　　　　　　　）
（3）（問題などが）厄介な （　：　　　　　　　　　　　）
（4）不足，乏しさ （　：　　　　　　　　　　　）
（5）を裏づける，を確証する （　：　　　　　　　　　　　）
（6）夜行性の （　：　　　　　　　　　　　）
（7）到来，流入 （　：　　　　　　　　　　　）
（8）地層 （　：　　　　　　　　　　　）
（9）最終的に （　：　　　　　　　　　　　）
（10）塩分（濃度） （　：　　　　　　　　　　　）
（11）懐疑的な （　：　　　　　　　　　　　）
（12）を困惑させる （　：　　　　　　　　　　　）
（13）満場一致で （　：　　　　　　　　　　　）
（14）を仮定する （　：　　　　　　　　　　　）
（15）を含む，を伴う （　：　　　　　　　　　　　）
（16）休眠［冬眠］している （　：　　　　　　　　　　　）

❶ unanimously	❷ residue	❸ salinity	❹ postulate
❺ thorny	❻ nocturnal	❼ majestic	❽ skeptical
❾ entail	❿ scarcity	⓫ ultimately	⓬ corroborate
⓭ baffle	⓮ dormant	⓯ stratum	⓰ influx

2 次の日本語の意味の単語を下の❶～⓬の中から選んで書きなさい。

(1) 悪化する，衰える　(　　：　　)
(2) とてもおいしそうな　(　　：　　)
(3) 威信のある，名声の高い　(　　：　　)
(4) 発生，起源　(　　：　　)
(5) を改善する　(　　：　　)
(6) 捕食者　(　　：　　)
(7) 前提，仮定　(　　：　　)
(8) 信用，信頼　(　　：　　)
(9) を公言する，を明言する　(　　：　　)
(10) 実行可能な，実現性のある　(　　：　　)
(11) 狂乱，取り乱した状態　(　　：　　)
(12) 常習的な，慢性の　(　　：　　)

❶ genesis	❷ mouthwatering	❸ credence	❹ frenzy
❺ deteriorate	❻ ameliorate	❼ viable	❽ predator
❾ inveterate	❿ prestigious	⓫ premise	⓬ profess

解答

1
(1) ❼ (→p. 228) (2) ❷ (→p. 233) (3) ❺ (→p. 237) (4) ❿ (→p. 240)
(5) ⓬ (→p. 245) (6) ❻ (→p. 248) (7) ⓰ (→p. 253) (8) ⓯ (→p. 257)
(9) ⓫ (→p. 261) (10) ❸ (→p. 264) (11) ❽ (→p. 269) (12) ⓭ (→p. 272)
(13) ❶ (→p. 276) (14) ❹ (→p. 280) (15) ❾ (→p. 284) (16) ⓮ (→p. 288)

2
(1) ❺ (→p. 229) (2) ❷ (→p. 232) (3) ❿ (→p. 236) (4) ❶ (→p. 244)
(5) ❻ (→p. 249) (6) ❽ (→p. 253) (7) ⓫ (→p. 256) (8) ❸ (→p. 260)
(9) ⓬ (→p. 273) (10) ❼ (→p. 277) (11) ❹ (→p. 281) (12) ❾ (→p. 284)

3 次の単語の意味に最も近いものをそれぞれ❶〜❹の中から1つ選びなさい。

（1）pasture
- ❶ spectrum
- ❷ outlet
- ❸ getaway
- ❹ grass

（2）prodigious
- ❶ impending
- ❷ optimum
- ❸ enormous
- ❹ unique

（3）novice
- ❶ beginner
- ❷ herd
- ❸ fungi
- ❹ yield

（4）perforate
- ❶ eradicate
- ❷ pierce
- ❸ deduce
- ❹ maneuver

（5）assimilate
- ❶ absorb
- ❷ curtail
- ❸ tumble
- ❹ commence

（6）catch on
- ❶ dominate
- ❷ poach
- ❸ undermine
- ❹ boom

（7）robust
- ❶ vigorous
- ❷ prudent
- ❸ crucial
- ❹ eminent

（8）prey on 〜
- ❶ hunt
- ❷ contend
- ❸ defy
- ❹ procure

（9）anomaly
- ❶ irregularity
- ❷ arsenic
- ❸ fracture
- ❹ landslip

（10）implicit
- ❶ renowned
- ❷ traumatic
- ❸ unexpressed
- ❹ decorative

（11）inevitably
- ❶ astoundingly
- ❷ inescapably
- ❸ substantially
- ❹ irreversibly

（12）propensity
- ❶ glut
- ❷ infestation
- ❸ burden
- ❹ tendency

(13) inherent   ❶ coherent   ❷ innate

                 ❸ bizarre   ❹ pervasive

(14) breakthrough   ❶ advance   ❷ feasibility

                 ❸ concession   ❹ balance

(15) insecticide   ❶ blight   ❷ consumption

                 ❸ larvicide   ❹ acuity

(16) payoff   ❶ tinge   ❷ distribution

                 ❸ reward   ❹ perspective

(17) beseech   ❶ implore   ❷ abate

                 ❸ substantiate   ❹ annihilate

(18) drawback   ❶ disadvantage   ❷ framework

                 ❸ sediment   ❹ gimmick

(19) scurry   ❶ incite   ❷ dash

                 ❸ fasten   ❹ stunt

(20) morsel   ❶ mouthful   ❷ analogy

                 ❸ scrounger   ❹ fallacy

(21) covertly   ❶ amazingly   ❷ unwittingly

                 ❸ secretly   ❹ inadvertently

(22) formidable   ❶ versed   ❷ daunting

                 ❸ haphazard   ❹ obligatory

自然・環境

確認テスト

解答

3　（1）❹（→p. 228）（2）❸（→p. 232）（3）❶（→p. 236）（4）❷（→p. 240）

　（5）❶（→p. 244）（6）❹（→p. 248）（7）❶（→p. 252）（8）❶（→p. 252）

　（9）❶（→p. 256）（10）❸（→p. 257）（11）❷（→p. 261）（12）❹（→p. 264）

　（13）❷（→p. 264）（14）❶（→p. 268）（15）❸（→p. 268）（16）❸（→p. 273）

　（17）❶（→p. 276）（18）❶（→p. 277）（19）❷（→p. 280）（20）❶（→p. 284）

　（21）❸（→p. 288）（22）❷（→p. 289）

教育・心理・社会

教育・心理・社会

テーマを知る

　教育・心理・社会では人の心理とその理由・行動などが扱われることが多い。心理学や社会学の実験内容とその結果が紹介された後，結果が何を示唆するのか説明されるという形式がよく見られる。一般的に良いと思われているものが実は悪い面も持つ，あるいはその逆もあるという論調も少なくない。あまりなじみのない話題が取り上げられることもあるが，前提知識を要求するようなものは多くないため，文章のスタイルに慣れておくことが対策となる。日ごろからニュースで取り上げられる社会問題に目を向け，英語で記事を読んでみてもよいだろう。

注目用語

paradigm shift パラダイムシフト

広く普及し当然と考えられていた考え方である paradigm（パラダイム）が覆されること。「教育・心理・社会」では通説を覆すパラダイムシフトを扱った英文がしばしば見られる。

methodology 方法論

科学的手法について分析や考察を行う学問が methodology（方法論）である。研究や実験にはその方法について，研究者が見落としたあるいは無視した arbitrariness（恣意性）や bias（傾向，偏見）に対する批判，それによる実験結果に対する疑問がしばしば投げかけられる。そういった批判的思考から新しい発見が生まれることもある。

キーワード・表現

教育・心理・社会

Moral Licensing

Researchers have found that sometimes when we do something good, it can make us more likely to do something we should not afterward.

1   [1]**Virtuous** acts make people feel good about themselves. However, researchers have found that the [2]**contentment** people experience from doing the right thing tends to make them feel they have acquired a free pass to behave in morally questionable ways. Researchers have found that

5   making charitable contributions, for example, can increase people's tendency to commit tax fraud.

   This phenomenon is known as moral licensing, and it can range from relatively [3]**innocuous** things like [4]**bingeing** on chocolate because you've successfully adhered to a strict exercise regimen to morally

10   [5]**objectionable** behaviors like discriminating in hiring decisions. For instance, researchers found that after research subjects completed a survey where they disagreed with [6]**blatantly** [7]**sexist** statements like "most women are not really smart," they were more likely to select male candidates in hiring decisions for [8]**stereotypically** [9]**masculine**

15   occupations.

   One implication of this research is that efforts at encouraging [10]**diversity** in [11]**corporate** environments could easily [12]**backfire**. Having made efforts to set up [13]**inclusion** [14]**initiatives** and promote diversity, a firm could find that moral licensing has caused employees to use their

20   cooperation with the initiatives as a [15]**justification** for discriminatory behavior. For instance, [16]**compulsory** attendance in diversity workshops could cause employees to do small things that make them feel like they are treating minorities well, and then [17]**engage in** behavior like [18]**passing over** minorities at promotion time.   (220 words)

モラル・ライセンシング

研究者たちは，私たちは何か良いことをすると，やってはいけない何かを後でする可能性が高くなることがあると発見した。

^{1}高潔な行いは人々を，自分について肯定的な気分にさせる。しかしながら，研究者たちは，正しいことをすることによって人が経験する^{2}満足感によって，その人が，道徳的に疑問があるような行動を自由にする許可証を得たような気分になる傾向があることを発見した。研究者たちは，例えば慈善的な寄付をすることによって，人は税金詐欺をする傾向が強まる可能性があることを発見した。

この現象は，モラル・ライセンシングとして知られていて，厳しい運動療法をうまく守れたから，チョコレートを^{4}思い切り食べるというような比較的^{3}害のないものから，雇用を決定するときに差別をするなどの道徳的に^{5}好ましくない行動に至るまで，さまざまである。例えば，研究者たちは，被験者たちが「ほとんどの女性はあまり利口ではない」というような^{6}あからさまに^{7}性差別主義的な意見に反対するような調査を終えた後には，^{8}型通りに^{9}男らしい職業に対して，男性の候補者を選ぶ傾向がより強くなるということを発見した。

この研究が暗示していることの1つは，^{11}企業環境において^{10}多様性を奨励する努力は，簡単に^{12}裏目に出る可能性があるということだ。^{13}多様性受け入れの^{14}取り組みを確立し，多様性を促進する努力をすることによって，社員がモラル・ライセンシングによって，その取り組みへの協力を差別的行動の^{15}正当化に利用していることを会社は発見するかもしれない。例えば，多様性の研修会に^{16}強制的に参加させられることによって，社員たちは自分たちが少数者たちを正しく扱っているという気分になるようなささいなことをし，その後で昇進のときに少数者^{18}を除外するというような行動^{17}に携わる可能性がある。

多様性と包摂性

diversity and inclusion（多様性と包摂性）は，SDGs（p.19参照）を達成するための鍵となる理念の1つである。多様性は，さまざまな人種・国籍・ジェンダー・宗教などの属性を持つ人々が存在すること，包摂性は，そうした多様性を尊重して認め合い，すべての人に平等な機会を与えることを言う。この理念，あるいはequity（公正さ）を加えたdiversity, equity, and inclusionという理念の実現をcorporate social responsibility（企業の社会的責任，CSR）とする企業も増えている。

Moral Licensing

1 ☐☐ **virtuous** [vɔ́:rtʃuəs] ❶	▶ honorable, noble 形 高潔な，徳のある 名 virtue ⇔ wicked（不道徳な）
2 ☐☐ **contentment** [kənténtmənt]	▶ content, satisfaction 名 満足（感） 形 content ⇔ discontent, discontentment
3 ☐☐ **innocuous** [ɪná(:)kjuəs]	▶ harmless, benign 形 無害な，当たり障りのない ⇔ harmful, detrimental
4 ☐☐ **binge** [bɪndʒ]	▶ eat or drink too much in a short period of time 動 暴食する，暴飲する〈on 〜を〉 ● 現在分詞は bingeing または binging
5 ☐☐ **objectionable** [əbdʒékʃənəbl]	▶ unpleasant, offensive, obnoxious 形 好ましくない，不快な ⇔ pleasant, agreeable, favorable
6 ☐☐ **blatantly** [bléɪtəntli]	▶ flagrantly 副 露骨に，あからさまに 形 blatant
7 ☐☐ **sexist** [séksɪst]	▶ treating people unfairly because of their sex 形 性差別的な　名 性差別主義者 名 sexism
8 ☐☐ **stereotypically** [stèriətípɪkəli]	副 型通りに，紋切り型に 名 stereotype　形 stereotypical
9 ☐☐ **masculine** [mǽskjʊlən] ❶	▶ manly 形 男らしい，男性的な 名 masculinity ⇔ feminine
10 ☐☐ **diversity** [dəvɔ́:rsəti]	▶ variety 名 多様性，多様さ 形 diverse　動 diversify
11 ☐☐ **corporate** [kɔ́:rpərət]	形 企業の，法人の，会社の 名 corporation ● 主に大企業について用いる語

12 ☐☐ **backfire** [bǽkfàɪər]	▶ have the opposite result from what was expected **動** 裏目に出る ● 不完全燃焼した燃料がエンジン内で逆流することが本義
13 ☐☐ **inclusion** [ɪnklúːʒən]	▶ incorporation **名** 含めること，包含，包摂 **動** include **形** inclusive ⇔ exclusion（排除）
14 ☐☐ **initiative** [ɪníʃɪəṭɪv]	▶ a new plan to solve a particular problem **名**（新しい）計画，構想，イニシアティブ
15 ☐☐ **justification** [dʒʌ̀stɪfɪkéɪʃən]	▶ a good and acceptable reason for doing something **名** 正当化，正当な理由〈for ～に対する〉 **動** justify **形** justifiable
16 ☐☐ **compulsory** [kəmpʌ́lsəri]	▶ mandatory, obligatory **形** 強制的な，義務的な **動** compel **名** compulsion ⇔ voluntary（自発的な）
17 ☐☐ **engage in ～**	▶ take part in, be involved in ～に携わる，～に従事する
18 ☐☐ **pass over ～**	～を（昇進などの）対象から外す ● be passed over for promotion（昇進を見送られる）
☐☐ **upright** [ʌ́pràɪt]	▶ honorable, righteous, upstanding **形** 清廉潔白な，正直な

Grade Inflation

Some experts suggest that the reason more people are graduating from college is that teachers are giving high grades more easily than in the past.

1　　　It has sometimes been ¹**hailed** in the media as a success story that the percentage of students who achieve ²**bachelor's degrees** has risen dramatically in the US since the 1990s. However, some researchers attribute the cause to a phenomenon known as grade inflation. Initially
5　³**perplexed** by increases in graduation rates despite the fact that students appeared to be spending less time studying, the researchers eventually came to attribute the trend to an easing of academic standards. Once rare on college ⁴**transcripts,** A grades have become so common that employers who want to utilize them in hiring decisions frequently
10　⁵**grumble** that grades are losing their meaning as an indicator of academic performance.

　　It is possible that grade inflation comes from governments, ⁶**appalled** by college ⁷**dropout** rates as high as 40 percent, having used graduation rates as a benchmark in funding decisions for post-⁸**secondary**
15　institutions. Some experts ⁹**speculate** that colleges which are being held ¹⁰**accountable** for their graduation rates have found that the easiest way to boost them and ensure continued ¹¹**handouts** is to pressure ¹²**faculty** members to assign higher grades.

　　A less ¹³**cynical** theory, however, is that educational reforms affecting
20　high schools are helping them ¹⁴**churn out** graduates who are better prepared for the ¹⁵**rigors** of college academics. Debate on the question remains ¹⁶**heated**, and further research is needed to solve this important ¹⁷**conundrum**.

🇬🇧 (222 words)

成績のかさ上げ

大学を卒業する人が増えているのは，教師が以前よりも簡単に高評価を与えているからだと示唆する専門家もいる。

アメリカでは [2]**学士号**を取得した学生の割合が 1990 年代以来劇的に増加したことが，成功の物語としてメディアで時折 [1]**歓迎されてきた**。しかし，成績のかさ上げと言われる現象が原因だと言う研究者もいる。最初は学生たちが勉強に費やす時間が減っているようだという事実にもかかわらず卒業の割合が増加していることに [3]**困惑した**研究者たちは最終的にその傾向は教育水準の緩和のせいだと考えるようになった。かつては大学の [4]**成績証明書**においてまれだった A の評価があまりにも普通になったために，その評価を雇用の決定に役立てたいと思う雇用者たちは，成績評価が学業成績の指標としての意味を失いつつある**と**しばしば [5]**不平を言う**。

成績のかさ上げは，[8]**中等教育後**の教育機関への助成金給付を決定する基準として卒業率を利用してきたため，40％もの大学の [7]**退学率**に [6]**愕然とした**政府からもたらされた可能性がある。卒業率に [10]**責任がある**とされる大学が，その卒業率を引き上げ，[11]**補助金**の継続を確実とするための最も簡単な方法は，[12]**学部**の教職員に，より高い成績をつけるように圧力をかけることだということに気づいたのだ [9]**と推測する**専門家もいる。

しかし，もう少し [13]**皮肉っぽくない**説は，高校に影響を与えている教育改革が，大学の学業の [15]**厳しさ**により準備ができた卒業生 [14]**を大量生産する**助けになっているというものだ。この問題についての論争は今も [16]**白熱しており**，この重大な [17]**難問**を解決するにはさらなる研究が必要だ。

Grade Inflation

1 ☐☐ **hail** [heɪl]	▶ praise, welcome, acclaim 動 を歓迎する，を称賛する〈as ～と〉 ● hail A B（A を B と称賛する）という用法もある
2 ☐☐ **bachelor's degree**	学士号 ●「修士号」は master's (degree)，「博士号」は doctorate または PhD
3 ☐☐ **perplex** [pərpléks] ❶	▶ confuse, puzzle, baffle, bewilder 動 を当惑させる，を混乱させる 形 perplexing 名 perplexity
4 ☐☐ **transcript** [trænskrìpt]	▶ an official document that records a student's grades 名 成績証明書
5 ☐☐ **grumble** [grʌ́mbl]	▶ complain, moan 動 と不平を言う，と不満を述べる 名 不平，不満
6 ☐☐ **appall** [əpɔ́ːl]	▶ horrify, frighten, terrify 動 を愕然とさせる，をぞっとさせる 形 appalling
7 ☐☐ **dropout** [drɑ́(ː)pàut]	▶ someone who quits school before graduation 名 退学者 ● drop out（退学する）
8 ☐☐ **secondary** [sékəndèri]	形（学校・教育が）中等の ● 日本の中学校・高校に相当する。post-secondary「中等教育後の」は大学を指す
9 ☐☐ **speculate** [spékjulèit]	▶ conjecture, surmise 動 と推測する，と考える 名 speculation 形 speculative
10 ☐☐ **accountable** [əkáunṭəbl]	▶ responsible, answerable, liable 形 責任のある，説明責任のある〈for 行為などの〉 名 accountability ⇄ unaccountable
11 ☐☐ **handout** [hǽndàut]	▶ subsidy, grant 名 補助金 ●「施し」というネガティブな響きがある

12 ☐☐ **faculty** [fǽkəlti]	▶ department 图 学部，（学部の）教員陣
13 ☐☐ **cynical** [sínɪkəl]	▶ ironic, sarcastic 形 皮肉な，冷笑的な 图 cynic（皮肉屋），cynicism（冷笑的言動）
14 ☐☐ **churn out ～**	▶ grind out ～を大量生産する，～を粗製乱造する
15 ☐☐ **rigor** [rígər]	▶ austerity, harshness, severity 图（しばしば the -s）厳しさ，過酷さ 形 rigorous
16 ☐☐ **heated** [híːṭɪd]	▶ excited, feverish, vehement 形 白熱した，興奮した 動 名 heat
17 ☐☐ **conundrum** [kənʌ́ndrəm]	▶ enigma, puzzle, dilemma 图 難問，謎
☐☐ **thesis** [θíːsɪs] ❶	▶ dissertation 图（学位請求）論文 ● 一般的な「論文」は paper，treatise など
☐☐ **higher education**	高等教育 ● 大学での教育を言う。「初等教育」は primary [elementary] education

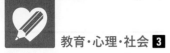

教育・心理・社会 **3**

The Bobo Doll Experiment

In a famous experiment, researchers showed that children tended to play more aggressively after watching adults acting violently toward a doll.

1　The question of whether watching violent movies or TV programs can ¹**prompt** aggression in the real world is a contentious one. One piece of evidence that is frequently ²**cited** by those who believe observing violence can be ³**detrimental**, though, is the 1961 Bobo doll experiment.

5　Researchers divided preschool-age subjects into groups. One set of children observed an adult playing peacefully with a building set, while another group saw an adult ⁴**pummeling** an ⁵**inflatable** clown named Bobo and striking it with a ⁶**mallet**, as well as being ⁷**verbally** aggressive. After a brief ⁸**interval**, the children were provided with a ⁹**selection** of

10　toys, some of which invited aggression, such as a mallet, a dart gun, and a Bobo doll, as well as more ¹⁰**sedate** toys, like crayons and plastic animals.

　Children who had been ¹¹**exposed** to violence ¹²**exhibited** a strong tendency to imitate what they had observed. This contradicted the then-¹³**prevailing** theory that behaviors were learned ¹⁴**exclusively** through

15　punishment or reward rather than observation. Furthermore, since children appeared ¹⁵**inclined** to emulate aggression modeled by adults, the experiment suggested that disciplining children using ¹⁶**corporal punishment** may actually increase children's aggressive tendencies.

🇺🇸 (188 words)

ボボ人形実験

ある有名な実験で，研究者たちは，子供は大人が人形に暴力をふるうのを見た後，より攻撃的に遊ぶ傾向があることを示した。

　暴力的な映画やテレビ番組を見ることは実生活で攻撃性 [1]を引き起こすかどうかという問題は議論を巻き起こすものだ。けれども暴力を見ることは [3]有害になり得ると信じる人々がしばしば [2]引用する 1 つの証拠は，1961 年のボボ人形実験である。

　研究者たちは，小学校入学前の被験者たちをグループに分けた。一方のグループの子供たちは，大人が静かに建築おもちゃセットで遊んでいるのを見たのに対して，別のグループは大人が [5]空気を入れて膨らますボボという名前のピエロの人形 [4]を続けざまに殴ったり，[6]木槌で殴ったりし，[7]言葉でも攻撃するのを見た。短い [8]中断の後，子供たちは [9]いろいろなおもちゃを与えられたが，その中には木槌やダート銃，それにボボ人形といった攻撃性を呼び起こすようなものもあれば，クレヨンやプラスチックの動物など，もっと [10]穏やかなおもちゃもあった。

　暴力に [11]さらされた子供たちは，自分たちが見たものをまねる傾向を強く [12]示した。これは，当時 [13]主流であった，行動は観察ではなく，[14]もっぱら処罰か報酬によって学習されるという理論に相反した。さらに，子供たちは大人が見せた攻撃性を手本として模倣する [15]傾向があるように見えたため，実験は [16]体罰を使って子供にしつけをすることは，実際には子供の攻撃的な傾向を増長することを暗示した。

裁判官の木槌

古いアメリカ映画などで，裁判長が Order! Order!（静粛に願います）などと言って木槌で机をたたくのを見たことのある人もいるだろう。この木槌は gavel（ガベル）と呼ばれる。ガベルは裁判長や議会の議長が注意喚起を求めたり裁定を下したりするときに使う道具だが，今では実際に用いられる場面は少なくなっている。米国下院では，新旧の Speaker of the House（議長）が交代する際，象徴的な意味を込めてガベルの受け渡しをすることがある。今でもガベルが使われているのは競売で，落札者が決まり auctioneer（競売人）がガベルを打ち下ろす光景は一般的である。「落札価格」を hammer price と言うのはここから来ている。

The Bobo Doll Experiment

1 ☐☐ **prompt** [prɑ(:)mpt]	▶ arouse, induce, provoke 動 を誘発する，を促す
2 ☐☐ **cite** [saɪt]	▶ quote, refer to 動 を引用する，を引き合いに出す 名 citation
3 ☐☐ **detrimental** [dètrɪméntəl]	▶ damaging, harmful, inimical 形 有害な 名 detriment ⇔ harmless, innocuous
4 ☐☐ **pummel** [pʌ́məl]	▶ beat, batter 動 を続けざまに殴る
5 ☐☐ **inflatable** [ɪnfléɪtəbl]	形 （空気などを入れて）膨らます必要のある 動 inflate　名 inflation
6 ☐☐ **mallet** [mǽlɪt]	名 木槌 ●「金槌」は hammer
7 ☐☐ **verbally** [vɜ́ːrbəli]	▶ orally 副 言葉で，口頭で 形 verbal　●「書面で」は in writing
8 ☐☐ **interval** [ɪ́ntərvəl] ❶	▶ pause, intermission 名 （時間の）間隔，合間，小休止
9 ☐☐ **selection** [səlékʃən]	▶ range, choice 名 品ぞろえ，精選品
10 ☐☐ **sedate** [sɪdéɪt]	▶ calm, placid, serene 形 穏やかな，落ち着いた
11 ☐☐ **expose** [ɪkspóʊz]	▶ subject 動 をさらす，を遭わせる〈to 危険などに〉 名 exposure

12 □□ **exhibit** [ɪgzíbət] ❶	▶ show, reveal **動** (兆候・感情など) を示す，を表に出す **名** exhibition
13 □□ **prevailing** [prɪvéɪlɪŋ]	▶ common, popular, prevalent, predominant **形** 広く行き渡った，普及した，優勢な **動** prevail **名** prevalence
14 □□ **exclusively** [ɪksklú:sɪvli]	▶ only, completely, solely **副** もっぱら，独占的に **形** exclusive
15 □□ **inclined** [ɪnkláɪnd]	▶ likely **形** 傾向がある〈to do 〜する〉 **名** inclination
16 □□ **corporal punishment**	▶ physical punishment 体罰 ● corporal は「身体の，肉体の」という意味
□□ **tantrum** [tǽntrəm]	▶ temper **名** (子供の) かんしゃく，不機嫌 ● throw a tantrum (かんしゃくを起こす)
□□ **unruly** [ʌnrú:li]	▶ recalcitrant, uncontrollable, wild **形** 言うことを聞かない，手に負えない **反** docile, obedient (従順な)
□□ **defiant** [dɪfáɪənt]	▶ rebellious **形** 反抗的な **動** defy **名** defiance
□□ **acquisition** [æ̀kwɪzíʃən]	**名** (技術・知識などの) 習得，獲得 **動** acquire
□□ **cognitive** [ká(:)gnəṭɪv]	▶ perceptive **形** 認知の，認識の **名** cognition

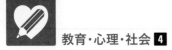

教育・心理・社会 **4**

WEIRD Psychology Experiments

Since most psychology experiments use white, educated subjects from wealthy Western countries, findings based on them may not be useful for people in other cultures.

1　WEIRD is an [1]**acronym** for Western, Educated, Industrialized, Rich, and Democratic, and is sometimes used to characterize the subjects of [2]**innumerable** psychology experiments carried out in the Western world. While it has long been [3]**presumed** that the findings of psychology studies
5　were universally [4]**applicable**, the fact that a [5]**disproportionate** number of research subjects are "WEIRD" indicates that many findings may be [6]**slanted**.

　Since the society we are raised in affects the [7]**paradigms** that influence our [8]**interpretations** of the world around us, it can impact
10　everything from [9]**ethics** to visual perception. For instance, it has been observed that WEIRD subjects are more susceptible to optical illusions than some indigenous peoples are. Furthermore, the [10]**overwhelming** majority of subjects are youthful college students. This may mean that studies of cognitive function are biased toward youthful brain types,
15　which could even mean that the standards by which we [11]**diagnose** [12]**senility** are [13]**skewed**.

　As well as the subjects, the [14]**methodologies** and concepts used may be affected by WEIRD influences. For example, concepts such as "shame" may lack direct equivalents in other languages or have differing
20　[15]**connotations**. As researchers become [16]**cognizant** of their own and their subjects' biases and tendencies, it is becoming apparent that the psychology profession will need to make adjustments to research techniques and standards.　　　　　　　　　　　　　　　(212 words)

WEIRD（風変わり）な心理学実験

心理学実験の大多数が裕福な西洋諸国の白人で教養のある被験者を使用するため，彼らに基づく研究結果は他文化の人々には役立たないかもしれない。

WEIRD は Western（西洋の），Educated（教養のある），Industrialized（工業化した），Rich（裕福な），そして Democratic（民主的な）の ¹頭字語である。そして時には，西側世界で実施される ²数え切れないほどの心理学実験の被験者の特徴を表すのに使われることがある。長いこと心理学研究の研究結果は普遍的に ⁴適用できる ³と見なされているものの，⁵不均衡な数の被験者たちが WEIRD だという事実は，多くの研究結果が ⁶偏ったものだということを表しているのかもしれない。

我々が育てられた社会は我々の周りの世界の ⁸解釈に影響を及ぼす ⁷枠組みに影響するのだから，それは ⁹倫理から視覚的な認識に至る，すべてのものに影響を与える可能性がある。例えば，WEIRD な被験者たちは一部の先住民よりも目の錯覚を起こしやすいことがわかっている。さらに，被験者の ¹⁰圧倒的多数が若い大学生である。このことは認知機能の研究が，若者の脳のタイプに偏っているということを意味し，つまりは我々が ¹²老衰 ¹¹を診断する基準が ¹³ゆがんでいるということさえあり得るのである。

被験者と同様に，使用される ¹⁴手法と概念も WEIRD の影響を受けるかもしれない。例えば，「恥」などの概念は他の言語で直接対応する同義語がなかったり，異なる ¹⁵意味を持っていたりするかもしれない。研究者たちが自分たちと被験者たちの偏りや傾向に ¹⁶気づくにしたがって，心理学界が調査技術や基準に関して調整が必要だということが明らかになりつつある。

略語あれこれ

単語の頭文字を組み合わせた abbreviation（略語）は読み方によって 2 種類に大別される。1 つは USA（= United States of America）のように「ユーエスエイ」とアルファベットをそのまま発音するもので，initialism（頭文字略語）と言う。もう 1 つは OPEC（= Organization of the Petroleum Exporting Countries）のように「オウペック」とそれ自体を単語のように発音するもので，acronym（頭字語）と呼ばれる。CD-ROM（= compact disc read-only memory）のように，initialism と acronym が組み合わされた略語もある。パッセージの WEIRD は，形容詞 weird と同じ発音の acronym ということになる。

WEIRD Psychology Experiments

1 ☐☐ **acronym** [ǽkrənɪm]	名 頭字語
2 ☐☐ **innumerable** [ɪnjúːmərəbl]	▶ countless, numberless, umpteen 形 数え切れない，無数の ● in-（否定）＋numer（数える）＋-able（可能な）
3 ☐☐ **presume** [prɪzjúːm] ❶	▶ assume, surmise 動 と見なす，と推定する 名 presumption 副 presumably（たぶん，おそらく）
4 ☐☐ **applicable** [əplíkəbl]	▶ relevant 形 適用できる，当てはまる 動 apply
5 ☐☐ **disproportionate** [dìsprəpɔ́ːrʃənət]	▶ out of proportion 形 不均衡な，不釣り合いな 副 disproportionately ⬌ proportionate, proportional
6 ☐☐ **slanted** [slǽntɪd]	▶ biased 形 偏向した，偏った ● slant は「傾斜；を傾斜させる」が本義
7 ☐☐ **paradigm** [pǽrədàɪm]	名 パラダイム，理論的枠組み ● paradigm shift（パラダイムシフト。思考の枠組みなどの抜本的変化）
8 ☐☐ **interpretation** [ɪntə̀ːrprɪtéɪʃən]	▶ explication 名 解釈 動 interpret
9 ☐☐ **ethics** [éθɪks]	▶ morality 名 倫理，道徳 形 ethical ● 複数扱い。「倫理学」の意味では単数扱い
10 ☐☐ **overwhelming** [òuvərhwélmɪŋ]	▶ vast, massive 形 圧倒的な 動 overwhelm 副 overwhelmingly
11 ☐☐ **diagnose** [dàɪəgnóus]	動 を診断する 名 diagnosis ● be diagnosed with cancer（がんと診断される）

12 ☐☐ **senility** [sinílэti]	名 老衰, もうろく 形 senile ● 身体的な衰えは frailty, infirmity などと言う
13 ☐☐ **skewed** [skju:d]	▶ distorted 形 (報道・情報などが) ゆがめられた 動 skew
14 ☐☐ **methodology** [mèθədá(:)lədʒi]	名 (研究などの) 手法, 方法論 形 methodological
15 ☐☐ **connotation** [kà(:)nətéɪʃən]	▶ implication 名 言外の意味, 含意 動 connote ⇔ denotation (明示的意味)
16 ☐☐ **cognizant** [ká(:)gnɪzənt]	▶ aware 形 知っている, 認識している 〈of 〜を〉 名 cognizance
☐☐ **predisposition** [prì:dìspəzíʃən]	▶ inclination, tendency 名 傾向, 性質 〈to, to do 〜しやすい〉 動 predispose
☐☐ **adolescence** [ædəlésəns]	▶ puberty 名 思春期 形 名 adolescent (思春期の (人))
☐☐ **intuition** [ìntjuíʃən] ●	▶ instinct, hunch 名 直観 [感] 形 intuitive
☐☐ **cerebral** [sérəbrəl]	形 脳の, 大脳の 名 cerebrum (大脳) ● cerebral cortex (大脳皮質)

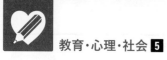

教育・心理・社会 **5**

Tribal Membership for Native Americans

Some Native American tribes have kicked out members, claiming that they do not belong, based on DNA testing or historical documents.

1   Traditionally, Native American tribes sometimes resorted to ¹**banishment** for members who had committed serious ²**offenses**, such as murder or drug ³**dealing**. In recent years, however, the practice has become more common.

5   Tribal membership is often based on Native American ⁴**ancestry**, but since ⁵**intermarriage** with non-Natives is common, the issue of how much Native American blood is necessary is a rather ⁶**murky** one. In recent years, many previously impoverished tribes have gained wealth through legal ⁷**exemptions** that allow them to operate casinos on tribal
10   lands, and this influx of gambling ⁸**revenue** has been ⁹**correlated** with a rise in tribe members being disenrolled. Tribal leaders claim that they are simply removing individuals with ¹⁰**tenuous** claims of Native status who were seeking tribal benefits such as free education and ¹¹**stipends** they do not deserve. Disenrolled individuals, on the other hand, have ¹²**leveled**
15   accusations of corruption and greed at tribal leaders.

Adding to the controversy is the fact that disenrollment can be based on DNA testing. While using such apparently ¹³**objective** evidence seems attractive as a ¹⁴**quantitative** approach to membership, some experts have serious ¹⁵**qualms** about the reliability of the tests. Furthermore, many
20   argue that tribal identity consists more of shared traditions, ¹⁶**worldviews**, and a sense of community, and that a person's genetic ancestry is relatively inconsequential.   (213 words)

アメリカ先住民部族の所属資格

一部のアメリカ先住民の部族は，構成員を DNA テストや歴史文書に基づいて構成員ではないと主張し，彼らを追放した。

　伝統的に，アメリカ先住民の部族は，時に重大な²犯罪，例えば殺人や麻薬³売買などを犯した一員を¹追放するという手段に訴えることがあった。しかしながら，近年その慣例はより一般的になってきた。

　部族の構成員の資格は，アメリカ先住民を⁴祖先に持つことを根拠とすることがしばしばであるが，部族民以外との⁵結婚はよくあることなので，どれだけのアメリカ先住民の血が必要であるかというのは少々⁶微妙な問題である。近年，かつては貧しかった部族の多くが，自分たちの部族の土地でカジノの運営ができる法的⁷免除措置を通して富を得るようになり，この賭博⁸収益の流入が名簿から抹消される部族民の増加と⁹相互に関係している。部族の首長たちは，無償の教育や受け取る資格のない¹¹給付金などの部族の恩恵を得ようとしていた，先住民であるという¹⁰根拠の薄弱な主張を持った個人を排除しようとしているだけだと主張している。他方，抹消された個人たちは，不正行為や強欲に対する非難を部族の首長たちに対して¹²向けている。

　部族からの排除が DNA テストに基づいている可能性があるという事実が，さらに物議を醸している。そのような一見したところ¹³客観的な証拠を使うことは部族民としての資格への¹⁴定量的なアプローチとして魅力的に見えるが，鑑定の信頼性について深刻な¹⁵疑念を持つ専門家もいる。さらに，大勢の人が，部族のアイデンティティーは，共有の伝統，¹⁶世界観，それに共同体意識からなり，人の遺伝上の祖先というものは比較的重要度の低いものだと論じている。

異なる集団の間の結婚

inter- は「〜間の」を意味する接頭辞だが，intermarriage では「異なる集団の間の」という意味で用いられている。異集団間の結婚の具体例としては，interracial marriage（異なる人種間の結婚），interfaith marriage（異なる宗教間の結婚），international marriage（異なる国の間の結婚）すなわち「国際結婚」などがある。国際結婚は transnational marriage（国を超えた結婚）とも言う。他にも，民族，文化，社会階級などを超えた結婚も intermarriage に含まれる。mixed marriage という表現もあり，通例「異なる人種［宗教］間の結婚」に限定して用いられる。

Tribal Membership for Native Americans

1 ☐☐
banishment
[bǽnɪʃmənt]

▶ expulsion
名 （国・共同体などからの）追放
動 banish

2 ☐☐
offense
[əféns]

▶ crime, violation
名 犯罪，違反
動 offend

3 ☐☐
dealing
[díːlɪŋ]

▶ trade, transaction, buying and selling
名 売買，取引
● 動詞は deal in ～（～を売買する）

4 ☐☐
ancestry
[ǽnsèstri]

▶ ancestors, descent, lineage
名 祖先，家系
● people of Asian ancestry（アジア系の人々）

5 ☐☐
intermarriage
[ìnʧərmǽrɪdʒ]

名 異なる集団間での結婚
動 intermarry

6 ☐☐
murky
[mə́ːrki]

▶ unclear, obscure, vague
形 曖昧な，わかりにくい
●「（水が）濁った，（空気などが）曇った」が本義

7 ☐☐
exemption
[ɪgzémpʃən]

名 （義務などの）免除
形 動 exempt（免除された；に免除する）
● exemption from tuition fees（学費の免除）

8 ☐☐
revenue
[révənjùː] ●

▶ income, profit, earnings
名 収益，収入
⇔ expenditure, expense

9 ☐☐
correlate
[kɔ́(ː)rəlèit]

動 を互いに関連させる〈with ～と〉
名 correlation 形 correlative
● be correlated with ～（～と相関関係がある）

10 ☐☐
tenuous
[ténjuəs]

▶ weak, flimsy, uncertain
形 （関係などが）希薄な，（根拠などが）薄弱な
●「とても細い」が本義

11 ☐☐
stipend
[stáɪpend]

名 （定期的に支給される）給付金，俸給

12 ☐☐ **level** [lévəl]	▶ aim, direct **動** （批判など）を向ける〈at ～に〉
13 ☐☐ **objective** [əbdʒéktɪv] ❶	**形** 客観的な **名** objectivity　**副** objectively **⇄** subjective
14 ☐☐ **quantitative** [kwá(:)ntətèɪtɪv]	**形** 定量的な，量の **名** quantity **⇄** qualitative（定性的な，質の）
15 ☐☐ **qualm** [kwɑːm] ❶	▶ misgiving, doubt, scruple **名** （通例 -s）疑念，気のとがめ〈about 自分の行為についての〉
16 ☐☐ **worldview** [wə́ːrldvjùː]	▶ outlook **名** 世界観
☐☐ **genealogy** [dʒìːniǽlədʒi]	▶ family tree **名** 系譜，系図 **形** genealogical　**名** genealogist（系図学者）
☐☐ **forebear** [fɔ́ːrbèər]	▶ ancestor, forefather **名** 祖先，先祖 **⇄** descendant（子孫）
☐☐ **punitive** [pjúːnətɪv]	▶ penal **形** 罰の，処罰の ● punitive measure（懲罰措置）

Agriculture Gag Laws

Some states in the US have "ag-gag laws," which prevent animal rights activists from recording the conditions that animals experience inside agricultural facilities.

1   In recent decades, photographs and videos depicting animal suffering in **¹slaughterhouses** or **²factory farms** have been **³instrumental** in influencing public opinion. Shocking **⁴footage** of animals in extremely filthy or **⁵cramped** conditions has sometimes swayed public opinion in

5   favor of **⁶legislation** to protect animal rights or led to consumer **⁷boycotts** of animal products. The livestock industry, however, has lobbied the government to pass legislation to prevent the **⁸surreptitious** recording of images in animal facilities. These laws have become known as agriculture gag laws, or ag-gag laws for short.

10   People in the agriculture industry often argue that the images have been obtained under false **⁹pretenses**, often by **¹⁰activists** **¹¹posing** as ordinary people seeking employment in the industry. One state's law, therefore, makes it a criminal offense to possess "records obtained by theft or **¹²deception**" from an agricultural facility. In other places, **¹³whistle-**

15 **blowers** can be held **¹⁴liable** for damages of up to $5,000 per day if they are found guilty of recording in an agricultural facility.

      Animal rights activists maintain that such laws are **¹⁵unconstitutional** as they infringe on freedom of speech. As a result, courts in several states have **¹⁶struck down** ag-gag laws, and efforts are underway to have them

20 **¹⁷repealed** in states where they remain **¹⁸on the books**.   ⬛ (207 words)

ℓ.11   under false pretenses：身分を偽って，虚偽の名目で

農業箝口令

アメリカの一部の州には「農業箝口令」があるが，それは動物の権利の活動家たちが農業施設内の動物の状態を撮影できないようにするものだ。

　最近数十年で，¹食肉処理場や²工場畜産場で苦しんでいる動物を描く写真や動画は世論に影響を与えるのに³役立ってきた。極端に不潔で⁵窮屈な状態の動物を映した衝撃的な⁴映像は，時に動物の権利を守るための⁶法律制定に賛成するよう世論を動かしたり，消費者による畜産物の⁷ボイコットに導いたりしたことがある。しかし，畜産業は，動物施設における⁸密かな撮影を防ぐ法案を通過させるよう政府にロビー活動をしてきた。これらの法律は，農業箝口令，または略して ag-gag 法として知られるようになった。

　農業に携わる人々は，これらの映像は，この産業界で職を求めている普通の人々の¹¹ふりをした¹⁰活動家が，偽りの⁹見せかけを使って得られたものだとしばしば主張する。したがって，ある州の法律では，農業施設から「盗みまたは¹²詐欺によって得られた記録」を所有することを犯罪としている。また別の場所では，¹³内部告発者たちは，農業施設で撮影したことで有罪となれば，1 日につき最高 5,000 ドルの賠償金の支払い¹⁴義務を負う可能性がある。

　動物の権利の活動家たちは，そのような法律は言論の自由を侵害するため，¹⁵憲法に違反していると主張する。その結果，いくつかの州の裁判所では ag-gag 法¹⁶を無効とし，それらが依然として¹⁸有効とされている州ではそれら¹⁷を廃止する努力がなされている。

---

gag は「ギャグ」のみにあらず

gag には「ギャグ」の意味もあるが，辞書では名詞「猿ぐつわ」，動詞「(人) に猿ぐつわをかませる」が第一義として挙げられることが多い。そこから比喩的に「言論の封殺」「(人) の口を封じる」の意味が生じた。例えば，裁判所が発する gag order は裁判の内容に関する「口外禁止命令」，gag the media は「メディアから言論の自由を奪う」という意味である。パッセージの ag-gag laws は，家畜の飼育施設で見聞きした情報を外部に漏らすことを違法とする法律を言う。

Agriculture Gag Laws

1 ▢▢ **slaughterhouse** [slɔ́:ʈərhàʊs]	▶ abattoir 名 食肉処理場，畜殺場
2 ▢▢ **factory farm**	工場畜産場，工場式農場 ● 「工場畜産」は factory farming と言う
3 ▢▢ **instrumental** [ìnstrəméntəl]	▶ helpful, useful, important 形 役立つ，重要な〈in 〜に〉 ⇔ obstructive（妨げとなる）
4 ▢▢ **footage** [fʊ́ṭɪdʒ]	名 （ある出来事の）映像,（映像に記録された）場面
5 ▢▢ **cramped** [kræmpt]	▶ confined, restricted, overcrowded 形 窮屈な，狭苦しい ⇔ spacious（広々とした）
6 ▢▢ **legislation** [lèdʒɪsléɪʃən]	▶ law, lawmaking 名 法律，立法 形 legislative（立法の）　名 legislature（立法機関）
7 ▢▢ **boycott** [bɔ́ɪkɑ̀(:)t]	名 ボイコット，不買運動　動 をボイコットする ● a boycott of the Olympic Games（オリンピックのボイコット）
8 ▢▢ **surreptitious** [sə̀:rəptíʃəs]	▶ secret, clandestine, furtive, undercover 形 密かな，秘密の 副 surreptitiously
9 ▢▢ **pretense** [prí:tens]	名 見せかけ，ふり 動 pretend ● under false pretenses（身分を偽って）
10 ▢▢ **activist** [ǽktɪvɪst]	名 （政治・社会運動などの）活動家 名 activism（積極的行動主義） ● environmental activist（環境活動家）
11 ▢▢ **pose** [poʊz]	▶ pretend, feign, sham 動 ふりをする〈as 〜の〉，装う〈as 〜を〉 ● 人をだます目的で正体を偽ることを言う

12 ☐☐ **deception** [dɪsépʃən]	▶ deceit, fraud, trickery **名** 詐欺，だますこと **動** deceive **形** deceptive
13 ☐☐ **whistle-blower** [hwíslblòʊər]	**名** 内部告発者 **名** whistleblowing ● 「～を内部告発する」は blow the whistle on ～
14 ☐☐ **liable** [láɪəbl] ❶	▶ responsible, accountable, answerable **形** 義務を負う，（法的）責任がある〈for ～に対して〉 **名** liability
15 ☐☐ **unconstitutional** [ʌ̀nkà(:)nstətjúːʃənəl]	**形** 憲法違反の，違憲の **名** unconstitutionality ⇄ constitutional
16 ☐☐ **strike down ～**	▶ annul, repeal, rescind （法律）を無効とする
17 ☐☐ **repeal** [rɪpíːl]	▶ abolish, rescind, revoke, annul **動**（法律）を廃止する
18 ☐☐ **on the books**	（法律が）施行されて，有効で
☐☐ **husbandry** [hʌ́zbəndri]	▶ farming, agriculture **名** 農業 ● animal husbandry（畜産）
☐☐ **infiltrate** [ɪnfíltreɪt]	▶ penetrate **動**（組織など）に潜入する，を潜入させる〈into ～に〉 **名** infiltration, infiltrator
☐☐ **inhumane** [ìnhjuméɪn]	▶ cruel, brutal, savage **形** 非人道的な，残酷な **名** inhumanity ⇄ humane

A Shortage of Black Commanders

Historically, it has been more difficult for Black soldiers in the US military to receive promotions, but efforts are underway to remedy the problem.

1   Blacks have long served in America's armed forces with honor and ¹**distinction**, making up over 20 percent of the nation's ²**enlisted** soldiers. However, they ³**constitute** just 11 percent of active-duty Army officers. Furthermore, at the higher levels of the ⁴**chain of command**, only two of 5   the Army's 96 ⁵**infantry**, ⁶**artillery**, and ⁷**armor** units are led by Black ⁸**commanders**. At the very top ranks, just two of 41 four-star generals or ⁹**admirals** in the military are Black.

This problem has long historical roots. America's military was ¹⁰**segregated** until 1948, and disproportionately heavy ¹¹**casualties** among 10   Blacks during the Vietnam War, as well as ¹²**systemic** racism throughout the military, have discouraged Blacks from enlisting in combat units. Even the current generation of Black officers say that while ¹³**overt** racism has declined ¹⁴**drastically**, they can still face discrimination at promotion time.

15   Experts say that the situation could have ¹⁵**dire** consequences for morale and unit ¹⁶**cohesion**, and there are no quick solutions. Training a colonel to lead a brigade takes 20 years, so any efforts at inclusion could take decades to ¹⁷**bear fruit**. The Army is, however, making ¹⁸**concerted** efforts to recruit more Black officers and encourage them to choose 20   combat assignments, as well as taking photos off of the ¹⁹**personnel files** that are sent to promotion boards to prevent discrimination based on skin color.

(220 words)

ℓ.17 brigade：旅団（複数の大隊から成り，アメリカ陸軍では，司令部と，最低 1 つの歩兵隊または機甲部隊から構成される）

黒人司令官不足

歴史的に見ると，アメリカの軍隊で黒人の軍人が昇進することはより難しかったが，この問題を改善するための取り組みがなされている。

黒人は，名誉と ¹栄誉を受けつつもう長くアメリカの軍隊で任務に就いてきた。その割合はこの国の ²入隊者の 20％以上である。しかし，彼らは現役の陸軍将校のうちたった 11％ ³を占めるのみである。さらに，組織のより高位の ⁴指揮系統で見ると，96 ある陸軍の ⁵歩兵隊，⁶砲兵隊，それに ⁷機甲部隊のうち，黒人 ⁸司令官が指揮するのはたった 2 隊である。最も高い階級では，軍隊の 41 人の大将，⁹提督のうち黒人はたった 2 人である。

この問題は長い歴史に根づいている。アメリカ軍は 1948 年まで ¹⁰人種差別が行われており，ベトナム戦争中の黒人の不釣り合いに多い ¹¹犠牲者や軍隊全体における ¹²制度的人種差別のために，黒人たちは戦闘部隊に入隊することをためらってきた。現世代の黒人将校たちでさえも，¹³公然の人種差別は ¹⁴劇的に減少したとは言え，いまだに昇進時においては差別に直面すると言っている。

専門家たちは，この状況は士気と部隊の ¹⁶結束に ¹⁵悲惨な結果をもたらす可能性があり，早急な解決法はないと言っている。旅団を指揮する大佐を養成するには 20 年かかるため，いかなる多様性を受け入れる努力も ¹⁷実を結ぶには何十年もかかる可能性がある。しかし，陸軍はもっと多くの黒人将校を採用し，彼らに戦闘任務を選ぶように勧める ¹⁸一致協力した努力をしており，また肌の色に基づいた差別をなくすため，昇進委員会に送られる ¹⁹人事記録簿から写真を取り除いている。

A Shortage of Black Commanders

1 ☐☐ **distinction** [dɪstíŋkʃən]	▶ honor, credit, merit 名 栄誉, 名誉
2 ☐☐ **enlisted** [ɪnlístɪd]	形 下士官と兵卒の 動 enlist（入隊する） ● officer（将校）と対比して用いる
3 ☐☐ **constitute** [kɑ́(:)nstətjùːt] ❶	▶ comprise, form, make up 動（割合など）を占める, を構成する 名 constitution（構成）
4 ☐☐ **chain of command**	▶ the line of authority along which instructions are passed 指揮系統
5 ☐☐ **infantry** [ínfəntri]	名 歩兵隊
6 ☐☐ **artillery** [ɑːrtíləri]	名 砲兵隊
7 ☐☐ **armor** [ɑ́ːrmər]	名 装甲, 機甲部隊 ●「（戦士が身に着ける）甲冑」が本義
8 ☐☐ **commander** [kəmǽndər]	名 司令官, 指揮官 ● commander in chief（最高司令官）
9 ☐☐ **admiral** [ǽdmərəl] ❶	名 提督
10 ☐☐ **segregate** [ségrɪgèɪt]	動 に人種差別を行う, を人種で区別する 名 segregation ⬌ integrate
11 ☐☐ **casualty** [kǽʒuəlti]	▶ fatality, victim 名 犠牲者, 死傷者 ● casualty rate（死傷率）

12 ☐☐ **systemic** [sɪstémɪk]	形 組織的な，制度的な ● systematic は「系統立った」，systemic は「システム全体に及ぶ」というニュアンス
13 ☐☐ **overt** [ouvə́ːrt]	▶ obvious, plain, undisguised 形 公然の，明白な ⇄ covert（内密の）
14 ☐☐ **drastically** [drǽstɪkəli]	▶ radically, dramatically 副 劇的に，徹底的に 形 drastic
15 ☐☐ **dire** [daɪər]	▶ dreadful, terrible, frightful 形 悲惨な，恐ろしい
16 ☐☐ **cohesion** [kouhíːʒən]	▶ unity 名 結束（力），団結 形 cohesive
17 ☐☐ **bear fruit**	▶ produce a successful result 実を結ぶ，成果を上げる
18 ☐☐ **concerted** [kənsə́ːrtɪd]	▶ coordinated, collaborative, united 形 一致協力した，歩調を合わせた ⇄ separate（別個の）
19 ☐☐ **personnel file**	人事ファイル，人事記録簿
☐☐ **echelon** [éʃəlà(ː)n]	▶ level, rank, rung 名 （組織の）階層，階級 ● the upper echelons of the military（軍の上層部）
☐☐ **disparity** [dɪspǽrəṭi]	▶ discrepancy, imbalance, gap 名 不均衡，格差 ⇄ parity ● racial disparity（人種間格差）

The Importance of Diversity

Although some people worry that diverse workforces will have more conflicts, research shows that having team members with different backgrounds can be beneficial.

1   While diversity has been repeatedly demonstrated to be a [1]**catalyst** for innovation and [2]**enhanced** decision-making that leads to increased profits for companies, business leaders tend to instinctively feel that [3]**homogeneous** teams with a strong [4]**rapport** produce the best results.
5   Researchers, though, have uncovered evidence that the success of diverse teams [5]**stems from** the very tension and [6]**apprehension** brought on by the lack of cohesion that leaders sometimes fear.

In one experiment, subjects consisting of either four friends or three friends and a stranger were [7]**tasked** with solving a hypothetical murder
10 mystery. The diverse groups successfully worked out the correct answer 75 percent of the time, as compared with just a 51 percent success rate for homogeneous teams. In a surprising [8]**twist**, though, the friends were more confident they were right, while diverse teams felt that [9]**dissension** between members had led to flawed decisions. It seems, therefore, that
15 despite their [10]**collaborative** strengths, [11]**tightknit** groups are vulnerable to [12]**presumption** and [13]**complacency**.

Research also indicates that people tend to overestimate the degree of conflict that diversity causes. Therefore, when diverse groups are brought together, attempts are frequently made to minimize differences. However,
20 [14]**provided that** it does not lead to [15]**hostility** or relationships that impede the smooth running of the team, it may be better to celebrate and encourage dissension and diverse perspectives.   (219 words)

多様性の重要さ

多様性のある労働環境の方が対立が多くなると懸念する人もいるが，研究によって異なる背景を持つチームメンバーがいることは有益な場合があることが示された。

多様性は会社を増収に導くようなイノベーションや意思決定の [2]強化の [1]きっかけであることが繰り返し実証されてきた一方で，ビジネスリーダーたちは，強い [4]信頼関係を持つ [3]均質なチームが最高の結果を生むと本能的に感じがちである。けれども研究者たちは多様なチームの成功は，リーダーたちが時に恐れるまとまりのなさによってもたらされる，まさにその緊張と [6]不安 [5]から生じることを示す証拠を明らかにした。

ある実験においては，4人の友人，または3人の友人と1人の他人のどちらかから成る被験者グループが，仮想の殺人事件を解決するという [7]課題を与えられた。多様なグループが75%の確率で正しい答えをうまく導いたのに比べて，均質なチームの成功率は51%にすぎなかった。けれども，友人グループは自分たちの正しさにより自信を持っていたのに対して，多様なチームは，メンバー間の [9]意見の不一致が欠陥のある決断を導いたと感じたという驚くような [8]意外な展開を見せた。したがって，[10]協調性という強みにかかわらず，[11]強く結びついたグループは [12]憶測や [13]自己満足に陥りやすいようだ。

研究はまた，人々が，多様性が引き起こす対立の程度を過大評価する傾向にあることを示している。したがって，多様なグループが集まると，しばしば，違いを最小化するための努力がなされる。しかし，[15]敵意や，チームの円滑な運営を妨げるような関係に至らない [14]限りは，意見の不一致や多様な視点は喜んで受け入れ，奨励する方が良いのかもしれない。

The Importance of Diversity

1 ☐☐ **catalyst** [kǽṭəlɪst]	▶ impetus, stimulus 名 きっかけ〈for 〜の〉，触発するもの［人］〈for 〜を〉 ●「触媒」が本義
2 ☐☐ **enhanced** [ɪnhǽnst]	形 強化された，向上した 動 enhance 名 enhancement
3 ☐☐ **homogeneous** [hòʊmədʒíːniəs]	▶ uniform 形 均質の，同種の 名 homogeneity ⇔ heterogeneous
4 ☐☐ **rapport** [ræpóːr]	▶ harmonious relationship 名 信頼関係〈with 〜との〉
5 ☐☐ **stem from 〜**	▶ come from, derive from, originate from 〜から生じる，〜に由来する
6 ☐☐ **apprehension** [æprɪhénʃən]	▶ anxiety, fear, misgiving, unease 名 不安，懸念 形 apprehensive
7 ☐☐ **task** [tæsk]	▶ charge 動 に任務［課題］を課す〈with 〜の〉 ● 通例受身形で用いる
8 ☐☐ **twist** [twɪst]	名 （状況などの）意外な展開，急変 ● a twist of fate（運命のいたずら）
9 ☐☐ **dissension** [dɪsénʃən]	▶ disagreement, discord, conflict 名 不和，意見の相違〈between 〜の間の〉
10 ☐☐ **collaborative** [kəlǽbərèɪṭɪv]	▶ joint, cooperative 形 共同の，協力する ● collaborative project（共同プロジェクト）
11 ☐☐ **tightknit** [tàɪtnít]	▶ close-knit 形 （集団内の人々が）固く結ばれた，緊密な関係の

12 ☐☐ **presumption** [prɪzʌ́mpʃən] ❶	▶ assumption, conjecture, supposition 名（根拠のない）推測，憶測 動 presume　形 presumptive
13 ☐☐ **complacency** [kəmpléɪsənsi]	▶ self-satisfaction, smugness 名 自己満足，独りよがり 形 complacent
14 ☐☐ **provided (that) ...**	▶ on condition (that), providing (that), given (that) もし…ならば，…という条件で
15 ☐☐ **hostility** [hɑ(:)stíləti]	▶ animosity, antagonism, enmity 名 敵意，反感 形 hostile
☐☐ **distrust** [dɪstrʌ́st]	▶ mistrust 動 を疑う，を信じない　名 不信，疑惑 形 distrustful　⇄ trust
☐☐ **disparate** [díspərət]	▶ dissimilar, contrasting 形 異質の，まったく異なる
☐☐ **friction** [fríkʃən]	▶ conflict, disharmony, tension 名（人間関係の）摩擦，あつれき ●「（物の）摩擦」が本義

Double Majors

According to researchers, students who major in more than one subject tend to be more innovative and earn higher salaries.

1   While most American college students concentrate on just one main area of study for their [1]**undergraduate** degrees, pursuing a "double major," in which one takes enough courses to graduate in more than one academic [2]**discipline**, has become increasingly [3]**prevalent** in recent
5   decades. Not only can it give you a [4]**leg up** on peers with single majors when job hunting, but research has shown some additional clear benefits to it.

The researchers who conducted the study worried that [5]**variables** such as race and gender, a family history of [6]**entrepreneurship**, or traits like an
10 [7]**extroverted** character might influence their research, so they were careful to [8]**factor out** these things. Then, they measured innovation [9]**capacity** through [10]**appraisals** of ability to [11]**network**, persuasiveness, ability to work on diverse teams, and risk-taking. They concluded that individuals who studied in multiple [12]**domains** were [13]**conspicuously**
15 more [14]**innovative**.

A few years ago, a researcher who [15]**crunched** numbers using [16]**census** data also found that there are [17]**perceptible** differences in the salaries of double majors. [18]**Liberal arts** majors who [19]**tacked on** STEM degrees enjoyed a 9 percent salary [20]**premium**, while those adding
20 business majors earned 7.9 percent more. Although double majors can delay graduations and raise tuition expenses, it seems they may pay off in the long run.

(208 words)

・・・
ℓ.18 STEM：科学，技術，工学，数学（science, technology, engineering, and mathematics）の
    頭文字

ダブル・メジャー（複数専攻）

研究者たちによると，複数の専攻を学ぶ学生はより革新的でより高い給料を得る傾向がある。

　アメリカのほとんどの大学生は [1]学部の学位取得のため1つだけの主専攻に集中するが，1つ以上の学問 [2]領域で卒業するのに十分な課程を取る「ダブル・メジャー」を追求することが，最近の数十年でどんどん [3]広まってきた。そうすることで就職活動において，主専攻が1つの仲間よりも [4]優位に立つことができるだけでなく，はっきりとした付加的利益があることを研究は示してきた。

　この研究を実施した研究者たちは，人種や性別，[6]起業家を輩出する家系，あるいは [7]外向的な性格などの特質といった [5]変数が，彼らの研究に影響を与えるのではないかと心配したので，これらの事柄 [8]を取り除くように注意した。それから，彼らは [11]人脈を作る力や説得力，さまざまなチームで活動する能力，それに危険に立ち向かう姿勢などの [10]評価を通してイノベーション [9]能力を測った。彼らの結論は，複数の [12]分野で学んだ個人の方が [13]著しく [14]革新的であるということだった。

　数年前，[16]国勢調査のデータを使って [15]大量の計算をしたある研究者も，ダブル・メジャーの人の給料には [17]目に見える違いがあることを見つけた。[18]文系専攻に理系の学位 [19]を加えた人は，給料に9％の [20]加算を受けている一方，ビジネス専攻を加えた人たちは 7.9％余分に稼いでいた。ダブル・メジャーによって卒業が遅れたり学費が高くついたりすることがあるが，長い目で見ると元が取れるようだ。

Double Majors

1 □□ **undergraduate** [ʌ̀ndərgrǽdʒuət] ❶	名 学部学生 ● 「大学院生」はアメリカでは graduate student，イギリスでは postgraduate (student) と言う
2 □□ **discipline** [dísəplɪn]	▶ field, area, subject 名 (学問の) 分野，学科 形 disciplinary
3 □□ **prevalent** [prévələnt] ❶	▶ widespread, prevailing, common 形 広く行き渡った，一般的な 動 prevail 名 prevalence
4 □□ **leg up**	▶ advantage 優位，有利な立場 〈on ~に対する〉 ● have a leg up on ~ (~より優位にある)
5 □□ **variable** [véəriəbl] ❶	名 変動要因，変数 動 vary ⟷ constant (定数)
6 □□ **entrepreneurship** [ɑ̀:ntrəprənə́:rʃìp]	名 起業，起業家活動 名 entrepreneur (起業家) 形 entrepreneurial
7 □□ **extroverted** [ékstrəvə̀:rtɪd]	▶ outgoing, sociable 形 外向的な 名 extrovert (外向的な人) ⟷ introverted
8 □□ **factor out ~**	~を考慮から外す ⟷ factor in ~ (~を考慮に入れる)
9 □□ **capacity** [kəpǽsəti]	▶ ability, capability, competence 名 能力，才能 ⟷ incapacity
10 □□ **appraisal** [əpréɪzəl]	▶ assessment, estimation, evaluation 名 評価，査定 動 appraise
11 □□ **network** [nétwə̀:rk]	動 人脈を作る 名 networking ● 通例ビジネス目的の人脈を作ることを言う

12 ☐☐ **domain** [doʊméɪn]	▶ area, field, sphere **名** 分野，領域
13 ☐☐ **conspicuously** [kənspíkjuəsli]	▶ remarkably, strikingly, noticeably **副** 目立って，際立って **形** conspicuous
14 ☐☐ **innovative** [ínəvèɪţɪv] ●	▶ enterprising **形** 革新的な，創造力のある **動** innovate **名** innovation, innovator
15 ☐☐ **crunch** [krʌntʃ]	▶ calculate **動** （大量の数字・データ）を計算する，を処理する ● number cruncher は「数値計算の専門家」の意味
16 ☐☐ **census** [sénsəs]	**名** 国勢調査 ● take a census（国勢調査を行う）
17 ☐☐ **perceptible** [pərséptəbl]	▶ appreciable, discernible **形** 知覚できる，それとわかるほどの **動** perceive **副** perceptibly **↔** imperceptible
18 ☐☐ **liberal arts**	（大学の）一般教養 ● 歴史・文学・哲学・言語など，文系を中心とした基礎科目
19 ☐☐ **tack on ～**	▶ add, attach ～を加える，～を付け加える
20 ☐☐ **premium** [prí:miəm] ●	**名** 割増金
☐☐ **multifaceted** [mʌltɪfǽsɪţɪd]	▶ many-sided, multifarious **形** 多面的な，多角的な
☐☐ **interdisciplinary** [ìnţərdísəplənèri]	**形** 学際的な，複数の学問分野にまたがる ● interdisciplinary studies（学際的研究）

The Financially Fortunate Have Fewer Children

Although it may seem logical that richer people would have more children, researchers have found that as societies become wealthier, the number of children tends to go down.

1　　It should come as no surprise to most people that there is an inverse correlation between wealth and ¹**fertility rate**. ²**Affluent** people usually ³**forgo** large families. From a Darwinian perspective, where ⁴**dominant** members of a species ⁵**invariably** ⁶**propagate** more and increase their

5　impact on the ⁷**gene pool**, this development appears illogical. Anna Goodman of the London School of Hygiene and Tropical Medicine set out to determine the biological ⁸**rationale** behind this ⁹**contemporary** ¹⁰**demographic** trend. Ecologists ¹¹**posit** couples have two ¹²**reproductive** strategies: either produce numerous offspring and invest little in each, or

10　have fewer offspring and invest more, under the ¹³**pragmatic** assumption that with more ¹⁴**perks**, they will do better in life and ¹⁵**eventually** produce more offspring of their own.

　　To get a better picture of demographic developments, Goodman turned to a Swedish study that correlated economic standing and birth rate

15　over the ¹⁶**span** of generations. The findings showed that, ¹⁷**on the face of things**, the offspring of the affluent were indeed more competitive throughout life. However, the ¹⁸**progeny** of the wealthy continued to have few children. This is a riddle to biologists, though there is a ¹⁹**side effect** that can be viewed as a blessing. As more countries become developed

20　and birth rates decline, demographers ²⁰**project** that population growth will ²¹**level off**.　　　　　　　　　　　　🇬🇧 (212 words)

裕福なほど子供は少ない

お金持ちの人ほど多くの子供を持つのは理にかなっているように思われるが，社会が豊かになるにつれて子供の数は減少する傾向にあることを研究者たちは発見した。

　富と [1]出生率に逆相関関係があることはほとんどの人には意外ではないはずだ。[2]裕福な人たちはたいてい大家族になるの [3]を控えている。種の中で [4]優勢なものは [5]必ずより [6]繁殖し [7]遺伝子プールへさらに強い影響を与えるというダーウィン説の観点で考えると，この展開は筋が通らないように見える。ロンドン大学衛生熱帯医学大学院のアナ・グッドマンはこの [10]人口統計に見られる [9]現代の傾向の背後にある生物学上の [8]論理的根拠の究明を始めた。生態学者は夫婦には [12]子作りにおいて2通りの方策がある [11]と仮定する。それは，たくさん子供をもうけて一人一人の子にはあまりお金をかけないか，あるいは，子供がより多くの [14]特典を手にすることでより望ましい生活を送り，[15]ひいては子供が多くの子孫を残せるという [13]現実的な推測により，子供は少なくして1人の子にたくさんお金をかけるかである。

　人口発展の背景をより詳しく知るために，グッドマンは数世代の [16]期間にわたって経済的地位と出生率の関係づけを行ったスウェーデンでの研究を参照した。その結果は [17]一見したところでは富裕層の子孫は生涯を通してより競争力があることを示した。しかし，富裕層の [18]子孫が少数の子供を持つ状態は続いた。恩恵と見なせる [19]思わぬ結果はあるけれどもこれは生物学者にとって謎である。多くの国が発展し出生率が低下するにつれて，人口統計学者たちは，人口増加は [21]横ばいになるだろう [20]と予測する。

少子化の特典

perk は，給与，保険，勤務時間などの基本的な労働条件以外に，雇用者が従業員に与える特典を指す語。また，「ある立場にいる人が特権的に得られる利益」という意味でも用いられる。この英文では，兄弟姉妹が大勢いると一人一人のパイの取り分は小さいが，兄弟姉妹が少なければそれだけ取り分が大きくなる，という意味合いで perks が使われている。

The Financially Fortunate Have Fewer Children

1 ☐☐ **fertility rate**	▶ birthrate, natality 出生率 ⬌ mortality rate, death rate
2 ☐☐ **affluent** [ǽfluənt]	▶ rich, wealthy, opulent 形 裕福な 名 affluence
3 ☐☐ **forgo** [fɔːrgóu]	▶ do without, refrain from, forbear (from) 動 を差し控える，をなしで済ませる
4 ☐☐ **dominant** [dá(:)mɪnənt]	▶ ascendant, prevailing, powerful 形 優勢な，支配的な 動 dominate（を支配する）　名 dominance（支配）
5 ☐☐ **invariably** [ɪnvéəriəbli]	▶ always, consistently, constantly 副 必ず，常に 形 invariable（不変の，一定の）
6 ☐☐ **propagate** [prá(:)pəgèɪt]	▶ breed, reproduce, engender 動 （動植物などが）繁殖する，（思想など）を広める 名 propagation（繁殖，普及）
7 ☐☐ **gene pool**	遺伝子プール，ある集団の全個体が持っている 遺伝子の全体
8 ☐☐ **rationale** [ræ̀ʃənǽl]	▶ reason, reasoning, explanation 名 論理的根拠，根本的理由 動 rationalize（を論理的に説明する）
9 ☐☐ **contemporary** [kəntémpərèri]	▶ modern, current, present 形 現代の
10 ☐☐ **demographic** [dèməgrǽfɪk]	形 人口統計の 名 demographics（人口統計），demography（人口統計学），demographer（人口統計学者）
11 ☐☐ **posit** [pá(:)zət]	▶ postulate, assume, presume 動 を事実と仮定する

12 ☐☐ **reproductive** [rìːprədʌ́ktɪv]	▶ procreative, propagative **形** 生殖の，繁殖の **名** reproduction
13 ☐☐ **pragmatic** [præɡmǽṭɪk]	▶ practical, realistic, businesslike **形** 現実的な，実際的な **名** pragmatism（現実主義，実際的な処理）
14 ☐☐ **perk** [pəːrk]	▶ perquisite, privilege, benefit **名**（地位に伴う）特典，給与以外の手当，給付
15 ☐☐ **eventually** [ɪvéntʃuəli]	▶ finally, ultimately, in the end **副** 最終的に，結局（は）
16 ☐☐ **span** [spæn]	▶ period, term, spell **名**（一定の）期間
17 ☐☐ **on the face of things**	▶ apparently, seemingly, at first sight 一見したところ
18 ☐☐ **progeny** [prá(ː)dʒəni]	▶ children, offspring, descendants **名** 子孫，子供たち ● 集合名詞
19 ☐☐ **side effect**	▶ aftereffects, byproduct 思いがけない結果，副作用 ● 悪い意味で用いられることが多いが，ここでは中立的
20 ☐☐ **project** [prədʒékt] ❶	▶ predict, estimate, forecast **動** を予測する，を推定する **名** projection
21 ☐☐ **level off**	▶ level out 横ばい状態になる，安定する

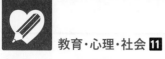
教育・心理・社会 **11**

The Joy of Giving

Experiments have revealed that giving away money can increase happiness, while being stingy may increase stress.

1   It turns out that money can ¹**confer** happiness, especially when you ²**give** it **away**. In a study published in *Science*, participants were given either five or twenty dollars in the morning with the ³**stipulation** that they had to spend the money by 5 p.m. They were ⁴**assigned** to one of two

5   groups, those who were told to spend the money on themselves, and those who were asked to buy a gift for someone else or donate the money to a charity. At the end of the day, the second group, who were stipulated to be ⁵**charitable**, reported that they were happier. A mere five or twenty dollars is hardly ⁶**big-time** ⁷**philanthropy**, but having even a ⁸**token** amount of

10 money ⁹**at your disposal** can be ¹⁰**uplifting** if it is shared.

   ¹¹**Stinginess** also has a return, though not a positive one. Participants in another study played a game in which they could share money with other players. Those who, ¹²**of their own volition**, chose to share little or nothing, reported feeling shame, which was shown to ¹³**elicit** release of

15 higher levels of cortisol, a stress hormone.

   Researchers believe that giving to others creates closer ¹⁴**bonds**, gives us a sense of ¹⁵**fulfillment**, and ¹⁶**innately** lowers our body's stress responses. It seems that ¹⁷**altruism** and ¹⁸**generosity** have their benefits, and not just for the ¹⁹**recipients**.　　　　　　■■ (221 words)

与えることの喜び

お金をあげると幸福度が増し，けちだとストレスが増す可能性があることが実験によって明らかになった。

　お金は，特に人に²**あげる**ときに，幸せ¹**を与えてくれる**ことが明らかになっている。『サイエンス』で発表されたある研究で，被験者たちは午後5時までに使わなければならないという³**条件**で午前中に5ドルか20ドルを渡された。彼らは2つのグループ，つまり自分自身のためにお金を使うように言われたグループと，誰かのために贈り物を買うか慈善事業に寄付するよう求められたグループのいずれかに⁴**割り当てられた**。その日の終わりに第2のグループ，つまり⁵**他人のために使う**ように決められたグループは，実験を始める前より幸福だと報告した。わずか5ドルか20ドルは決して⁶**大きな**⁷**慈善行為**ではない。しかし，⁸**ごくわずか**であっても⁹**自由に使えるお金**があり，それを他人と分け合うならば，¹⁰**気分を高揚させる**ことができる。

　¹¹**出し惜しみすること**もまた前向きではないが，見返りがある。別の研究で被験者は他の参加者とお金を共有できるゲームをした。¹²**自らの意志で**他人とほとんど，あるいはまったく共有しなかった人は恥じらいを感じ，そのことがコルチゾールというストレスホルモンのより多くの分泌¹³**を誘発する**ことが示された。

　研究者たちは他人に与えるという行為はより親密な¹⁴**絆**を作り出し，私たちに¹⁵**充実感**を与え，¹⁶**本質的に**体のストレス反応を弱めると考えている。¹⁷**利他的行為**や¹⁸**気前の良さ**には恩恵があり，それは¹⁹**受けた人**ばかりではないようだ。

博愛主義と慈善

philanthropy は語源のギリシャ語の意味が love of man（人を愛すること）であることから，伝統的に「博愛」と訳される。しかし現在では「慈善，篤志」の意味で使われることが多く，philanthropist は「博愛主義者」というより「慈善家，篤志家」である。一方 charity は「個人の慈善行為」ではなく，「慈善事業，慈善団体」の意味で使われるのが普通。例えば，富豪が貧困層を支援するための基金を創設するのは philanthropy だが，大勢の人が寄付を行って災害の被災者を支援する活動は charity である。

The Joy of Giving

1 ☐☐ **confer** [kənfə́ːr] 🔊	▶ give, bestow, award 動 を与える
2 ☐☐ **give away 〜**	▶ donate, contribute, endow 〜を寄付する，〜を無料で与える
3 ☐☐ **stipulation** [stìpjuléɪʃən]	▶ regulation, provision 名 (契約などの) 条件，規定 動 stipulate ((契約などが) を要求する，を規定する)
4 ☐☐ **assign** [əsáɪn] 🔊	▶ appoint 動 を割り当てる，割り振る 〈to 〜に〉 名 assignment
5 ☐☐ **charitable** [tʃǽrətəbl]	▶ philanthropic, benevolent, beneficent 形 慈善的な，惜しみなく施しをする 名 charity (慈善事業，慈善団体)
6 ☐☐ **big-time** [bíɡtàɪm]	▶ major, leading, top-level 形 最大級の，最上級の
7 ☐☐ **philanthropy** [fɪlǽnθrəpi]	▶ charity, beneficence, benefaction 名 慈善，博愛 (行為)
8 ☐☐ **token** [tóʊkən]	▶ nominal 形 ごくわずかな，名ばかりの
9 ☐☐ **at *one's* disposal**	▶ disposable, at *one's* disposition 自由に使える
10 ☐☐ **uplifting** [ʌplíftɪŋ]	▶ exhilarating, invigorating 形 気分を高揚させる
11 ☐☐ **stinginess** [stíndʒinəs]	▶ meanness, miserliness 名 出し惜しみ，けち 形 stingy

12 ☐☐ **of *one's* own volition**	自らの意志で
13 ☐☐ **elicit** [ɪlísət]	▶ arouse, provoke, evoke **動** を誘発する，を引き出す **名** elicitation
14 ☐☐ **bond** [bɑ(:)nd]	▶ tie **名** 絆，結束 **動** 絆を結ぶ
15 ☐☐ **fulfillment** [fʊlfílmənt]	▶ satisfaction, contentment, accomplishment **名** 充実感，満足感，達成感 **動** fulfill（を達成する，を満たす）
16 ☐☐ **innately** [ìnéɪtli]	▶ inherently, essentially, intrinsically **副** 本質的に，本来的に **形** innate（本質的な，固有の）
17 ☐☐ **altruism** [ǽltruìzm]	▶ regard for others **名** 利他的行為，利他心 **形** altruistic（利他的な） **⇔** egoism（利己心）
18 ☐☐ **generosity** [dʒènərá(:)səti]	▶ benevolence **名** 気前の良さ，物惜しみしないこと **形** generous
19 ☐☐ **recipient** [rɪsípiənt]	▶ receiver **名** 受取人，受領者 **動** receive

Safeguarding Your Motivation

Research has found the motivation levels of one's coworkers can have a significant effect on one's own motivation.

1　　Research reveals that workplace colleagues have more influence on us than we consciously realize. They affect our thoughts, our creativity, and our job performance. We often choose our jobs based on considerations of salary and [1]**job title**, [2]**giving short shrift to** workplace environments. Yet
5　it is the environment that shapes who we become.

In one study, experimental participants were placed in the same room with a motivated individual. Participants were found to be [3]**inspired** by that individual and their job performance improved. When paired with unmotivated individuals, motivation and performance fell. Yet participants
10　[4]**were blind to** this effect, unaware of the influence their partners [5]**exerted** on them. Motivation, or lack of it, is [6]**infectious**. This effect is due to the [7]**intrinsic** tendency of people to [8]**mimic** the behavior of others, especially significant others. Imitating clients, bosses and loved ones makes us feel more [9]**intimate**, and it has physical payoffs as well,
15　including lower blood pressure and a reduction in stress. However, imitation has its [10]**downsides** when we copy negative behaviors.

Companies should not [11]**underestimate** the importance of these findings, especially those involved with [12]**innovation**. Creativity requires an open and explorative [13]**state of mind**, but it is very easily [14]**stifled** by a
20　[15]**nuisance** such as negativity in the workplace. [16]**Eliminating** negative factors before they have a widespread impact on [17]**morale** is imperative.

🏴 (221 words)

勤労意欲のための予防線

調査によって，同僚の意欲の度合いが，自分の意欲に大きく影響することがわかっている。

調査によれば，職場の同僚は，私たちが意識している以上に私たちに影響を及ぼしている。彼らは私たちの思考，創造性，そして仕事の実績に影響を与える。私たちはしばしば給与と **¹肩書き**を考慮して職業を選び，職場環境 **²はあまり考えない**。だが，環境こそが私たちを形成するのだ。

ある研究で，被験者が意欲的な人と同じ部屋に配置された。被験者はその人 **³に奮起させられ**，仕事の実績が上がった。意欲のない人と組み合わされたときには，意欲も成果も下がった。しかし，被験者はこの効果 **⁴に気がつかず**，仕事仲間が自分たちに **⁵及ぼした**影響にも気づかなかった。意欲のありなしは **⁶伝染し**やすい。この効果は他の人の行動，特に重要な人物の行動 **⁸を模倣する**という人間に **⁷もともと備わっている**傾向によるものだ。顧客，上司，大切な人たちを模倣することでより **⁹親密**に感じることができ，それは血圧の低下，ストレスの軽減など身体的に良い効果をも生み出す。しかし，模倣にはマイナスの行動を模倣する場合 **¹⁰悪い面**もある。

企業，特に **¹²技術革新**に関わる企業は，このような研究結果の重要性 **¹¹を過小評価**すべきではない。創造力には開かれた，探究する **¹³心理状態**が必要だが，それは職場での消極性のような **¹⁵迷惑なもの**によって簡単に **¹⁴抑圧されて**しまう。**¹⁷士気**に広く影響を与える前にマイナス要素 **¹⁶を排除する**ことが不可欠なのだ。

Safeguarding Your Motivation

1 ☐☐ **job title**	▶ position title 肩書き，役職名，職位
2 ☐☐ **give short shrift to ～**	～をいいかげんに扱う ● short shrift で「無配慮，粗雑な扱い」の意味
3 ☐☐ **inspire** [ɪnspáɪər] ❶	▶ motivate, stimulate 動 を奮起させる，（人）にやる気を起こさせる 名 inspiration（刺激，鼓舞）
4 ☐☐ **be blind to ～**	▶ be oblivious of, be unaware of ～に気がつかない
5 ☐☐ **exert** [ɪgzə́:rt] ❶	▶ exercise, wield 動 （影響力など）を及ぼす 名 exertion（行使，発揮）
6 ☐☐ **infectious** [ɪnfékʃəs]	▶ catching, easily transmitted 形 伝染しやすい 動 infect 名 infection
7 ☐☐ **intrinsic** [ɪntrínsɪk]	▶ inherent, innate, essential 形 もともと備わっている，本質的な，固有の ⇄ extrinsic（付帯的な）
8 ☐☐ **mimic** [mímɪk]	▶ imitate, copy, emulate 動 をまねる
9 ☐☐ **intimate** [íntəmət] ❶	▶ close, friendly 形 親密な 名 intimacy
10 ☐☐ **downside** [dáʊnsàɪd]	▶ disadvantage, drawback, deficit 名 悪い面，欠点
11 ☐☐ **underestimate** [ʌndəréstɪmèɪt] ❶	▶ belittle, minimize, sell ～ short 動 を過小評価する

12 □□ **innovation** [ìnəvéɪʃən]	名（技術）革新，刷新 形 innovative
13 □□ **state of mind**	▶ emotional [mental] state, spirit, mood （ある時点での）心理状態
14 □□ **stifle** [stáɪfl]	▶ curb, suppress, suffocate 動 を抑圧する，を窒息させる
15 □□ **nuisance** [njúːsəns] ●	▶ annoyance, bore, bother 名 迷惑なもの［人］，厄介なもの［人］
16 □□ **eliminate** [ɪlímɪnèɪt] ●	▶ remove, get rid of 動 を排除する 名 elimination
17 □□ **morale** [mərǽl] ●	▶ motivation, enthusiasm 名（軍隊・集団などの）士気，意欲
□□ **demote** [dìːmóʊt]	▶ lower, relegate, downgrade, degrade 動 を降格させる 名 demotion ⬌ promote（を昇進させる）
□□ **incentive** [ɪnséntɪv]	▶ motivation, stimulus, spur 名 誘因，刺激〈to do ～するための〉，報奨金
□□ **mentor** [méntɔːr]	▶ experienced and trusted adviser 名 良き助言者 ● have a (good) mentor（（良き）助言者を持つ）

12

Two-Year-Olds Copy Group Behavior

An experiment on two-year-olds has shown that they tend to copy what the majority of other children are doing.

1   When hearing the words "[1]**peer** pressure," many adults imagine [2]**juveniles** [3]**experimenting with** smoking and drinking. These behaviors, which are not [4]**condoned** by adults, are often [5]**examples set** by their groups. Daniel Haun of the Max Planck Institute for Evolutionary Biology

5   in Leipzig, Germany, observed two-year-olds carrying out a simple [6]**chore** and realized they are not [7]**exempt** from peer pressure.

Haun watched as the [8]**toddlers**, his subjects, learned to place a ball in one of three boxes. The two-year-olds watched as one individual placed the ball in one box, and then a separate group of three put their own balls

10   into another box. The subjects were then told to put their balls away, and the majority chose the box used by the group rather than the box used by the first individual. Peer pressure is not limited to humans. Haun carried out an identical experiment with chimpanzees. The [9]**primates** were even more prone to copy the choice of the group. Haun theorizes that copying

15   group behaviors may have been a survival strategy early in human history, since it could have been [10]**treacherous** to make mistakes, to [11]**stray** from the [12]**norm** or to [13]**alienate** members of their group.

Haun plans to carry out further experiments but change the circumstances somewhat, [14]**namely** to see if humans and chimpanzees

20   change their behavior to [15]**conform**, even if they know the group's actions are wrong. Similar studies show that older children will conform to a group, even when their actions are known to be incorrect or even [16]**unethical**.   🟦 (252 words)

集団の行動をまねる2歳児

2歳児を対象とした実験で，彼らは他の子供たちの大多数がしていることをまねる傾向があることが示された。

「¹同調圧力」という言葉を聞くと，多くの大人は喫煙や飲酒 ³を試みている ²若者たちを思い浮かべる。これらの行いは，大人が ⁴許さないものであるが，しばしばグループ内での ⁵手本となっているものである。ドイツのライプチヒにあるマックス・プランク進化生物学研究所のダニエル・ホーンは2歳児が単純な ⁶雑用を行うところを観察し，彼らが同調圧力から ⁷免れていないことに気がついた。

ホーンは被験者である ⁸よちよち歩きの幼児たちが3つの箱の1つにボールを入れることを覚える様子を観察した。2歳児たちは仲間の1人がボールをある箱に入れるのを見てから，別の3人のグループが自分たちのボールを別の箱に入れるのを見た。その後，被験者たちはボールを片づけるように指示されると，大多数は最初の1人が使った箱ではなくグループが使った箱を選んだ。同調圧力は人間に限ったものではない。ホーンは同じ実験をチンパンジーに行った。その ⁹霊長類は集団の決定をより模倣する傾向にあった。ホーンは人類史の初期において，間違えること，¹²規範から ¹¹外れること，あるいは集団の構成員 ¹³と不和になることは ¹⁰危険だった可能性があるので，集団の行動を模倣することは生き残り戦略だったのだろうと理論を立てた。

ホーンはさらなる実験を行う計画を立てているが，今度はいくらか状況を変えようとしている。¹⁴すなわち集団の行動が間違いとわかっている場合でも，人間とチンパンジーはそれに ¹⁵従うために行動を変えるかどうかを調べようとしている。類似研究では，年齢が上の子供は，自分たちの行動が間違っている，さらには ¹⁶道義的でない，と知っていても集団に従うことがわかっている。

仲間からの圧力

peer の語源はラテン語で「同等の」を意味する par で，par はそのまま「等価」という英語にもなっている。年齢・地位・能力・環境などの観点で同等と見なされる人々が peers（仲間）で，peer group（仲間集団）を形成する。peer group の構成員は，norm（集団の規範）に従い（conform）仲間の多数と同じように振る舞う圧力を感じる。それが peer pressure で，「同調圧力」とも訳される。青少年の喫煙や飲酒を思い浮かべるというのは，子供の peer group は大人に比べて社会的に狭く閉鎖された集団であるため peer pressure が強く，また子供の方が圧力に対する抵抗力が弱いので，悪習が広まる可能性が高いと考えられているからである。

Two-Year-Olds Copy Group Behavior

1 ☐☐
peer
[píər] ❶
▶ coequal, equal
名 仲間, 同じ地位にある人
形 peerless (比類のない, 無比の)

2 ☐☐
juvenile
[dʒúːvənàil]
▶ adolescent, minor, youth
名 少年少女　形 年少者向きの, 未熟な
⇔ adult, senile (老人)

3 ☐☐
experiment with ～
▶ take a shot at, attempt to *do*, try
～を試みる

4 ☐☐
condone
[kəndóun]
▶ overlook, excuse, pardon
動 を許す, (罪など) を大目に見る

5 ☐☐
set an example
▶ serve as an example [a model], make the pace
手本を示す, 模範となる

6 ☐☐
chore
[tʃɔːr] ❶
▶ errand, duty, job
名 雑用, (特に家庭内で清掃に関連する) ちょっとした仕事

7 ☐☐
exempt
[ɪgzémpt] ❶
▶ immune, excused, spared
形 免れた〈from ～を〉, ない〈from ～が〉
動 に免除する〈from 義務などを〉

8 ☐☐
toddler
[tá(ː)dlər]
▶ infant, tot
名 よちよち歩きの幼児
動 名 toddle (よちよち歩く ; よちよち歩き)

9 ☐☐
primate
[práimeit]
▶ highest class of animals, including man, apes and monkeys
名 霊長類, 霊長目の動物

10 ☐☐
treacherous
[trétʃərəs]
▶ dangerous, perilous, precarious
形 危険な, 不安定な, 裏切りの
名 treachery

11 ☐☐
stray
[strei]
▶ wander off, diverge, get sidetracked
動 外れる, それる〈from ～から〉
形 はぐれた, 道に迷った

12 □□ **norm** [nɔːrm]	▶ standard, convention, criterion, benchmark 名 規範, 基準 形 normal
13 □□ **alienate** [éɪliənèɪt]	▶ estrange, separate, break off 動 と不和になる, を遠ざける 名 alienation（疎外）　形 alien（なじみのない）
14 □□ **namely** [néɪmli]	▶ specifically, that is to say, to be specific 副 すなわち, より具体的には
15 □□ **conform** [kənfɔ́ːrm]	▶ comply, follow, obey 動 従う〈to 模範・規則などに〉 名 conformity（従順, 服従）
16 □□ **unethical** [ʌnéθɪkəl]	▶ dishonest, immoral, dishonorable 形 非倫理的な ⟷ ethical（倫理的な, 道徳上の）
□□ **agitate** [ǽdʒɪtèɪt] ❶	動 を扇動する 名 agitation
□□ **antipathy** [æntípəθi]	▶ dislike, abhorrence, aversion, loathing 名 反感〈to ～への〉 ⟷ sympathy（同情）
□□ **coerce** [kouə́ːrs]	▶ make, force 動 に強要する〈into ～を〉 名 coercion　形 coercive（威圧的な）
□□ **docile** [dɑ́(ː)səl]	▶ submissive, obedient 形 素直な, 従順な 名 docility

教育・心理・社会 **14**

Why Intelligent People Are Often Insecure

Praising people for their intelligence rather than their effort may cause them to lose confidence when they attempt to do difficult things.

1   In an [1]**ironic twist**, numerous studies show that intelligent children are often less confident than those with [2]**mediocre** [3]**aptitudes**, and it seems that praise may be the culprit. In one study, children of equal intelligence were divided into two groups, and both groups received praise
5   in the experiments, but the type of praise differed for each group. The group praised for their intelligence when solving easy problems would more [4]**readily** blame their failure in solving difficult problems on their innate [5]**deficiency**. Those praised for their efforts in solving easy problems saw their failures on difficult problems as a lack of [6]**self-**
10 **discipline**. They then tended to [7]**bear up** better during failure and try harder on ensuing problems, [8]**nosing out** the group praised for intelligence.

Thus, the kind of feedback we get from parents and teachers as children has an effect on whether we see our abilities as innate or a result
15 of our efforts. The results were even more significant for women, with the smartest women more likely to [9]**discredit** themselves after experiencing failure. Children who have been praised for their intelligence are more vulnerable to self-doubt, with failures [10]**eating away at** their confidence. Many intelligent adults need to reevaluate their self-assessments so that
20 they can [11]**recoup** their self-confidence and face any challenge.

🇬🇧 (214 words)

知能が高い人々の多くが自信を持てないのはなぜか

人々の努力よりも知能を褒めることは，彼らが難題に取り掛かる際に自信をなくす原因となるかもしれない。

[1]**皮肉な話**だが，数多くの研究が知能の高い子供はしばしば[2]**並の**[3]**素質**を持つ子供よりも自信がないことを示しており，褒められることがその原因のようだ。ある研究で，同程度の知能の子供たちを2つのグループに分け，どちらのグループも実験で褒められたが，褒め方がグループで異なっていた。易しい問題を解いたときに頭が良いと褒められたグループは，難しい問題を解くときに失敗すると，[4]**すぐにそれを**生まれつきの[5]**欠陥**のせいにした。易しい問題を解く際の努力を褒められた子供たちは，難しい問題を解くのに失敗すると[6]**自分の鍛錬**が足りないと考えた。それで失敗をしている間にも[7]**頑張って**，次の問題ではいっそう努力する傾向があり，頭の良さを褒められたグループ[8]**に僅差で勝った。**

このようにして，子供のころに両親や先生たちから受けるフィードバックは，自分の能力を生まれついたものと見るか努力の結果と見るかに影響する。その結果は女性の場合の方がより深刻で，非常に頭の良い女性たちは失敗すると自分[9]**を卑下し**がちだった。頭の良さを褒められてきた子供は，失敗が自信[10]**を徐々にむしばみ**，自己不信になりやすい。高い知能を持つ大人たちの多くは自己評価を見直して，自信[11]**を取り戻し**，どんな課題にも立ち向かえるようにする必要がある。

Why Intelligent People Are Often Insecure

1 ☐☐ **ironic twist** 	皮肉な展開
2 ☐☐ **mediocre** [mìːdióʊkər]	▶ average, commonplace 形 並みの、平凡な 名 mediocrity（平凡（な才能））
3 ☐☐ **aptitude** [ǽptɪtjùːd]	▶ gift, talent, flair 名 素質、才能 形 apt（利発な）
4 ☐☐ **readily** [rédɪli] ❶	▶ at once, right away, immediately 副 すぐに、直ちに 形 ready
5 ☐☐ **deficiency** [dɪfíʃənsi]	▶ shortage, incompleteness, inadequacy 名 欠陥、不足 形 deficient
6 ☐☐ **self-discipline** [sèlfdísəplɪn]	▶ self-improvement 名 自己訓練
7 ☐☐ **bear up** 	▶ endure, stand, tolerate 頑張る、耐える
8 ☐☐ **nose out ～** 	▶ edge out, beat out narrowly, win by an inch ～に僅差で勝つ
9 ☐☐ **discredit** [dɪskrédət]	▶ cast doubt on, disgrace 動 に疑いをかける、の信用を傷つける 形 discreditable（信用を傷つける（ような））
10 ☐☐ **eat away at ～** 	▶ erode, undermine, afflict ～を徐々にむしばむ、～をさいなむ
11 ☐☐ **recoup** [rɪkúːp]	▶ recover, regain, make up for 動 を取り戻す ● recoup one's losses（損失を取り戻す）

☐☐ **impeccable** [ɪmpékəbl]	▶ perfect, faultless, flawless **形** 完璧な,申し分ない ● impeccable manners（非の打ち所のない作法）
☐☐ **lament** [ləmént] ❶	▶ deplore, bewail, bemoan, mourn **動** を嘆く **形** lamentable
☐☐ **torment** [tɔːrmént] ❶	▶ torture, trouble, plague, persecute **動** を苦しめる **名** 苦痛 ● 名詞で be in torment は「苦悩する」の意味
☐☐ **intelligence quotient**	▶ a measurement of one's intelligence 知能指数,IQ
☐☐ **rave** [reɪv]	▶ extol, cry up, acclaim **動** を激賞する,を褒めちぎる **名** 激賞,べた褒め
☐☐ **overconfident** [òʊvərká(ː)nfɪdənt]	▶ conceited, self-assured **形** 自信過剰の **名** overconfidence
☐☐ **vex** [veks]	▶ annoy, irritate, torment, afflict **動** を悩ませる,をいらいらさせる ● a vexing issue（厄介な問題）
☐☐ **demeanor** [dɪmíːnər]	▶ behavior, conduct, bearing **名** 態度,振る舞い
☐☐ **fortitude** [fɔ́ːrtətjùːd]	▶ bravery, courage, endurance, patience **名** 不屈の精神 ● admirable fortitude（賞賛すべき強靭な精神）
☐☐ **plight** [plaɪt]	▶ bad state, difficulty, predicament **名** 窮状,苦境

The Wide Perspective of Sports Psychologists

Sports psychologists must consider a wide variety of factors in order to help athletes achieve the best performance possible.

1   Sports psychologists have traditionally worked with individual athletes to help them reach the [1]**pinnacle** of their performance. However, athletes do not live [2]**in a vacuum**. Many of today's psychologists intervene in the [3]**interpersonal dynamics** of an athlete or sports team,

5   which requires [4]**concord** with coaches, team members, family and sometimes even friends — any of whom can act as support or a [5]**hindrance**. This broader approach to mental well-being is paying off.

Coaches are instrumental in psychologically preparing the athlete and providing cohesion among team members: they are the ones who most

10 directly influence the emotional [6]**arena** throughout the training regimen. Psychologists help coaches create the right balance between the autonomy and the [7]**interdependence** of the athlete and key others. Sometimes, coaches have been too [8]**obtrusive**, too [9]**presumptuous** about their role, and have hampered athletes from achieving their best performance.

15 Friends and family can either provide stability or be mental [10]**drains**. For some sports psychologists, that sometimes means [11]**leveling with** [12]**intrusive** individuals directly, while other psychologists prefer helping athletes [13]**sort out** problems by themselves.

Psychologists must also consider the individual [14]**traits** and

20 [15]**idiosyncrasies** of the athletes themselves, as well as the [16]**distinctive** requirements of their sport. The approach to training for a weightlifter, who requires a quick [17]**spurt** of energy, is very different from that of an archer, who must [18]**buckle down** and calm his mind as he [19]**takes aim**. Psychologists must become intimately involved in the athlete's routine

25 and mental preparation in order to [20]**instill** concentration, confidence and [21]**composure**.   (249 words)

スポーツ心理学者に課される広い視野

スポーツ心理学者たちは，選手たちが可能な限り最高の成果を出す手助けをするために，さまざまな要素を考慮しなければならない。

　スポーツ心理学者たちは従来選手が成績の ^{1}頂点に達する手助けをするために選手個人と仕事をしてきた。しかし，選手たちは ^{2}孤立して生きているわけではない。現代の心理学者の多くは選手あるいはスポーツチームの ^{3}人間関係の力学に干渉している。このことはコーチ，チームのメンバー，家族，そして時には友人さえ——支援者または ^{5}妨害者となり得るあらゆる人たちとの ^{4}協調を必要とする。精神的健康へのこのより広い取り組みは成果を上げている。

　コーチは選手に心理面での備えとチームのメンバー間に結束を与える点で役に立つ。コーチはトレーニングの間中ずっと情緒の ^{6}領域に最も直接的に影響する人物なのである。心理学者は，コーチが選手とその他の主要関係者たちとの間の自律と ^{7}相互依存の適切なバランスを作り出す手助けをしている。時々，コーチは自らの役割以上に ^{8}出しゃばり過ぎたり ^{9}無遠慮過ぎたりして，選手が最高の成果を出す妨げとなる場合がある。

　友人や家族は安定を提供できる半面，精神的に ^{10}くたくたにさせる者にもなり得る。一部のスポーツ心理学者にとって，それは直接 ^{12}押しつけがましい個人に ^{11}率直にものを言うことに時にはつながる。その一方で，選手が自分で問題 ^{13}を解決する手助けをすることをよしとする心理学者もいる。

　心理学者は，選手の競技に ^{16}特有の要件とともに，個々の選手の ^{14}特徴と ^{15}特異性をも考慮しなくてはならない。エネルギーを素早く ^{17}一気に噴出する必要のある重量挙げの選手のためのトレーニングへの取り組みは，^{18}気持ちを引き締めて心を穏やかにして ^{19}的に狙いを定めなければならないアーチェリーの選手へのものとはまったく別のものだ。集中力と自信と ^{21}平静 ^{20}を徐々に教え込むために，心理学者は選手の日課と精神的な心構えに密接に関わるようにならなくてはならないのだ。

> ## 精神的流出
>
> drain は，水が流れ出す「排水管」のように，力・お金・時間・資源などをどんどん奪い取っていくものを指す。したがって，mental drain は「精神的エネルギーを奪い取るもの」，つまり「精神的に疲弊させるもの」という意味になる。友人や家族は支えにもなるが，時に出すぎた（intrusive）行動により選手にとって心理的負担にもなり得る。そこに積極的に介入する心理学者と，距離を置いて見守る心理学者とがいるわけである。

The Wide Perspective of Sports Psychologists

1 ☐☐ **pinnacle** [pínəkl]	▶ acme, apex, peak 名 頂点, 絶頂, 最高点
2 ☐☐ **in a vacuum**	▶ in isolation 孤立して
3 ☐☐ **interpersonal dynamics**	▶ relationship dynamics 人間関係の力学, 人が行動し相互に影響し合うあり方
4 ☐☐ **concord** [ká(:)nkɔ̀:rd] ❶	▶ adjustment, alignment, collaboration 名 協調〈with 〜との〉
5 ☐☐ **hindrance** [híndrəns]	▶ impediment, interference, obstacle 名 障害（物） 動 hinder
6 ☐☐ **arena** [ərí:nə]	▶ field, realm, sphere 名 領域, （さまざまな活動が行われる）場
7 ☐☐ **interdependence** [ìntərdɪpéndəns]	名 相互依存
8 ☐☐ **obtrusive** [əbtrú:sɪv]	▶ forward, pushy, officious 形 出しゃばった, 押しつけがましい 動 obtrude 名 obtrusion
9 ☐☐ **presumptuous** [prɪzʌ́mptʃuəs]	▶ audacious, brazen 形 無遠慮な, ずうずうしい 動 presume 名 presumption
10 ☐☐ **drain** [dreɪn]	▶ drag, strain 名 疲れ果てさせる人［もの］ 動 を疲れ果てさせる
11 ☐☐ **level with 〜**	▶ confide in, confess to 〜と率直に話をする

12 □□ **intrusive** [ɪntrúːsɪv]	▶ meddlesome, presumptuous, obtrusive **形** 押しつけがましい, 侵入的な **動** intrude
13 □□ **sort out ～**	▶ settle, resolve, clear up (問題など) を解決する, ～を処理する
14 □□ **trait** [treɪt]	▶ aspect, characteristic, attribute **名** 特徴, 特性
15 □□ **idiosyncrasy** [ìdiəsíŋkrəsi]	▶ singularity, eccentricity, uniqueness **名** 特異性, 特徴 **形** idiosyncratic
16 □□ **distinctive** [dɪstíŋktɪv]	▶ characteristic, special, unique **形** 特有の, 他との区別を示す **名** distinction (区別, 差異)
17 □□ **spurt** [spəːrt]	▶ burst, rush, spate **名** (力などを) 一気に集中して出すこと **動** (スポーツで, 特に終盤) 短時間に全力を出す
18 □□ **buckle down**	▶ concentrate, knuckle down 気持ちを引き締める, 身を入れる
19 □□ **take aim**	▶ target, set *one's* sights on 狙う, 狙いを定める
20 □□ **instill** [ɪnstíl]	▶ imbue, inculcate, infix **動** を徐々に教え込む, を浸透させる
21 □□ **composure** [kəmpóuʒər]	▶ calmness, tranquility, countenance **名** 平静, 落ち着き **動** compose ((心) を落ち着ける)

The Benefits of Negativity

This passage looks at some of the good points of being negative, such as depression helping people to empathize, and pessimism helping people prepare for setbacks.

1   Researchers at University College London determined that the majority of people have a persistent "[1]optimism [2]bias," meaning people tend to [3]overestimate potential positive [4]outcomes and underestimate the negative. Such an overly optimistic [5]outlook has its [6]pitfalls, for it can

5   [7]set up a person for being careless and naive. Moreover, blindly optimistic people are [8]ill-prepared for life's [9]ordeals, such as the death of a loved one or the breakup of an important relationship. As a result, overly optimistic people are apt to have [10]bouts of [11]depression.

    Depression is not always bad, however, for it provides an opportunity

10   to [12]reflect on our lives as well as our changing circumstances. People who have experienced depression are sometimes better [13]equipped to understand the feelings of others and are better able to [14]empathize.

    There is a [15]stigma against negative thinking, and it certainly does have its drawbacks. However, like many things in life, balance and

15   flexibility are important. Optimism feels good and can be a good [16]motivator, but pessimism can protect us by preparing us for potential setbacks. It can also spur us to work harder and avoid making mistakes. [17]Psychiatrists often stress that we must [18]face up to the world's realities with [19]tenacity, factoring in the bad as well as the good, in order to

20   [20]temper our expectations. (214 words)

後ろ向きの利益

この文章では，人々が共感する助けとなる憂うつや挫折に備える手助けをする悲観主義など，後ろ向きであることの良い点のいくつかを見ていく。

ユニヴァーシティー・カレッジ・ロンドンの研究者たちは，大多数の人には根強い「[1]楽観的 [2]偏向」，つまり，良い [4]結果が出る可能性 [3]を過大に見積もり，良くない結果の出る可能性を過小に見積もる傾向があることを見つけた。そうしたあまりに楽観的な [5]見通しには [6]落とし穴がある。人を不注意な世間知らず [7]にする可能性があるからだ。その上，むやみに楽観的な人たちは，愛する人の死や大切な人間関係の破綻などの人生の [9]試練に対し [8]準備ができていない。その結果，あまりに楽観的な人々は [10]一定の期間 [11]憂うつになる傾向がある。

しかし，憂うつは必ずしも悪いものではない。というのも，変化する環境とともに，自分の人生 [12]についてよく考える機会になるからだ。憂うつを経験した人は周りの人の気持ちを理解する [13]素地が身に付いて，人といっそう [14]共感できることもある。

消極的思考を [15]よしとしない考えがあり，確かに欠点はある。しかし人生の多くのことと同様に，バランス感覚と適応力が重要である。楽観主義は心地良く，また良い [16]動機づけにもなるが，悲観主義は起こり得る挫折に備えて私たちを守ることができる。私たちをもっと一生懸命働くよう鼓舞し，私たちが間違いを犯すのを防ぐこともできる。[17]精神科医がよく強調するのは，私たちが自分たちの期待 [20]を適度なものにするために，良いことも悪いことも考慮した上で世の中の現実に [19]粘り強く [18]立ち向かわなければならない，ということである。

The Benefits of Negativity

1 ☐☐ **optimism** [á(ː)ptɪmɪ̀zm] ❶	▶ rose-colored glasses 名 楽観（論），楽天（主義） 形 optimistic ⇄ pessimism
2 ☐☐ **bias** [báɪəs]	▶ prejudice, tendency, favoritism 名 （心理的な）傾向，偏見 形 biased（偏見を持った，偏った）
3 ☐☐ **overestimate** [òʊvəréstɪmeɪt]	▶ overplay, overprize, overvalue 動 を過大に見積もる，を過大評価する 名 overestimation
4 ☐☐ **outcome** [áʊtkÀm] ❶	▶ consequence, result, effort 名 結果，成果
5 ☐☐ **outlook** [áʊtlÙk] ❶	▶ forecast, foresight, prospect 名 見通し，（未来のことについての）展望
6 ☐☐ **pitfall** [pítfɔ̀ːl]	▶ hazard, snag, peril 名 落とし穴，思いがけない危険
7 ☐☐ **set up *A* for *B***	▶ make *A B*, render *A B* A（人）を B（状態）にする
8 ☐☐ **ill-prepared** [ìlprɪpéərd]	▶ unprepared, ill-conceived, incomplete 形 準備が整っていない，心構えが不十分な〈for ～への〉
9 ☐☐ **ordeal** [ɔːrdíːl] ❶	▶ trial, tribulation, a cross to bear 名 厳しい試練，苦難
10 ☐☐ **bout of ～**	▶ a spell of （病気など）の（短い）期間
11 ☐☐ **depression** [dɪpréʃən]	▶ despair, melancholy, the blues 名 憂うつ，うつ病，不況 動 depress 形 depressive

12 ☐☐ **reflect on ~**	▶ consider, contemplate, ponder 〜のことをよく考える，〜のことを思案する
13 ☐☐ **be equipped to *do***	▶ be ready to *do*, be prepared to *do*, be set up to *do* 〜するだけの実力を備えた
14 ☐☐ **empathize** [émpəθàɪz]	▶ sympathize, identify with, feel for 動 共感する 名 empathy
15 ☐☐ **stigma** [stígmə]	▶ shame, blemish, disgrace 名 汚名，不名誉 動 stigmatize 形 stigmatic
16 ☐☐ **motivator** [móuṭəvèɪtər]	▶ trigger, signal, incentive 名 動機づけ，やる気を引き出すもの［人］
17 ☐☐ **psychiatrist** [saɪkáɪətrɪst] ❶	名 精神科医，精神医学者 名 psychiatry（精神医学） 形 psychiatric
18 ☐☐ **face up to ~**	▶ confront, look squarely at 〜に立ち向かう，〜を直視する，〜を認める
19 ☐☐ **tenacity** [tɪnǽsəṭi]	▶ persistence, perseverance 名 粘り，根気 形 tenacious（粘り強い）
20 ☐☐ **temper** [témpər]	▶ allay, moderate, ease up 動（過度なもの）を調節する，を緩和する
☐☐ **bleak** [bliːk]	▶ grim, dark, hopeless 形（将来などが）暗い ● bleak future [prospect]（暗い将来［見通し］）

教育・心理・社会
確認テスト

1 次の日本語の意味の単語を下の❶〜⓰の中から選んで書きなさい。

（1）型通りに，紋切り型に	（	:		）
（2）皮肉な，冷笑的な	（	:		）
（3）木槌	（	:		）
（4）偏向した，偏った	（	:		）
（5）を互いに関連させる	（	:		）
（6）詐欺，だますこと	（	:		）
（7）砲兵隊	（	:		）
（8）自己満足，独りよがり	（	:		）
（9）目立って，際立って	（	:		）
（10）現実的な，実際的な	（	:		）
（11）ごくわずかな，名ばかりの	（	:		）
（12）を抑圧する，を窒息させる	（	:		）
（13）と不和になる，を遠ざける	（	:		）
（14）を嘆く	（	:		）
（15）頂点，絶頂，最高点	（	:		）
（16）（将来などが）暗い	（	:		）

---

❶ correlate　　❷ stifle　　❸ bleak　　❹ conspicuously

❺ pragmatic　　❻ stereotypically　　❼ pinnacle　　❽ mallet

❾ artillery　　❿ cynical　　⓫ lament　　⓬ deception

⓭ slanted　　⓮ complacency　　⓯ alienate　　⓰ token

2 次の日本語の意味の単語を下の❶～⓬の中から選んで書きなさい。

（ 1 ）裏目に出る　　　　　　　　　　　（　　：　　　　　　　　　　　　　　　　　）

（ 2 ）と推測する，と考える　　　　　　（　　：　　　　　　　　　　　　　　　　　）

（ 3 ）反抗的な　　　　　　　　　　　　（　　：　　　　　　　　　　　　　　　　　）

（ 4 ）言外の意味，含意　　　　　　　　（　　：　　　　　　　　　　　　　　　　　）

（ 5 ）（法律）を廃止する　　　　　　　　（　　：　　　　　　　　　　　　　　　　　）

（ 6 ）犠牲者，死傷者　　　　　　　　　（　　：　　　　　　　　　　　　　　　　　）

（ 7 ）均質の，同種の　　　　　　　　　（　　：　　　　　　　　　　　　　　　　　）

（ 8 ）優勢な，支配的な　　　　　　　　（　　：　　　　　　　　　　　　　　　　　）

（ 9 ）を降格させる　　　　　　　　　　（　　：　　　　　　　　　　　　　　　　　）

（10）仲間，同じ地位にある人　　　　　（　　：　　　　　　　　　　　　　　　　　）

（11）素質，才能　　　　　　　　　　　（　　：　　　　　　　　　　　　　　　　　）

（12）無遠慮な，ずうずうしい　　　　　（　　：　　　　　　　　　　　　　　　　　）

教育・心理・社会

確認テスト

❶ speculate	❷ casualty	❸ demote	❹ backfire
❺ connotation	❻ aptitude	❼ presumptuous	❽ defiant
❾ homogeneous	❿ peer	⓫ repeal	⓬ dominant

解答

1　（ 1 ）❻ (→p. 300)　（ 2 ）❿ (→p. 305)　（ 3 ）❽ (→p. 308)　（ 4 ）⓭ (→p. 312)

　　（ 5 ）❶ (→p. 316)　（ 6 ）⓬ (→p. 321)　（ 7 ）❾ (→p. 324)　（ 8 ）⓮ (→p. 329)

　　（ 9 ）❹ (→p. 333)　（10）❺ (→p. 337)　（11）⓰ (→p. 340)　（12）❷ (→p. 345)

　　（13）⓯ (→p. 349)　（14）⓫ (→p. 353)　（15）❼ (→p. 356)　（16）❸ (→p. 361)

2　（ 1 ）❹ (→p. 301)　（ 2 ）❶ (→p. 304)　（ 3 ）❽ (→p. 309)　（ 4 ）❺ (→p. 313)

　　（ 5 ）⓫ (→p. 321)　（ 6 ）❷ (→p. 324)　（ 7 ）❾ (→p. 328)　（ 8 ）⓬ (→p. 336)

　　（ 9 ）❸ (→p. 345)　（10）❿ (→p. 348)　（11）❻ (→p. 352)　（12）❼ (→p. 356)

3 次の単語の意味に最も近いものをそれぞれ❶〜❹の中から1つ選びなさい。

（1） innocuous
- ❶ procreative
- ❷ harmless
- ❸ overt
- ❹ punitive

（2） compulsory
- ❶ infectious
- ❷ impeccable
- ❸ mandatory
- ❹ cognizant

（3） grumble
- ❶ complain
- ❷ propagate
- ❸ coerce
- ❹ penetrate

（4） pummel
- ❶ segregate
- ❷ stray
- ❸ beat
- ❹ vex

（5） exclusively
- ❶ invariably
- ❷ namely
- ❸ solely
- ❹ readily

（6） ethics
- ❶ morality
- ❷ premium
- ❸ exemption
- ❹ outlook

（7） murky
- ❶ virtuous
- ❷ vague
- ❸ dire
- ❹ sedate

（8） qualm
- ❶ misgiving
- ❷ revenue
- ❸ adjustment
- ❹ bond

（9） cramped
- ❶ confined
- ❷ docile
- ❸ perceptible
- ❹ countless

（10） cohesion
- ❶ ordeal
- ❷ unity
- ❸ impetus
- ❹ altruism

（11） dissension
- ❶ echelon
- ❷ interdependence
- ❸ conundrum
- ❹ disagreement

（12） extroverted
- ❶ masculine
- ❷ massive
- ❸ prevalent
- ❹ outgoing

(13) crunch   ❶ calculate   ❷ appall

                ❸ mistrust   ❹ confer

(14) contemporary   ❶ demographic   ❷ conceited

                ❸ modern   ❹ accountable

(15) give away ~   ❶ expose   ❷ drain

                ❸ donate   ❹ exert

(16) elicit   ❶ motivate   ❷ provoke

                ❸ binge   ❹ forgo

(17) mimic   ❶ condone   ❷ rave

                ❸ hail   ❹ imitate

(18) treacherous   ❶ perilous   ❷ affluent

                ❸ applicable   ❹ mediocre

(19) deficiency   ❶ puberty   ❷ footage

                ❸ rapport   ❹ shortage

(20) intrusive   ❶ characteristic   ❷ meddlesome

                ❸ intimate   ❹ skewed

(21) bias   ❶ diversity   ❷ intuition

                ❸ prejudice   ❹ annoyance

(22) face up to ~   ❶ perplex   ❷ posit

                ❸ torture   ❹ confront

教育・心理・社会

確認テスト

解答

3 （1）❷（→p. 300）（2）❸（→p. 301）（3）❶（→p. 304）（4）❸（→p. 308）

   （5）❸（→p. 309）（6）❶（→p. 312）（7）❷（→p. 316）（8）❶（→p. 317）

   （9）❶（→p. 320）（10）❷（→p. 325）（11）❹（→p. 328）（12）❹（→p. 332）

   （13）❶（→p. 333）（14）❸（→p. 336）（15）❸（→p. 340）（16）❷（→p. 341）

   （17）❹（→p. 344）（18）❶（→p. 348）（19）❹（→p. 352）（20）❷（→p. 357）

   （21）❸（→p. 360）（22）❹（→p. 361）

さくいん

単語

A